GUV'NOR

VALERIE McLEAN & PETER GERRARD

—— MARRIED TO THE ——
GUV'NOR

SIDGWICK & JACKSON

First published 2003 by Sidgwick & Jackson
an imprint of Pan Macmillan Ltd
Pan Macmillan, 20 New Wharf Road, London N1 9RR
Basingstoke and Oxford
Associated companies throughout the world
www.panmacmillan.com

ISBN 0 283 07363 2

3 5 7 9 8 6 4 2

A CIP catalogue record for this book is available from
the British Library.

Typeset by SetSystems Ltd, Saffron Walden, Essex
Printed and bound in Great Britain by
Mackays of Chatham plc, Chatham, Kent

For Jamie and Kelly,

and in memory of my Lenny

— ONE —

As I stood in the City of London chapel at Manor Park I didn't think anything could be so final as watching that curtain slowly pull across, knowing my Lenny was behind it – disappearing out of my life for ever.

It was a beautiful sunny day, the sort of day he might have said, 'Let's shoot down to Clacton, babe.' Instead I was saying goodbye to the only man I'd ever loved. He used to drive me mad with his endless, 'Nice cup of tea, babe,' but I would've given anything just to go home and hear those words. Everything was just a blur, really.

I thought about the day when he said, 'Val, when the time comes I don't want no fuss – y'know, funeral and all that. Nice and quiet, eh? You and the kids, some of the family and a few mates.' I used to look at him and think: 'How can you talk so calmly about your own death?' But I carried on dusting around the room and just casually said, 'OK, Len, if that's what you want.' I watched him out of the corner of my eye and saw his mouth go down and his forehead furrow up. He thought about that for a bit, then came out with, 'On the other hand, babe, if you want a bit of a do – it's up to you.' I'm still dusting and fiddling around and I don't really know what I'm doing because my eyes have filled up with tears. I couldn't turn round and let him see them, but I managed to say, 'No, Len, you're probably right – a nice quiet send-off would be best.'

After twenty-nine years I think I knew Lenny better than he did himself most of the time, and I just couldn't keep it up. Kneeling down beside him, I took those big hands of his in mine and said, 'Lenny, please God it's going to be years before your time comes. But, if and when it does, I'll make sure your send-off stops the traffic in the East End. Remember Ronnie's? Remember how Ritchie went? Well, your day will be better than anybody's. We'll have the four black horses, English's best carriage and I promise you everybody will be there to see you off.'

As I was forcing myself to say things I couldn't even begin to think about, Lenny was squeezing my hand and nodding in approval. Then, with a big grin on his face he sat back in his armchair, hummed a little tune and drummed his fingers on the arms, obviously well pleased that I'd fallen in with what he really wanted, and knowing him as I did I could imagine that from then until the end he would visualize his own funeral over and over again in his head and love every minute of it.

Don't think that this was some sort of madness brought on by that horrible thing inside his head. He might have had cancer in his brain, but apart from occasional lapses he never lost that sharp mind that set him apart from most other men in his business. He knew what was wrong with him – he knew he was going to die, and deep down he knew that day was getting closer with every hour that passed. Yet watching him and listening to the things he said, I often got the impression that he saw what was happening to him as just another acting part. Only with this one he'd never see the final cut.

I'm not setting myself apart from the pain that everyone goes through when they lose someone they love, but to me, as I stood in that chapel it was as though no one could understand what I was going through. It was like my insides had been ripped out and I felt completely empty. I suppose you get totally selfish at a time like that and it was only much later that I considered I hadn't been alone in my grief. Jamie and Kelly had lost their dad in the prime of his life – they loved him to bits and now he was gone.

Family, close friends, people he'd worked with – whether in the same game as him or 'straight-goers', as he'd say – all of them had their personal reasons for being there, but though the thought comforted me later on, right at the time I felt very alone. It was like a dream I wanted to wake up from. It couldn't be happening. I wanted it all to stop and go back to normal. I felt like screaming, 'Don't take my Lenny away from me,' and inside I was, but instead I stood and watched those curtains quietly closing, holding on to my kids for support.

Before he went Lenny had said, 'Val, be brave – be strong, and one day I'll come back for you.' So for him and the kids I was outwardly strong and people must have thought, She's holding up well. If only they knew.

On the day of the funeral Lenny was already in English's chapel of rest. In our twenty-nine years together I could count on one hand the nights we'd spent apart, so I'd had a terrible night. When I woke up the sun was streaming through the window and I thought: 'What a lovely day.' Then like a punch in the stomach the thought flooded through me that in a few hours I was going to lose my husband for ever.

Not right then, but months later when I thought about it, I understood what Lenny used to say when he was in prison. He'd say, 'Val, the only way I can get away from thinking that I'll only ever see you and the kids through bars for the next twenty-five years is when I'm asleep. But I have to wake up and that's when it rips my guts out. Wake up – eyes open – empty mind, then bang – *murder – life – murder – twenty-five years.*' I sort of understood. Like people think they do when they say to somebody, 'Oh, I understand what you're going through – I know just how you feel.' I'm sure they mean it, like I did when I sympathized with Len in that prison visiting room, but I didn't have a clue, really. I didn't realize exactly what he meant until that morning when I was filled with so much pain I wanted to die myself.

I don't remember what was going on that morning. It was just a daze of people coming and going and flowers and cards being delivered. But what does stick in my mind is standing looking out of the bedroom we shared and of being aware that for people not involved, life was carrying on. We live on a busy street and things were going on that I'd watched a thousand times from that window. But now it was different. Cars were pulling away from the driving test centre, some builders were having a laugh taking stuff off their lorry, old ladies were chatting and it seemed like everybody I looked at didn't have a care in the world. That's what I mean about being selfish, because I couldn't help thinking: 'Don't they care? Don't they know what's happening today?'

After when I looked down to our front drive it was filled with beautiful wreaths. There was a big floral cup and saucer – because he loved his nice cup of tea. A life-sized petalled likeness of our dog Lady. It broke Lenny's heart when she got old and he had to take her to be put to sleep. Broke mine as well because we'd had her for eighteen years. There was a book in white flowers with, what else, 'The Guv'nor' picked out in tiny roses – a boxing glove, a cream cake. Every one of them carefully thought about as a tribute to Lenny.

Then up the drive and along the pavement outside our wall were so many friends they were standing shoulder to shoulder. I can't list all the names even though all of them are special. But I could see Lenny's mum's brother, Uncle Fred – old now. He'd been there for Lenny and the family since he was a baby and now he was here for him at the end. John Nash and his wife Linda, still supporting me like they'd always done. Alfie Hayes, Lenny's best mate since they were babies. John Huntley, who Lenny had taken under his wing when he was only a kid. His brothers Barry, all the way from Australia, and Kruger, and sisters Linda and Boo. Every face I looked at brought back another memory of Lenny.

Up the road and down the road all I could see was a solid line of black limousines with their drivers standing by the doors. They were causing a lot of traffic problems but it seemed like everybody was respectful because I never heard any horns blowing or nothing. Every now and then one of the drivers and some of the mourners would pull their sleeve up and check the time. I knew they were waiting for me but I couldn't move. Something inside me was saying, 'If I don't go out, it can't happen.' Then I thought of Lenny on his own ten miles away in the East End and I desperately wanted to be with him. Suddenly, from not wanting to walk out of our front door, the car couldn't go fast enough for me.

As we got near Hoxton little groups of people gave way to bigger and bigger crowds and my heart filled up with pride that they were all making the effort to say goodbye to my Lenny.

When he'd been taken away from our home the day before his funeral I thought my heart would break. Now, as we slowly drove towards the East End, I had this strange feeling inside me that I was going to meet him again. Once the hundreds of wreaths were placed on the carriage and the other cars, and that took about an hour, we set off for Manor Park Crematorium and we were together again and in mind and body. I was with him all the way.

The only part that really sticks in my mind – apart from the thousands of people – is that every half mile or so we'd pass another giant poster advertising *Lock, Stock and Two Smoking Barrels*. It was only afterwards that I found out that the boys from the film company had worked all night to get those posters up for the day. In fact they'd gone to a lot of effort to change them from ones with Lenny on them to others with Vinnie Jones – just so I wouldn't get upset.

After the service at the crematorium the journey home was something so different that even now, years after the day, I can still feel the pain. I know he'd been dead for a week but in a way I still had him. Now I had to face life without the man I'd grown up with since the age of seventeen. No more, 'Val, nice cup of tea.' No more, 'Val, me shoelace is broke,' 'Val, where's me shirt, lighter, training bag?' On the other hand no more, 'Babe, you know I love you. Come 'n' give us a cuddle,' or a kiss goodnight or a bunch of flowers. Just no more of what I'd grown used to over all those years.

There's no getting away from it – he was a nuisance all his life: but that was Lenny McLean, the man I'd chosen to spend my life with, and I loved him whatever. Like every married couple does we had our ups and downs. And those times when we argued or had a fall out, perhaps I didn't like him very much, but I always loved him. I know for sure that he felt the same about me because he made a point of saying it every day, and there are not many women who could say that about their husband.

Back home it seemed the strangest thing ever to be having a party and Lenny not to be there, because he loved nothing better than to have good friends around. I know it's an odd thing to call an after-funeral get-together a party, but there's no other way to describe it, really. In a way I suppose we were all celebrating his life rather than thinking that he'd gone for ever. If he was looking down on us I can only think he had a big grin on his face, because he was the centre of attention and that's where he always wanted to be. I thought I would hate every minute of it, but I found it comforting to be talking about Lenny to these friends who liked or loved him as much as I did.

There always has to be lighter moments even at a time like that and one of them sticks in my mind. At the end of the funeral service the vicar was supposed to invite close friends and family back to my house. Instead of that he got mixed up and said, 'Everybody's welcome to go back to Mrs McLean's home.' I can remember thinking, 'I hope we've got enough food and drink in,' because that could mean about a thousand people turning up. As it turned out most people were sensible and just wished me well at the crematorium and went off. But at the same time it did mean I didn't personally know some of the people that took up the vicar's offer. I didn't really mind.

One of these was a man who'd tagged along with Maureen Flanagan. She was one of the very first page-three girls and we'd known her since Lenny worked with her brother-in-law on the window cleaning years before. Though I'd never met this man, I'm sure he knew Lenny and I don't think he would take offence if I said he was eccentric to say the least. He had a long beige coat on, carried a gold-topped ebony cane and round his neck he wore enough solid gold chains to open a shop. On one of these he had an MBE that had been given to him by the Queen. The comical thing though was when him and Eric, another old friend, both the worse for wear, got together in the middle of everybody in my garden and sung 'Nessun dorma' at the top of their lungs, each one of them trying to outdo the other. They were doing it for Lenny, with their faces pointed up to the sky, and I couldn't help thinking it was touching and funny at the same time. God knows what the neighbours made of it, though.

But that little piece of forgetting why we were all there couldn't go on for ever and as I shut the door on the last to leave it swept over me that my life was never going to be the same again.

I can't say that that first night of being truly alone was any worse than those that came after. When I say alone I mean inside, because my Jamie and Kelly were there for me every minute. We all drew close and gave each other strength, but your kids, no matter how much you love them, are not the same as a partner to share your life with, so after I kissed them both goodnight and closed my bedroom door a wave of loneliness came over me.

I sat in bed cuddling a T-shirt of Lenny's, then leant over and turned on our clock radio that was on his side of the bed. As soon as I pressed the button Patsy Cline started to sing 'Crazy', Lenny's favourite song. I knew it couldn't be anything else but his way of letting me know he was still there. I cried myself to sleep but at the same time felt a lot stronger.

Perhaps if someone else had told me that story I might have thought they were crazy themselves, or wanting to believe something that wasn't there. But all my life

I've been able to sense or see things. I won't go so far as to say I'm clairvoyant, but perhaps I am a little bit.

I know all about coincidence, and perhaps that's all it is, but only the other week when Peter and me were working on this book we got round to talking about Lenny's ashes that I still keep in our bedroom. The reason for that is he never wanted them to be scattered because there was no one place that held any special significance for him. With some people it's where they used to go on holiday every year, or a football pitch or a racetrack. But as he often said, 'Val, I want to be with you,' and that's what I've done.

But part of me thinks it would be nice if he was laid to rest with his mother, and that's what upsets me when I think about it. Would I be being disloyal to his last wishes? Would he be wherever he is, thinking that I don't want him in my life? It's a very emotional thing to think about. So when I'm telling Peter how I feel and trying to find an answer I just couldn't help myself and started crying. I had the radio switched on in the kitchen, for a bit of background like you do, but I don't think either of us was listening to it. All of a sudden it was like the volume was turned up and there was Patsy Cline singing 'Crazy' again.

In the months after Lenny died I had a lot of dreams – if you want to call them that, to me they were very much more real. I was just laying in bed, not asleep but not properly awake either. I wasn't even thinking of Lenny at the time, when I felt a hand gently rubbing my shoulder. The pressure on my shoulder was so real it made me sort of roll over and look behind me and there he was standing by my bed. He was wearing a tracksuit and he looked at me for a second then said, 'Val, I've come to get you.' Even though I couldn't speak I wasn't shocked or nothing, it just seemed natural that he was there. Then he said again, 'I've come to take you with me.' This time I managed to say, 'I'm not ready yet, Len – it's not my time,' and he just looked at me again for a moment then he was gone. Strangely enough it didn't upset me, just left me feeling peaceful.

This happened more than once and it was always much the same. But after a couple of years had passed what he was saying was different. I woke up one night, or dreamed, or whatever and he was sitting on my side of the bed holding my hand. This time I spoke to him first, saying, 'You all right, Len?' and he smiled and said, 'Val, I couldn't be happier, but I've got to go,' and he was gone. Leaving me with my arm up in the air and my fingers clenched as though I had been holding something.

Afterwards I told myself that I was imagining things. But when I thought about it, it occurred to me that surely my brain would've told me that he wasn't happy and he wanted to stay with me, because I suppose that's what I'd want to hear. Instead of that it was the exact opposite. I don't make a big thing out of these things happening, I just accept them for what they are.

I remember one night years ago when we lived in Allen Road. We were both in bed and it was ten past three because I looked at the clock. What had woke me up was the sound of kids messing about outside. First I thought, 'Little buggers,' then as they sounded quite young it worried me a bit in case they were babies who'd sneaked out without their parents knowing. I put a dressing gown on, went outside onto our balcony that overlooked a kiddies' play park, and there was five or six girls, all running round in a circle laughing and singing – well, not singing proper songs, more la-la-lahing that kids do when they're playing. Funny thing was, they were all wearing white nighties. I suppose they were aged between seven and ten. I watched them for about four minutes, then they all ran off and through the solid wall that was down one side. Afterwards when I ran it through my head again I realized they weren't wearing nighties, but the long smock dresses kids wore years ago.

Another time, again we were in bed, I opened my eyes and Jamie was standing at the bedroom door. He was about five years old then, but as my eyes focused properly I saw that it wasn't Jamie but an older boy, perhaps eight or nine, dressed in a blue jumper and long green trousers – bit scruffy, really. I swung my legs out of the bed and sat on the edge looking at this boy, and he never took his eyes off my face. Strangely enough I wasn't a bit frightened or apprehensive. I don't know how long we stared at each other but after a while he just faded away. Made me feel a bit sad, really, because whoever the boy was, it seemed like he wanted something from me that I couldn't give him.

It was different when an old lady appeared sitting on the other side of the bed beside Lenny. I could see her but she didn't seem to notice me – just sat there with a little smile on her face. For all I knew it could've been somebody from Lenny's past, but I'd never know because he never saw her or anything else.

I've never made anything of this sort of thing. I don't go round telling people I'm some sort of medium or I can read the future, and to be honest until now it's not something I talk about. These things happen for whatever reason and that's the end of it. I've never even tried to find out more about what it means, though a friend of mine talked me into going to a Doris Stokes meeting. She was well famous as a medium at that time. Yet from the minute I sat down I knew, don't ask me how, but I knew she was lying. She was taking money right, left and centre, and, as far as I was concerned, telling vulnerable people what they wanted to hear.

So with this sort of background that's been part of my life for as long as I can remember, Lenny coming back to me occasionally or giving me messages when I needed them doesn't strike me as strange at all.

In some ways what made things worse for me when I was trying to come to terms with being without Lenny, was that he seemed to be everywhere. Most women who've lost their husbands are surrounded by memories indoors. The scent of their aftershave that hangs on in the wardrobe, a favourite jumper, an ornament they might have brought back off holiday together – painful, but nice in a comforting sort of way. But when they go out they can forget for a little while – not the person, but the pain.

In my case, because of Len's success everywhere I turned there he was smiling or scowling out at me from bookshop windows, posters and film advertisements.

Five months after Lenny died Peter and me were given a surprise presentation of a framed plaque to mark the fact that *The Guv'nor* was best autobiography of 1998. Of all places this party was held at night in London Zoo, and it did seem strange to be walking past all the caged animals and them all looking at us. My plaque was handed to me all wrapped up in nice paper and though I couldn't see it I knew it would have a picture of my Len on it. I thought, 'Please, God, don't let them make me open it in front of everybody,' because I couldn't bear having to see his face – it would've broken my heart.

It was a lovely idea and I wasn't ungrateful but it made me very conscious of what Lenny had missed out on. He should've been accepting that prize. He should've been standing there getting the standing ovations from all those people. It was what he'd dreamed of. He always wanted to be the best at whatever he did and he would've loved every second of it. He'd have made a speech full of his funny stories. He'd have given that audience twice their money's worth – probably sung 'Always Look On the Bright Side of Life' before finishing with, 'Never thought I'd get anything like this when I was sitting on that poxy murder charge.'

Though he often made a joke of it, that charge affected all of our lives more than he'd ever admit, but I'll come to that later.

I was accepting it on his behalf and I couldn't even look at it. Now I can, and every time I do it makes me feel proud of what he achieved. Not only because his book was number one, but because so many young lads seem to have picked up on the values he lived by and taken them on for themselves. I know this is true from all the letters I get and comments on the Internet like, 'This book has turned my life around,' and, 'I kicked drugs after reading about Lenny McLean,' and, 'When I'm thinking of going wrong I think what Lenny would have done, then straighten out.' And that's just three from thousands. In his own way Lenny saved all those mothers of these kids going through grief. Imagine how that makes me feel.

Though he made a success of his life in the end, he always felt that he'd wasted a lot of years through lack of education and messing about. If anyone had asked him if he regretted anything or would change the past if he could, his answer would be, 'Me? Nah. Blinding life. Rough start, but then I took over the reins and it turned out sweet as a nut.' But that was for the public. Inside he knew that he'd had the brain to have gone all the way in some legitimate business. But fighting and easy money got in the way until it was too late to go back. That's why he was genuinely passionate about young kids keeping away from crime and drugs and getting a good education. It wasn't just something to say and it wasn't just something to put in his book to make him look good – he really believed in it. So if half the kids who write to me manage to keep on the straight and narrow that's a wonderful tribute to my husband.

Talking of comments, sometimes I have to smile when some of these same youngsters ask me things like, 'Can you have a fight?', 'Did you ever go on a job with Lenny?', and similar sorts of things. What do they think I am? Some bleached-haired gangster's moll? Lenny might have been extraordinary but he would've hated it if I was any different from the very ordinary person that I am.

That some people might think I'm something I'm not doesn't annoy me or bother me, because they never get the chance to see people like me and other quiet wives like myself. How can they? The closest they get to the underworld in their lives is when they watch gangster films or television police series. And without fail the wives are portrayed as hard-as-nails tarts. So it's no wonder the public have this strange idea of me, even though it's a hundred miles from the truth.

I suppose somewhere out there some villains' wives are like that. But in my experience, and remember Lenny mixed with some very well-known faces, every wife I knew was basically ordinary, nicely dressed and kept herself well in the background.

Something that I never can get used to is how my Len's life has spread all round the world. Geography was never one of his strongest points and if someone said to him they'd been to Dubai or Tanzania he'd furrow up and say, 'Where the fuck's that?' Or if they said they'd had an eighteen-hour flight to Perth (Australia), he'd say, 'Blimey, I could've walked to Scotland in that time.'

Now people are talking about him in these places. One lady wrote to me to say that her son had asked her to send a copy to the North Pole where he was working in a research place. Even when Lenny was at his lowest, if you asked him how he felt he was always 'top of the world', and that's exactly one of the places his book ended up.

Strange, really, because London's East and West End was Lenny's world. Later in his life, if he could've done his work by making a few phone calls while he was sitting in our conservatory, it would've suited him down to the ground. He had a couple of working trips to America, and he took off to Scotland every now and then. But he never wanted to be away from me and the kids for too long and if he could have got out of going he would've like a shot. I suppose you could say he was a very big fish in a small pond, and most of his life he was quite happy with that.

He was known, or at least his name was, all over the country – Ireland as well, but that was mainly by people on the fighting circuit and a lot of them couldn't have put a face to the name. That all changed when he started doing a bit on television, especially when he appeared in *The Knock* and got written up in papers and magazines as the real thing. Then everybody wanted to know all about him, and believe me there was a lot to know. So when his book came out I wasn't a bit surprised that ordinary people were queuing up to clear the shelves every week. Almost on top of that came *Lock, Stock*, and for more reasons than just being in the film Lenny was a household name.

Though he didn't live long enough to see that he'd become what some people call 'an icon', before the end he saw enough to realize that he'd proved a point that had been in the back of his head since he was a baby of six years old. All his life he'd wanted to be somebody and, like I said before, the best at whatever he took on.

Because I've always been perfectly happy being who I am, it's always puzzled me why people are so desperate to be famous. I was happy being married to Lenny, but that was because he was a nice man and I loved him. Nothing at all to do with him being the well-known hard man that he was. I had a nice home, two smashing kids and everything I wanted. We might have rubbed shoulders with faces and film stars but none of that meant anything to me at all.

Do these people who want their picture in every paper want loads of money? Do they want to be flash? Look down on ordinary people who have to work hard every day just to get by? I really don't know what drives them on, but I do know it was none of these things as far as Lenny was concerned. Most of all he wanted respect, but then again he wanted that when he was window cleaning so it was nothing to do with making a name for himself for its own sake.

One thing about Lenny was that he never play-acted tough like too many of them do – he was what he was, tough inside and out. In fact he hated show-offs and the people who walked the walk, swaggering along splaying their feet and rolling their shoulders. I've heard him say to young fellas more than once, 'Oi, what's the matter with you? Straighten yourself up – walk properly,' and they always did. Made me laugh if I ever saw them walking with Len again, because they were so conscious of making an arse of themselves in front of him, who was tougher than anyone they'd ever known, that they walked as if they had a broom handle up their back.

It's funny, when he was on the streets – and come to that, right up until the day he died – nobody had a bad word to say against him. In fact if you listened to the talk everyone was his best mate. A nod to them on the door at the Hippodrome or wherever made Lenny a lifelong friend when they were trying to impress their mates. But before my husband was cold people were queueing up to have a go at him.

I was grieving – not for Lenny McLean the street-fighter, the toughest man in Britain, the film actor or what have you, but for the man I'd loved since I was only seventeen. Twenty-nine years we shared together, so I didn't need to hear that someone like John McVicar was writing in a magazine that Lenny brought his death on at forty-nine because he overdid the steroids. Who does McVicar think he is to dirty my Len's name and cause me even more pain? I don't remember him ever criticizing Len when he was alive.

Then there was others saying, 'Course, he was a right bully.' Bullying? They don't know the meaning of the word. But after what he'd been through my Len did, first hand, and he didn't have it in him to be like that. I said to Peter, 'Look the word up in the dictionary so's I know what I'm talking about,' so he did and it said, 'To treat cruelly the old, the young and the weak.' Do any of these things and Lenny would've knocked you spark out without a second's thought.

I was having a drink with some friends in the Blue Boy about a year ago, when some man said, 'You're Lenny's missus, ain't ya?'

I said, 'I'm his widow, actually, can I do something for you?'

He said, 'Nah, I just wanted to say your old man was a bit of a bully.'

I thought, 'Thank God my Jamie's not here or there'd have been murders,' but I kept calm and made an allowance that this idiot had drunk a few too many. 'Why do you say that, then?'

'Well,' he said, 'I was in my mate's shop a few years ago, then Lenny came in and started banging on the counter and shouting, "I want everybody out in an hour – or else," frightening everyone to death.'

I said, 'That wouldn't have been a double-fronted shop in Soho, would it?'

'Spot on, yeah. Why?'

I said, 'I bet your mate didn't tell you that he was squatting there, did he? And I bet he didn't say that because of him decent people who'd laid out a lot of money buying the place couldn't start earning a living until your no-value mate was chucked out. Lenny was asked to do a favour for people who was too straight to do it themselves. Now if you don't mind I don't want to talk to you any more,' and turned my back on him. Then he wanted to apologize but I thought, 'No, he's probably told that story to a thousand people and rubbished my Lenny's name – so get lost.'

As far as I know all those who scream bully are bullies themselves who don't like being straightened out.

Another time I was in a pub with my girlfriend and a man came up to me and said, 'I know you, don't I?'

I said, 'Do you? Sorry, but I don't know you,' and turned away. I thought he was trying to chat me up and I wasn't a bit interested in that sort of thing.

'No,' he said, 'I mean I know who you are – Lenny McLean's wife, and d'you know what? He knocked me out one night.' I thought, 'Bloody hell, here we go again,' but instead of having a dig at Lenny he said, 'I deserved it. I was drunk, making a right c— er, fool of myself and I was asking for trouble – didn't 'alf 'urt, though.' Then he said something like, 'Sorry Lenny died an' all that,' shook my hand and walked away. Made me laugh the rest of the night that somebody had been pleased to get one of Len's right-handers. Couldn't have been much of one, though, or he'd still be lying there.

As if I didn't have enough heartache in those first weeks after I lost my husband, it seemed like certain people couldn't wait for him to die so they could come after me. They watched the funeral on television, and then got on to their solicitors over some passing remark or name-mention Lenny had put in his book. I felt they showed no respect for my feelings, no decency to allow me to grieve in peace – just the desire to grab some money with him out the way.

Believe me, as ill as he was, up to the day he died Lenny was still capable of knocking anybody who came looking for trouble spark out. But then these people must've known that anyway and wouldn't have dared to open their mouths if he was still around.

Remember, I'm not talking a year or two years after the funeral – this was weeks after, when I was completely numb. My brain had switched off and all I could think about was how could I get through the rest of my life without my husband.

What it was, with Lenny's book being such an instant success, a lot of people thought that millions of pounds were flying about and wanted to get their hands on some of it. Somebody in the book business told me that, 'Where there's a success, there's a writ,' like it was comical and something to be expected. But it wasn't funny to think that because of a word out of place in his book, certain people thought they could sue and take some of the legacy my husband left me.

A few people tried it on, but there was one in particular who I won't even hint at because I know he does nothing else but study the papers and magazines looking for his name to be mentioned so he can make some easy money. If you said he'd sneezed he'd say, 'No, I didn't – I coughed,' then sue you. And to be honest I just don't want the bother of it, though I'd love to expose these people.

When Lenny was working on his book about seven years ago the furthest thing from his mind was that one day what he was honestly putting down would come back to give me a load of aggravation. He put a lot of effort into getting his book just right and often, at the end of the day, he'd say to me, 'This ain't half hard, babe,' then sit for ages looking thoughtful.

I'd say, 'How can it be hard? You're doing what you like best, talking about yourself, so how hard can that be?' I was only having a laugh with him, but instead of joining in he'd give me a look and shake his head as much as to say, 'You don't understand.' And I've got to say I didn't at the time, but I do now.

It is hard putting your own life under a magnifying glass. I don't mean remembering the details, that's easy enough because one thought sort of leads you on to the next one, but it's hard reliving all your old dreams and happy times, sad times. Seeing in your head people who've gone and you'll never see again. Seeing places and things that have changed or disappeared – that's what makes it hard. Most people never put themselves through the emotion of that. They might smell a rose and think of their grandma, or come across a crayon drawing and think back to when their kids were little babies, but those thoughts only pop in and out every now and then. To do it day after day is emotionally draining, specially in my case when most of my thoughts were about the man I spent well over half my life with.

They say that someone never dies as long as they're remembered, and I'm finding that's true. I never have forgotten Lenny, not for a minute – and I'm sure I never will – but thinking about him as much as I have been doing, so that I can get all the facts right, has brought him back – and for that it's been worth all the tears.

— TWO —

I knew all about Lenny's childhood and his life as a young boy because he poured it all out to me not long after we first met. I don't mean all at once because I think he found it difficult to talk about a lot of it.

Some things he was proud of, some things he bragged about, but a large part of those days he kept inside until he knew he could trust me. Now, comparing our early lives, the difference was like night and day. His was dark and troubled and hardly a childhood at all, while my own was bright and happy. I know it's not really true, but as far as I can remember the sun seemed to shine every day for me.

Something we did share right from the start was having a stepfather, but the difference between what we experienced was unbelievable. I don't remember my real dad, who was Henry Smith, because I was only about two when he died of a brain haemorrhage when he was only twenty-three. Strangely enough I don't remember my stepfather arriving in the house either, even though I must have been about five or six at the time and we'd been on our own for three or four years.

I was born in my grandad's house in Hackney Road, that's just off Bethnal Green Road. Mum and my dad had got married about five years before, when she was seventeen and he was eighteen. My sister Marie was born a year after that, so at least she could have this vague memory of him. It's strange to think that there was this man who must have loved me, cuddled and bounced me up and down on his knee, then went out of my life without leaving the tiniest memory. Sad, really. When you're a baby you just accept what's going on around you and don't even think about it.

So though I didn't have a real dad for those first years, I wasn't any different from my other friends because living with Grandad, he filled the gap – like he was the father figure that all kids need. He was my mum's dad and a lovely man.

Being only a kid I never gave any thought to how he made a living, but I did know that all the family on my real dad's side was what they called on the knocker. Or if you wanted to make it sound a bit more posh, wardrobe dealers. That's where they'd travel around knocking on doors and buying second-hand clothes and shoes. Whatever someone might want to get rid of after their husband or wife had died. Sounds one step up from a rag-and-bone man, but it was a good living and in those days a very respectable business. Especially if, like my grandad, you had a market stall to sell the stuff from. His was up Brick Lane and I used to love going up there with him.

I couldn't have thought such a thing then, but markets like that was the heart of the East End. To me, being there was like a kid today going to Alton Towers. Remember in the early fifties life was a bit dull and grey, so anything that brightened it up was exciting. The crowds of people, the smells, the colours and the noise made me dizzy half the time.

There were loads of immigrants coming into the country about that time, and what they'd do was come off the ships and make a bee-line for the market to get kitted out in cheap clothes ready for our weather. Keeping myself well hidden behind the suits, jackets and piles of shirts and vests, I'd peer out at all these strange men that were holding stuff against themselves for size, then waving their arms around trying to make themselves understood. Most of them were Indians or black men, and that was a novelty in itself. As they walked off in their baggy coloured outfits, or dresses as I thought they were, and clutching black pinstripes under their arms, Grandad would say, 'See 'im – he's come from Africa where the lions and tigers live,' or 'He's come from India that's got all them elephants,' and my mouth would just drop open.

Years and years later Reggie Kray phoned up to speak to Lenny. He was out so we just chatted for a bit. The East End is such a small place that when people from there are talking the conversation always comes round to, 'Who are you? Where did you live?' and so on. So after Reg asked me and I told him I was a Smith he wanted to know what my dad's name was. When I said Henry he said, 'I don't believe it. He was a good friend of mine,' and he said, 'I'll tell you something else, me and you have met before but I'll bet you don't remember.'

I did a few quick figures in my head and said, 'I don't think so. I was only about sixteen or so when you went away, so unless you sneaked out for a bit I don't see how we could've met.' He laughed at that. That was in the days when he could laugh and before he became a bit of a nuisance and drove us all mad. 'No,' he said, 'I was joking, really, I knew you wouldn't remember because you were only weeks old when I first saw you.' I didn't know what to say. Here I was, thirty-odd years on, and talking to someone who wasn't family, who'd spent a lot of time with my dad.

According to Reggie, him and Ronnie had known

Henry for years, even though he was three or four years older than they were. Dad must have had a good head on him when it came to buying and selling, because he used to take the twins' brother Charlie out with him. The twins often went as well, but really I don't suppose they was much help because from what Mum said there wasn't a day's work in either of them.

All this was really before they got themselves into too bad trouble, so it's not like my dad was part of the Kray gang or anything like it. He was just doing what East Enders have always done, and that was sticking with his own. Among the people I came from, and them I've been involved with all my life, being 'at it' was a way of life. It was then and it's still the same today. Straight-goers, meaning people who work at a job every day and never step out of line, live in a different world from everybody I know. I mean, you can be friendly enough with them but that's as far as it goes. When it comes to a bit of business you never touch them because that trust isn't there.

I know my dad did his share of thieving and bits and pieces like everybody else, but as far as I know he never got done for violence or anything like that.

So what with them being friends Dad would often pop in to Vallance Road, and of course the Krays would come to Grandad's house for a cup of tea and sort out the gear they'd bought that day. That's where Reggie had seen me, laying in my cot – same as Marie when she'd been born because, as he said, Henry was full of it when his little girls were born, and wanted to show them off to everybody.

Going back to those first few years when I said I didn't remember my stepfather turning up – I really didn't. He was just there and I accepted him straight away. What sticks in my mind is that every Friday night on his way home from work as a carpenter, he'd bring in a big box of fruit and a bag of sweets. When Mum and him got married I've no idea. Perhaps they slipped off to the registry on their own, though it is in my head that it must have been the day when Mum picked me up from school and told me that she'd been to change my name and I was to be called Valerie Lewis from now on.

She must have told the headmistress because next day when the teacher was ticking off the attendance register she called out Lewis and nobody moved. She said it again and we all looked round at each other, and then she said, 'Valerie Smith, will you answer your name.' It never really worked because none of my little friends understood what it was all about.

Although I was as much in the dark as they were, I must've taken it seriously because I can remember saying to Mum, 'Nobody won't stop calling me Smith,' and she'd say, 'Well, you've just got to tell them that's not your name any more.' But I didn't.

I suppose what was in my mum's mind was that she wanted a complete family. She'd changed her name so I can only think she didn't want us to be different from her and her new husband. I think she was wrong because in a way it was wiping out the memory of a good man. Might have been different if he was a drunk who knocked her about, then you could understand it. On the other hand they say don't criticize someone until you've walked in their shoes, and what I say I would or wouldn't have done today doesn't take on board what she went through then.

She'd lost one man she'd loved when she was really no more than a baby, then fallen in love with another man and wanted everything to be just right. Even if that meant not allowing my sister and me to visit my real dad's family. We still went, though, just learned not to mention it indoors.

Later on Denise was born, followed by Debbie, and as far as everyone was concerned we were just one family. Me and Marie as blonde as you like and the other two dark-haired, and I don't remember either of them questioning why we were so different. In fact they never knew that we were half-sisters until they were in their very early teens, and they should never have found out how they did.

I'd met Lenny by then and I've got to say he wasn't always the man that he eventually grew into. We weren't married then and Lenny was round our house when a bit of a row blew up between my younger sisters and me. Nothing really, can't even remember what it was over. Bit of name calling, a few doors slammed, so I thought it best if we cleared off out of it. But Lenny, being Lenny, always had to have the last word, so as I've pulled the front door shut he's bent down and shouted through the letterbox, 'You two can fuck off 'cos you ain't even Val's real sisters.'

Sometimes I never really knew what was going on inside his head. I don't think he meant it cruel or spiteful – he was just stating fact as far as he was concerned – but he was right out of order. I needn't go into all the ins and outs that came afterwards, and only Debbie and Denise could tell you how it affected them. But without excusing Lenny, really our mum should've sat those girls down years before and told them how it was. Either way I don't think they ever forgave Lenny for that day's work.

Having said a lot about my real dad who I never knew, I've got to say that my stepfather, and that's a word I never used, was a dad in every sense. It can't be easy taking on a ready-made family when you're only in your late twenties, but he did and I don't think I ever heard him complain.

It splits your head in two when you think too hard about real fathers and any other kind. You want to know about the one that gave you life, if you like, because you're part of him and that makes you what you are. But that shouldn't take anything away from the 'father' that looked after you from a baby. Where mine's concerned, I've got to say I love him and give him all respect for what he did.

What made my life so nice until I met Lenny was that it was just about as ordinary as you could get. I don't have to look any further than Lenny's early years to see that what makes sad but interesting reading for other people was a nightmare for him that not only changed his life but what went on inside his head for ever. So as far as my early days are concerned I can't get anywhere near what was so readable in his book – and I thank God for that.

That I was nearly taken away by an old man and possibly murdered when I was about five didn't really have any lasting effect. At least not until I was an adult and reading about that sort of thing in the papers and thinking how easy it happens no matter how parents warn their kids.

I don't even know what I was doing outside the school gates at that age, but there I was scuffing my red shoes against the wall when this man stopped and said, 'Hello, Blondie.' I thought that was funny so I said hello back. Then he opened his coat and tucked into his waistcoat was a tiny black puppy. The oldest trick in the book. More babies must have been lured away by fluffy animals or the promise of one than anything else, and I was no different.

What he said was could I show him a shop where he

could get a box to put this puppy in. There was a sweet shop just round the corner so when I told him that, he said to me that if I'd take him there he'd get me some sweets and let me hold the puppy, but I had to hold his hand in case I left him behind.

Everything that I'd ever been told by my mother went right out the window and I grabbed his hand and set off. Then I heard screaming from the playground – and I mean really high-pitched screaming. It was Marie, my older sister, and she was running along inside the chain-link fence telling me to run away. Her screaming frightened me so I let go and ran back to the gate crying, then everything got all jumbled up as teachers ran out, the police were called and Mum was brought from where she worked just down the road. I don't remember what happened after that, apart from everybody keep asking me, Why had I done it? Why had I gone with him? The answer to me was simple. I was going to get sweets and pat that little dog – what better reason?

On one hand today I can laugh about how naive I was, but on the other it makes me feel sick inside about what might have happened to me – but more, that it's happened to thousands of little kids over the years. Why do people go on and on about how the streets were safer in those days? Because they weren't.

Something else that happened when I was a bit older wasn't all that serious, but it's stuck in my head ever since. Like a lot of kids I was always fascinated by fire. I'd nick matches and sit on the wall outside lighting them one by one.

One time when I was sitting in front of the coal fire indoors I threw one of my shoes on the fire and sat and watched it flare up. When I'd got over the smack round the ear my mum gave me when she saw what I'd done, I couldn't for the life of me explain why I'd done it.

The thing I'm talking about has to do with me being a Catholic, though to be honest the name is only something to say or put down on forms in the space that says Religion. Other than that it didn't really affect my life apart from going to Sunday school and to the main church on and off up until I was in my teens.

I've always believed in God and in a lot of ways that helped me and Lenny in those last months of his life. But I've never taken it any further than that. I'd never say anything about any religion people believe in, because it's nice if they have something like that in their lives. But if I remember rightly, all that Catholic stuff that was drummed into me was more about frightening you to death than about love and all that.

It's a long time ago but I can remember being told that I was full of sin and my soul, whatever that was, was all black because of all the bad things I'd got up to. God could see everything and more than once I was conscious of looking over my shoulder when I was doing something I shouldn't.

Anyway, my friend and me went into our local church for something to do. I don't think I've been in a Catholic one since I met Lenny, but I'm told that nowadays they've got little electric candles in a box and when you put your money in one lights up. It's a nice idea because you're doing it to remember someone you've lost or is ill or whatever. Back then, all those years ago, it was the real thing and you lit a proper candle with a taper. Well, that drew me like a moth, but instead of lighting a candle Valerie thinks it would be more fun to set light to a pile of prayer books. They must have been as dry as bones because they flared up and the two of us couldn't put out the flames. Somebody shouted and we both legged it up the aisle and ran home.

Later when we were just sitting down to have our tea

there was a knocking on the door and Mum brought the priest through and he had a face on him like a smacked arse. I shit myself but tried not to let it show.

He looked like a big black crow and he towered over me and said, 'Valerie Lewis, you were seen setting fire to the House of God.'

I crossed my fingers under the tablecloth, looked him straight in the eye and said, 'No, it wasn't me because I've been over the park all day.'

He asked me again about half a dozen times and each time I swore it wasn't me. Then him and Mum went into the kitchen and when they came back I was told to get my coat on and follow him. So I did, all the way round to the church, with Mum trailing behind. I thought about having a little cry because that usually worked when I was in trouble, but I had a feeling it would be a waste of time, so just bit my lip as we marched along.

When we got to the church he let me go in first, then kept pushing me all the way down the aisle that I'd run up a few hours before. He said, 'Right, stand by the altar, look up and don't look away.' I looked up and there was the Virgin Mary staring down at me. I don't know how long he kept me standing there, but it seemed like ages before he said, 'I'm asking again – did you burn the prayer books and cloth?'

I didn't even think about it, just said, 'No, I didn't. I was over the park,' and that was that.

He never said sorry to me, but he said to Mum that he was sorry, a mistake must have been made because – and said in a loud voice, 'No child would risk the fires of hell by lying in front of the Virgin.'

I thought, 'Well, this one just has,' but put a look on my face that said I was the victim, and it was never spoken about again. I know I seemed to have all the bottle in the world to say what I did in that situation, but it did bother me inside. Even today I can't pass that church without feeling guilty and looking the other way.

There's no doubt about it, I was a right tomboy most of my early life. I could run faster than most boys we used to knock about with, and some of them couldn't touch me when it came to swimming either. We were always round the local baths because there wasn't much else to do if you didn't have a lot of pocket money, and what with there being four of us girls we didn't see too much of that.

We got our sweets and money for pictures and all that, but I don't suppose Dad was earning fortunes, so there wasn't much spare for us to waste. To get in the baths was only coppers, so we all ended up there when we had nothing to do.

And that's when I first met Lenny. Well, not met as to speak to him, but first saw him. I don't think I was all that impressed, come to think of it. One of the boys in our group was Tony McLean, and he lived just round the corner from me. Nice boy – not boyfriend or anything like that, because we were only about twelve or thirteen, and unlike today it would be a few years before any of us looked at the opposite sex as anything other than a friend.

Funny thing is, though Tony was Lenny's cousin, he never said anything about him, though as I found out years later, the two of them were up to all sorts even at that age – most of it on the other side of the law.

I couldn't help noticing Lenny at the baths that first time because he was big for his age, and like he would do for the rest of his life, he was giving it the big 'un so all the other kids would look at him.

One of the rules was that nobody was allowed to jump in the water in case somebody got hurt. So who was taking a long run and chucking himself in with a big splash? Yes, Lenny. I mean I wasn't bothered but he never even looked at me, and when we spoke about it years later he didn't have a clue what I was talking about. He must've had a bit of a name then because he was surrounded by a mob of kids of his own age, and he seemed to be number one. And if he wasn't, I'm pretty sure he thought he was. Come to think of it, Tony didn't even say, 'That's my cousin over there,' or go up and speak to him, so perhaps they'd had a fall-out at that time. Either way I wouldn't see him again for about four years.

From then until that day that happened, my life carried on in its usual ordinary way. I studied hard at school, took the usual exams and got good results, but I often ask myself why I'd bothered. There just didn't seem to be many options for girls back then. That was in the mid-sixties and everything was happening. Miniskirts, beehive hairstyles, Mary Quant, the Beatles – swinging Britain: really exciting times, people are always saying, though it all sounds more exciting reading about it in books and magazines now than it ever felt back then. I mean it was different from the years before, but somehow it bypassed all us working-class kids.

It makes me laugh when some old hippy comes out with, 'If you remember the sixties you wasn't there and it wasn't happening.' Well, I was there and most of the time stuck in one boring job after another. I wasn't stupid by a long way, but around the East End the best on offer was either secretary – and that was stretching your ambitions, more like pool typist/tea maker – or some sort of factory job in the rag trade. I tried them all. Kids today aim high and most of the time they get there, and even if they don't, falling short of their ambition's still a hundred times higher than we could ever dream about.

In my day I think air hostess was the job most young

girls dreamed of. Even before we left school me and my mates would talk about it and try and imagine what it would be like to be one of those posh-looking girls wearing a smart uniform, travelling all over the world, then marrying a pilot.

That thought came back to me more than once when I was staring out of the window of a little grey office in Old Street. Trainee typist banging out the quick brown fox jumped over the lazy dog a million times a day whenever things were quiet. Drove me round the bend. I was pleased when I got the sack for messing about.

From there I went to a coat factory up Bethnal Green Road and spent all day machining buttonholes and hems – just as boring but at least there was a load of other girls to have a laugh with. I was there for a good while before they sacked me, again for messing about. I don't want to sound flash but I think the problem with me was that I was too intelligent for the rubbish jobs I was doing, yet there wasn't really much better on offer. So as soon as I got bored with a job, which was in about five minutes, I would do something stupid because I didn't know what to do next to have a laugh and brighten the place up. Then I was on my way again.

Next was a bag shop in an arcade up Liverpool Street, but that didn't last long. That job was one of the few I didn't get the sack from, because I left when Mum got me fixed up at another clothes place where she'd always worked – the one round the corner from my infant school. And that's where I stayed for years until I got the sack for, guess what? Messing about, but by then I was married and never worked again.

After Mum and Dad had got married we'd lived in a few places, though never really far from where we'd started. The furthest we went was to the Kingsmead Estate on Hackney Marshes, but by the time I was in my mid-teens we were back in Hoxton, and though I didn't know it, living not far from the man who I'd eventually spend thirty years of my life with.

As you're growing up you lose touch with some friends, make new ones, lose touch then meet the old ones again, and it goes round like that. So because I hadn't seen Tony McLean for a few years didn't mean anything, really. I'd heard he'd been getting into bits and pieces of trouble, but then so were half the young fellas we knew so I never gave it much thought.

Nowadays kids seem to go out every night of the week, but then it was either Friday or Saturday night that was something to look forward to. I don't know if there was such a phrase as 'on the pull' as they call it now, and I don't think I was ever conscious of going out with the intention of meeting boys, but it's only natural at that age that the idea's in the back of your head, so we all made a special effort at the weekend when it came to dressing up for a night out.

My wages weren't all that, but for the sake of a pound a week in some shop up Roman Road, you could get a complete outfit for less than seven pounds. This particular Saturday I'd been up the Roman and picked out a lovely beige suit, then gone next door and bought, on the drip, red shoes, red handbag to go with it. Handbag? Seems funny now even to me, but girls then couldn't go anywhere without clutching a bag that matched their outfit.

Our meeting place for wherever we were going to any weekend was the Standard in Kingsland Road. My local, if you like, though I didn't drink very much and only used the place while we made up our minds where to go.

My friend Carol was sitting in the corner when I walked in. She'd already got me a Babycham so I didn't have to go up to the bar, though I noticed there was a new barman. I found out later he wasn't working there, just helping out because he was a mate of Sid the guv'nor's son. He was making himself busy, and I don't mean with serving drinks. He had a towel draped over his shoulder like he'd been in the business for years, but he never stood still for a minute. He was talking to this one and that one, balancing glasses on his arm and every now and then he'd burst into an Elvis song.

There was something familiar about how he was giving it the big 'un but I couldn't place it so turned my back on him and talked girl stuff with Carol. I showed off my new outfit and she sat there balancing her new beehive hairdo. It must have been two foot high and so hard with lacquer you could've knocked a nail in with it. My hair was long and natural because that's how I liked it, but I said hers was lovely – and it was for those days when hair like that was all the rage.

While we were chatting she kept looking over my shoulder and giggling. In the end I said to her, 'What is the matter with you, Carol?' and she said, 'Don't look round, but I think you've got an admirer.'

Course I looked round straight away and the fella behind the bar was giving me the eye. I said, 'You silly cow, it's you he's after,' but she said, 'No, he keeps winking at me and nodding his head at you.' I felt myself colouring up. I mean I'd been out with boys before but being looked over like that was embarrassing, though, if I admitted it, a bit flattering because he was handsome-looking.

I gave Carol some money for a couple of drinks, save me making a show of myself going to the bar, and when she came back she said, 'I know who he is, it's Lenny McLean – bit of a tearaway from what I've heard.' Then she said, 'I'm going for a wee, you coming?'

I said, 'No, I'm all right, I'll mind your coat,' so she took it off and ten seconds later this Lenny was beside me saying, ''Allo, darling, are you on your own?'

I said, 'You know I'm not. My mate's in the ladies.' From then until Carol came back he tried his best to get me to ditch her and go up West with him, but I wouldn't have none of it.

Playing hard to get was what it was all about then – so to get rid of him without slamming the door completely shut, I agreed to his suggestion that we meet up the following Saturday. I could always go somewhere else next weekend if I changed my mind between now and then.

According to Lenny years later, it seems I made a bigger impression on him than he did on me. He counted the hours all week leading up to that Saturday, and it would be nice to say the same thing, but I can't. Perhaps boys fall into what they think of as love a lot quicker than girls, and let's face it he only talked to me for about five minutes – but for me it was just another week sewing clothes. It wasn't even as if we'd made a proper date – it was just left like if I showed up in the Standard, we might go out somewhere together.

Thinking about it now, one half of me says if I'd known then what I was letting myself in for I'd have been a hundred miles away that next Saturday, then eventually married a plumber, a cab driver or a carpenter like my dad. But if I'm honest with myself, the other half of me says I made the right decision. It led to a life of ups and downs, good times and bad times, but one that I wouldn't have changed for the world.

— THREE —

I couldn't help giving Lenny a bit of thought that week because wherever I went it seemed like Carol had been there before me to tell people I was going out with Lenny McLean. I'm telling them all, 'No, I'm not – I hardly know him,' and they're sucking their breath in and shaking their heads like a garage bloke does just before he says you need a new engine because a bracket's rattling – and telling me some story or other that they'd heard about Lenny. He'd done prison time, he was always bashing people up, he was flash, a bully and his dad Jimmy McLean was a right so and so. I could believe the flash bit, but all the rest seemed a bit over the top from what I'd seen of him.

I'd better explain the Jimmy McLean remark. It would be nearly thirty years later before we found out that back then Jim Irwin, Lenny's stepfather, called himself McLean outside the house. Why I don't know, perhaps he used it as an alias, because he was a right dodgy character.

Anyway, it's pretty obvious that I turned up, but I might not have if my friend Carol hadn't had a cold so didn't want to go out – leaving me on my own. I told myself I'd meet him, but if he showed off I'd have one drink then tell him I had to sit with my gran, who was ill, then leave and go home.

My kids think nothing of going out clubbing at ten

o'clock at night, but when I was seventeen you was thinking about going to bed at that time. So at seven o'clock I pushed open the door of the Standard, and though I didn't know it then, stepped into a new life for myself.

I had to give him ten out of ten for effort because I hardly recognized him. He had a suit on (his brother's, as it happens, I found out later), his hair was all slicked down and his shoes were gleaming. I saw him before he saw me, and I don't know what he was thinking but he seemed miles away. Then, as he looked towards the door, his face broke out into a big smile that lit his eyes up. That did it for me, and, silly cow that I am, my stomach flipped over and I started to fall in love with him from that moment on.

After we had a couple of drinks and Lenny suggested we went up Tottenham Court Road to the Tottenham Royal, I thought I'd better say what I was thinking before any sort of relationship we might get going got off the ground. I said, 'I've been hearing a lot of stories about you.'

Even then he used to pull his mouth down and furrow his eyebrows. 'Nah,' he said. 'What? That I'm good-looking and sing like Elvis?' But he knew what I really meant.

'People say that you're always fighting and beating fellas up.'

This time he didn't make a crack, but looked serious. 'I don't care what people say, but listen, Valerie. On my mother's life I never have a go at no one unless they ask me for it.' And funnily enough, looking into those brown eyes, flecked with green, I believed him.

After that first night we started seeing each other two or three times a week. Nothing serious really, just keeping each other company – going to the pictures, dancing or to local pubs. I don't think we talked about anything of much sense at all. He was two years older than me and worked at the Guildhall, though he didn't even say whether he was a lecturer or a sweeper-up, though if I'd been asked to guess, it wouldn't have been hard.

Seems odd now that we didn't pick each other's brains about what our lives were like when we weren't together, but it didn't seem important when we were just out having a laugh. And that's what you got with Lenny. He was a complete fool. Not so much telling jokes, more like doing impressions of film stars, little tricks or just falling over in a funny way – like doing a handstand on a garden wall, then deliberately falling arse over head. Silly boys' stuff, but you couldn't help laughing.

He never lost that way about him, and it's that side that I'll remember. Not the big tough guy, not the unbeatable fighter that made his name, not the actor or any of that stuff, but his boyish sense of humour that was still making me laugh through my tears days before he died.

I told my sister Marie that I was seeing a boy, but I never mentioned it to Mum, for no other reason than, I suppose, young girls like to keep little secrets – make whatever they are a bit more special. Then one morning she said, 'Your dad says he saw you with a man up Kingsland Road. You were holding his hand. Who is he, then?'

I just said, 'Oh, him, he's just a friend I see sometimes,' and let it go at that. About a fortnight later I asked her if it would be all right if Lenny stayed the night because we were going to a party and wouldn't get home until about two o'clock.

She made a face, saying, 'But we've never met him and don't know nothing about him.'

As quick as you like I said, 'He works in the Guildhall,' and straight away Mum had him marked down as somebody in a suit and on the way up in the world, so everything was OK.

Come that Saturday night I managed to bribe my younger sisters to move out of their bedroom and sleep on the floor of mine and Marie's, so as Lenny could have their room, so it was all above board, if you know what I mean.

Next morning I overslept and by the time I walked into our living room Lenny was already up. Dad was sitting bolt upright on the edge of his armchair. Mum was screwing a tea towel into knots and her lips had disappeared altogether, while Lenny was lying across the settee like he'd lived there for years. As I sat down he said to me, 'Morning, babe. You look beautiful,' then turned back to Dad and said, 'Like I was saying, I got sent down and the poxy manager got away with a suspended.' Nobody moved a muscle as he carried on. 'Piece of piss, though – did it standing on my head. Ever done any yourself, Len? No? Well, let me tell you, if you can have a fight there ain't nothing to worry about. Val's probably told you already that I'm a bit lively with me hands – and there was this time when one of the warders says to me . . .'

I couldn't believe what I was hearing. Valerie hadn't said anything to her mum and dad because Valerie had never heard any of this sort of talk before. I mumbled something, shot out of the door and sat on the stairs with my fingers in my ears and humming at the same time to drown out the sound of Lenny's voice. Every time I took them out to check, he was still going on about the same thing. I dashed upstairs, dragged a brush through my hair, smudged my mouth with lipstick and flew down again. Lenny was just offering to get Dad a nice line in men's coats – 'If you know what I mean, Len.'

I grabbed him by the arm, saying, 'We said we'd meet

Carol and her boyfriend at eleven, we're going to be late.' As I'm pulling him out of the chair he's saying, 'You sure? I don't remember.' I pushed him out of the front door as Mum pulled me back inside, screaming in a whisper, 'You, my girl, can get rid of him and get yourself back here in ten minutes or I'll swing for you,' and she slammed the door.

As I stood at the gate my eyes just filled up with tears. Lenny said, 'What's the matter, Val?' and really did look as though he didn't have a clue.

'You're what's up. You and all those lies you just told my parents.'

'Lies, babe? Every word was the truth – honest,' as though that made all the difference.

'Well, you might have told me you'd been in Borstal and all the other stuff before you told them.'

And he looked at me like I was gone out, saying, 'Well, you never asked, did you?' I think the penny dropped then because he said, 'Come over a bit strong, did I? Well, I was nervous and when I get like that my mouth won't stop flapping.'

I hated having to say what I had to, but I said it anyway. 'I like you a lot, Lenny, but my mum's indoors waiting to tear my head off because of you. And I know just what she's going to say, so I'll say it first. I think we should call it a day.'

He looked like I'd slapped him and said, 'Hold up. Meet me later and I'll tell you everything you need to know about me, then make up your mind.'

But I knew I couldn't fight my mum so I just said, 'Sorry, Lenny, it's for the best,' and went indoors forcing myself not to look back at him standing there.

Mum was on me like a ton of bricks. 'What the bloody hell do you think you're playing at bringing somebody like that into my house?'

All I wanted to do was go upstairs and bury my head under a pillow, but I couldn't help myself arguing back. 'What do you mean, somebody like that? He's just ordinary and he's a nice person when you get to know him.'

She came back at me with, 'Oh yes? It didn't sound like it to me. He's not for you and I don't want my daughter going out with a man that's been in Borstal, so don't ever let me hear that you've been seeing him again – understand?' I didn't answer, just walked out slamming the door without listening to what else she was shouting after me. Dad never really said much at all – typical man, left it to Mum who said enough for both of them. But I did notice that a couple of times when I said I was going round the Standard to see a friend, Dad just happened to pop in for cigarettes, crisps or something.

After a while the fuss died down and we all went back to normal. Well, the rest of the family seemed to, and on the outside it must have appeared that I accepted the way things were, but inside I really missed Lenny and thought that he might have at least made the effort to see me in secret. But it was like he had disappeared – apart from the couple of times I saw him sitting on the wall of the Guildhall, and as I was on a bus I couldn't do much about it.

I lost count of the times I wished that we had got to know each other a bit better before he met my family. If I'd known about what he'd got up to and about being sent away and all that, it wouldn't have bothered me, but at least I could have warned him about what my parents were like and that they wouldn't want to hear all that talk.

But it always comes back to the same thing – what was done was done and I couldn't change it so I just had to carry on with my life, but it left a gap with him not being around. Don't get me wrong, I wasn't sitting in my room with the curtains pulled shut moping or nothing, but I did have this sort of empty feeling for ages. I mean fellas fall in love with every girl they meet, or they think they do, so I had this mental picture of Lenny up West with some girl on his arm, without a second's thought for me.

Girls are different, and I was no exception. We can like somebody a lot but when we admit to being in love like I did, it's something that comes from right inside and not said lightly.

I was seventeen so it's obvious I'd been on dates with boys, but that was kids' stuff. Usually with a crowd of other friends having a bit of laugh – a bit of fun. At the most a quick kiss on the doorstep and that was that. I honestly never felt or said I loved any of them, but Lenny was different. Why, I don't think I could've explained, but in the short time we'd known each other I'd seen something that he kept hidden from most people. They saw this big toughie and, I suppose, a bit of a cocky fella, but I saw somebody who was funny and gentle and, believe it or not, somebody who was quite shy and sensitive – though that was the last thing he'd ever want said about him.

Still, because of my family I'd been the one to tell him it was all over, so I had to live with that.

Ages after, I was having a drink with Carol, and a girl she knew but I didn't came and sat with us. Carol introduced us then said to this friend, 'I see your brother up the market the other day an' he was in a bit of a mess. Somebody run him over?'

She said, 'No, but it looked like it with his face all knocked about. What happened was, you know what he's like with all those Mod clothes he wears? Well, he was coming past the White Swan when three Rockers set about him for nothing. I mean really kicked the shit out of him. Lucky, though, some bloke jumped out of a Mini, run over and laid into the three of them. Young Jimmy said he'd never seen nothing like it – smashed all of them up then drove him home. Turns out the fella was Lorraine McLean's brother.'

I hadn't really been listening properly because I didn't know who she was talking about, but as soon as she said McLean my stomach turned right over. Course, then I wanted to know all the details about what this fella had done, though I didn't say I knew him. But there wasn't much else to say, apart from this girl adding that he was good-looking and she wouldn't mind a date with him – and that gave me a little pang of jealousy – silly cow.

Months had gone by without a word about him, then I heard that story and two nights later somebody touched me on the shoulder when I was in the pub, and a familiar gruff voice said, 'All right, babe? Remember me?' It was Lenny and I wanted to hug him there and then but instead of that, being a girl, I was a little bit cool. I didn't want to be like that but I couldn't help it.

Course he picked that up straight away and thought I had the hump with him. So he pulled a chair round, sat down and said, 'Listen, Val. I've missed you every single day since you told me to clear off.' It wasn't like that at all but I let it pass. 'But if you just let me explain a few things you'll see I ain't such a bad fella.' As he's said that he put both his hands over mine and I couldn't help seeing his knuckles all broken up. I said, 'Been fighting again?' because I knew he had the week before, and he pulled them back saying, 'Fighting? Me? Nah. That was getting a piano out of a block of flats.' He should've been proud that he helped that boy out, but instead told a white lie in case I thought less of him for having a punch-up.

This was a Saturday night and though Dad had given

up sticking his head in the bar to check I was behaving, I couldn't be sure he wouldn't. So I said to Lenny, 'If you've got something to say meet me over the park – ' Victoria Park – 'about eleven tomorrow, but we better not be seen together tonight.'

He said, 'That's a shame because I wanna stay with you, but to be honest I only slipped in to see Sid for two minutes. I've got a bit of business up West later so I can't stop anyway,' and off he went with that big grin on his face.

It was years before I found out that his bit of business, as he put it, was chucking something through the windows of high-class shops and stealing suits and coats. If I'd known right then what he was up to I think I would've been horrified. As it was, much later when he did tell me I was so used to his ups and downs it didn't mean a thing.

That night I laid in bed and thought, 'Unless he tells me he's a murderer or something, I don't care what else he's done, I'm not going to lose him again.'

When we talked about that time a long time after, like you do, it turned out he'd laid in bed practising what he was going to say to me the next day because, as he put it, it was so important to him that he should convince me he was worth going out with. When I told him what had been going through my head he said, 'Fuck me, Val. I wish I'd known – I never got a wink of sleep that night.'

Why I'd said we shouldn't see each other again had never been about whether I liked him or loved him. It was all about going against my parents. Nowadays kids seem to do what they like, and if their parents don't approve – well, that's just tough. But then, it didn't matter if you were eight or eighteen, you did what you were told and never really considered arguing back. And there was never any question of saying, 'Well, I'll move out and into a flat.' One, you couldn't afford it then, and two, it just never happened.

Now, by arranging to meet Lenny I knew I was going to come up against my mum, but I'd cross that bridge when the time came.

Nothing could have prepared me for what Lenny poured out to me that Sunday. In my mind was the thought that he'd broken one window too many, larking about like kids do, and been sent to approved school for a month. Wasn't all that unusual around where I lived. He'd square up his past to me – it wouldn't be much. I'd then explain it to Mum and we'd all move on. Wasn't quite like that, though.

It was a lovely day and by eleven it was really hot. He was waiting for me as I walked towards the fountain and, bless him, he was holding a little bunch of flowers and most of them were dying in the heat. Knowing young blokes, I couldn't believe he'd had the nerve to stand in the middle of the park holding flowers. On the other hand I didn't know hardly anything about the reputation he had that would've stopped any likely lads taking the piss.

We walked over to a bench and sat down. The first thing he said to me was, 'Mum and Dad OK?' As if he cared, but he was being polite.

I said, 'They don't know I'm here, but yes they're both fine.'

'Your dad's a sound geezer. Funny thing us both having the same name, s'pose that's why we got on like a house on fire before all that . . . Y'know.'

That made me smile inside, and I don't know why I said what I did because I never thought of him like that but I came out with: 'He's not my real dad, you know – he's my stepfather.' I couldn't believe Lenny's reaction.

'You're joking, ain't ya? You sure?' I didn't need to

answer that. 'What is he, all front? Bastard behind his front door?'

I was so shocked – Lenny was so, I don't know really, angry? Taken aback?

He'd stood up and was walking backwards and forwards. Upset me a bit because I didn't know what he was getting at. I told him that my dad – wish I'd never said 'step' – was a really nice man and always had been – bit strict sometimes, but then that was dads for you. As usual my eyes had filled up by then and Lenny crouched down in front of me, held my hands saying, 'Oh, babe, I'm sorry. I shouldn't have said that – course he's a lovely man. It's just my big mouth. Only I've got a stepfather as well and see this –' and he pulled his trouser leg up. 'Look at my knee. And see that – see this.' And as he's talking he's touching and pointing at different scars on his face and leg. 'That's what stepfather means to me. A beast – a bully – somebody who don't deserve to live.'

I still didn't know why he was so upset, but that was half eleven, and by half five he'd made me realize I knew nothing about life at all, and all I wanted to do was cuddle this big lump of a young man who'd suffered the sort of things I couldn't even imagine.

I could remember screaming at my mum when I was a kid that I hated her and was going to run away after she'd slapped the back of my legs, even though I deserved it. The sting lasted twenty seconds and I'd cry for twenty minutes more – hurt pride more than anything. But that was as far as any violence, if you can call it that, went in all the years of my growing up. Dad never laid a hand on any of my sisters, or me, so what I was listening to was right outside my experience.

I didn't get the whole picture, there was more to come as time went on, but it's that particular day and what I learned that has always stuck in my mind. It just went on and on.

Thirty-five years later I can still hear him, 'See, I was different from you, Val. I knew my real dad. He used to take me out, kick a ball around with me on the grass outside the flats. Not just me, my brothers and sisters, Linda, Lorraine, Barry an' little Raymond in his pram.'

I said to Lenny, 'I thought your little brother was called Kruger.'

And he burst out laughing. 'Fuck me, no, Val. Mum and Dad wouldn't have hung a name like that on the poor little sod. No, it was a nickname 'cos as a baby he looked like an old German bloke that lived in the flats.'

That broke his mood for a minute, but he carried on after a bit. 'Sometimes it's hard to think that my young life was so good. We'd get sweets and cuddles and Mum was happy, and it seemed like we were always laughing. Then my dad, that smashing man, was dead and I didn't even know what it meant. You know what? I used to hide in the cupboard and cry my eyes out nearly every day because I thought I was too big for all that. I wasn't even five and I had pain inside me that somebody ten times older shouldn't have to feel. If I saw a man in the street with one of them trilby hats on, I'd run after him and look up into his face. Don't laugh, Val – I must've made myself a right nuisance until I got the idea he was gone for good. I suppose what came after was worse because I'd known good times. Perhaps I could've taken it better if I didn't know any different.'

He told me all about his mum and about Jim Irwin turning up and how he resented him from day one, and even more once they got married. How he hated the fact that this man even called himself Dad. So what he told me after wasn't a surprise, really. Shouldn't have happened, but if somebody's a bully they're not going to be happy with some kid pulling his face every time he looks at you. Sounds like I'm making excuses for him, but I couldn't do that. No baby should ever get hurt like Lenny did, and if I'd been his mum I'd have stuck a knife in Jim Irwin. I can say that because I know if anybody harmed my Jamie or Kelly even now, I'd swing for them.

I think Lenny started to think he was saying too much because he suggested we went and got some hot dogs off a stall by the gates. I knew my Sunday roast was in the dustbin by then, so I was up for that. One was enough for me; Lenny had four.

We wandered back to the bench and he started all over again. 'Can you imagine any man who's a proper man hiding in a cupboard until a kid puts his hand on the biscuit tin because he thinks no one's there, then jumping out and punching him in the back of the head? Well, that was my stepdad. He belted and punched all of us, Mum and the girls – didn't make no difference to 'im. But for some reason he picked me out for the worst treatment and almost every day I got more'n my share of his feet an' knuckles.

'Another time I was up on tiptoes looking over the balcony and shouting down to my mate Alfie. Next thing I'm flying over the edge. I'm in midair looking straight down on concrete twenty foot under my nose. I just screamed my head off. What he'd done was come out the front door, grabbed me by the arse and collar and swung me right over the top. Wasn't going to chuck me over, but I didn't know that. He terrified that little kid out of his skin because he woke him up with his shouting.'

In a funny sort of way Lenny wasn't even talking to me – he was talking to himself as though he'd never really put all those thoughts together in his head before. And though he was talking about himself he kept saying,

'That little kid. That baby. That boy never stood a chance,' like he was talking about someone else. And it wasn't as if he was telling me these things so I'd think he was a tough guy to have taken what he did – it was more like he was thinking out loud.

I didn't realize it then, and wouldn't for years, but I'd just spent hours listening to the reasons for why Lenny became the man he did. I think all his life he wanted to prove that his stepfather Jim Irwin was wrong. Dozens of times a week that little baby was punched to the ground and told he was thick, stupid and a waste of time who'd never come to anything. That beast and excuse for a man tried to knock every little bit of spirit out of him from the age of six, but he never managed it. As little as Lenny was, and remember he was up against a man in his early thirties who was big and strong, every time he was knocked down he got up again to take some more.

I don't really think that he was aware of the effect it had on him in later life. Though he said often enough that every punch he gave in every fight he had was for that boy he used to be, but I think it went much deeper than that. His insecurities, his many needs, his fearsome aggression against bullies, his loyalty to friends and his love for all of us – I could go on and on, but bottom line, every part of his make-up could be traced right back to what he went through as a child.

When the sun went in about six and he saw me shiver, he laughed and said, 'Blimey, Val, you never asked for all that lot, did you – an' I never meant to say half of it, and I never have to anybody else. So how did I do? Am I in with a chance of seeing you again?' He made it sound a bit jokey, but he was studying my face as he said it. What could I say? I just felt very protective towards him, and that was a laugh because he towered over me and he must have weighed a good twelve and a half stone – but behind all that I could see a very vulnerable person and I thought: 'If you look after me in your way, I'll look after you in mine.' So I just put my arm through his as we walked across the park towards where he'd parked his car.

Before he dropped me off, well round the corner from where I lived, he said, 'Val, you can tell from what I said I ain't no angel, but I'm not a bad person. Tell your mum that and she'll be OK.' Some hope.

As soon as I walked in the door she was off. 'Where have you been? What time do you call this? . . . Dinner's wasted . . . No consideration . . .'

I took all that, but I was thinking: 'I'm a woman now.' Not according to the law, because twenty-one was when you got the key to the door, as they said. But inside I was and I wasn't going to act like a child or be spoken to like one, so when Mum stopped for breath I came right out with it. 'I've been for a walk with Lenny McLean.'

Then she went right into one. 'I've told you . . . no good . . . bad lot . . . end in tears . . .'

I just cut her off, saying, 'Mum, you've only spoken to him for an hour. He's not a bad person,' thinking of what he'd said. 'And there's a lot of things you don't know and I don't want to talk about – but I'm going to see him if you like it or not.' Then we both made for the door to be the first one to slam it to show how each of us felt.

We barely spoke for the next few weeks and avoided each other as much as we could. She didn't ask me anything and I never volunteered anything, but slowly, like the time before, things got back to normal and I assumed that she accepted the way things were.

In the meantime Lenny couldn't wait to take me round to meet his mum. I wasn't keen at first – not to meet his mum, but that I'd have to come face to face with this horrible man he'd told me about. But I think Lenny understood that, so that night he said, 'Come on, let's go and see my mum and have a nice cup of tea.' He added, 'Irwin's away for a bit so it'll only be us.'

On the way he was saying that he'd told her all about me, how beautiful I was – how nice – how clever, and I'm thinking: 'I don't know what she'll make of me, because it would take some doing to live up to all these things.' As it turned out she was the loveliest person you could wish to meet. Funnily enough I could see a lot of myself in her, and now looking back through the old photographs, I can see we were very similar at the same age – both blonde with blue eyes. It was obvious she'd been very attractive when she was younger, but by the time I met her she looked tired and what she'd been through – though she didn't know I knew – was in her eyes, same as Lenny's. We chatted away like we'd known each other for ages, while Lenny hovered about, pleased that we were getting on.

It was a long time before I met Jim Irwin and that suited me, but it couldn't be avoided. He turned up unexpectedly one night when I was there, and I've got to say he was very polite to me. I don't know what I expected, really – him to punch me in the head or jump out of a cupboard at me? I did notice there was always a bit of an atmosphere when he was around.

Without knowing the background somebody else might not have picked up on it, but it struck me that before his mum Rose or Lenny spoke or answered something, they'd glance at each other like the two of them had some sort of secret. I might have read too much into it but I don't think so.

It was Lenny's suggestion after we'd been in the Standard for a couple of hours one day that he should meet Mum and Dad again. As he said, 'They can't go on for ever pretending I don't exist, and anyway I should think they want to meet me but don't like to say.' He was so right about some things, but that didn't mean he couldn't be wrong sometimes. He said, 'Look, babe, I'll get a bit of Chinese to break the ice and I promise to say nothing except, "Hello, Mrs Lewis . . . Thank you, Mrs Lewis . . ." On my life.'

It had been a good few weeks so I thought, 'Why not?' Nothing had been said for ages and like he said, the sooner we all got together the better.

I suppose it was a bit too much to hope that everything could be put right over a portion of Bombay duck, and I almost changed my mind when we drew up outside with the exhaust blowing like an aeroplane, and I saw the curtains move.

As I put the key in the door it went flying open on its own, Mum's arm came out, grabbed me by the collar and pulled me inside. I felt the seam of my coat go and the heel broke off my shoe – that's how hard she got hold of me – then she's screaming at Lenny, 'Get away from here. Keep away from my girl – you're no good.'

I'm behind her looking out and Lenny just stood there with his mouth open. It's funny now, though it wasn't then. Lenny held up these two bags of food and said, 'But I've got us all some Chinese,' as if this made all the difference in the world. It didn't.

Mum said, 'You eat it, and I hope it chokes you,' and unlike her added, 'Now bugger off.'

That was the first but not the last time I saw Lenny change from the person I knew into someone I didn't. He went white round the mouth and seemed to double in size as he said, 'An' fuck you, an' all,' and threw both bags at Mum. They burst open and we both got covered – walls as well. Dad rushed out shouting, 'What's going on? What's going on?' and shoved Lenny away. Next thing Lenny's punched him twice in the chest to keep him off. Not hard enough to really hurt him, but it didn't matter, it was just tearing me apart that the two people I loved were having a fight. As Mum went to help Dad, Lenny backed away, then picked up two of Mum's flowerpots and threw them straight through the window.

That's when the police arrived. It wasn't my family that called them, but the five of them looked as though they were ready for trouble. Three of them pulled out truncheons as they jumped out of the van. One of the others rushed at him, but quick as you like Lenny grabbed him by the arm, swung him round and got him in a neck lock. Talk about stalemate. All I could see was the top of this copper's head under Len's arm, and he's shouting to the others, 'C'mon, then, try me if you want. But every time you whack me with them truncheons your mate 'ere's gonna get my knuckles on the top of his crust.' The coppers didn't know what to do and just stood there with their mouths open. Minutes seemed to tick by then Lenny said, 'What's it to be, then?' I didn't catch what one of them said but Len let go of the man, shoved him away and put his hands up in the air, like he was saying 'no trouble'. Straight away they surrounded him, pulled his hands down behind his back and slipped handcuffs on.

He called out, 'I'm sorry, Val – sorry – love you.' But Mum screamed at him, 'Don't you dare. I hope they send you back to prison where you belong,' shoved me back inside the door and pulled it shut with her outside. That way I couldn't hear what was said between her and the policeman. I flew into the kitchen for a cloth and the dustpan and brush, hoping that if I got the mess cleaned up before she came back in it wouldn't seem so serious. Then I remembered there was glass all over the front room, so knew there wasn't much chance of that.

Ten minutes later, when Mum was knocking on the front door to be let back in, I'd got most of the mess cleaned up, but she didn't even look. Just marched straight through to the kitchen. I couldn't run anywhere to avoid a row so I followed her.

Instead of kicking off in a blazing row she just sat at the table and looked at me for a bit, then she said, 'Y'know he's in prison by now, don't you?' I believed her. 'Those coppers are coming back in the morning. They want me to make a statement saying your precious boyfriend hurt your dad and smashed all the place up. One of them's told me he'll probably get three years.'

I felt sick, but I thought, 'If I don't try and stand up for him he's got no chance,' so I told her some of the things Lenny had told me that Sunday. Not all, but I let her see that because of his past he couldn't help going off when somebody had a go at him. She never said anything, just sniffed every now and then so I knew I wasn't getting anywhere. When I'd said as much as I could she just said, 'You better get yourself to bed, you've got work in the morning. Your dad and me have got things to talk about.'

Next day I even asked one of the girls I worked with what it was like visiting prison, because I knew her boyfriend was inside. That's how convinced I was that that's what I'd be doing for the next three years – because I intended sticking by him no matter what.

When I got home about five there was a new piece of glass in the window. Then sticking out of the wastebin in the kitchen was a bunch of flowers, and laying on the wooden draining board was a big card. I had a quick peek and carefully printed inside was just Thank You – nothing else, apart from the five one-pound notes that fell out.

Apart from hello, Mum didn't say a word, just kept

her lips all pursed up until I went out to meet Carol. Halfway down the road Lenny stepped out of a doorway in front of me, saying, ''Lo, Val. Give us a slap if you want to, but don't say you don't want to see me again.' He looked so miserable I couldn't do nothing else but give him a little cuddle, and that was us together for the next twenty-nine years. Should've been sixty, but I can't go all over that again.

As he told me, after he's been released from Old Street police station at half nine that morning, he'd got a warning but told no charges were being pressed against him. I could've run home there and then and given my mum and dad a kiss, but I didn't.

Once he was out Lenny had shot round to his Uncle Fred and that lovely man had given him five pounds for wallpaper, and on top of that had arranged for a builder to sort the window. The card and flowers was Lenny's idea, and he was so pleased with himself I didn't have the heart to tell him where they ended up.

Mum never, ever mentioned that business again, but she never forgave him either. Not for that day's work or for getting involved with her daughter – not ever. Hurt me a lot over the years, but I couldn't force them to like him.

Like I said before, most of the time Lenny was just full of fun and silliness. But then something would set him off and he became a different person. The first time this happened when I was with him frightened me to death. Not for myself, but at the violence in him.

We were round the pub and we had a row. What started it I don't even remember, but it was one of those silly things young people take all serious, with the result that he said, 'Fuck this, I'm taking you home if you're going to be in a mood.' I've said, 'Suits me,' and we banged out of the bar. He did take me home but instead of walking beside me he took off in front, leaving me traipsing well behind him.

As he turned the corner two young fellas came up behind me. As one of them said, 'Hello, Blondie, all on your own?' I jumped, but when I turned round I vaguely recognized one of them so knew they weren't out to attack me or nothing.

I said, 'I'm with my boyfriend, actually, not that you'd guess.'

They laughed and said, 'That's a shame – nice girl like you.'

With that a blur came past me and before my eyes these two fellas were knocked arse over head both at the same time, and Lenny's beside me, screaming, 'I'll give you chattin' up young gels in the street, you bastards.' But they were up and running. Afterwards I tried to explain they hadn't said anything out of order, but he wouldn't have it, just kept saying, 'I know their game.'

I'd never seen such violence like that close up before. Wouldn't be the last, even though I didn't know it at the time. I couldn't get over the speed of how it happened. One minute he's a mile up the road, the next he's catching one with his left and the other with his right – all at the same time. So that was that.

A week later I'm in the Standard waiting for Lenny – late as usual – and these same two fellas came in. They saw me and came over. They said they were sorry if they'd upset me but hadn't meant any harm, and what was up with my boyfriend that he'd given them a beating for nothing. I never even got a chance to answer that question before they're both on the floor again. Lenny had come in the back door and thought they were chatting me up again. I was so embarrassed I just walked out and left him to it.

As time went on I slowly began to realize that fighting was a way of life for Lenny. If he was fronted up or somebody who didn't know what he could do took the piss, or shoved somebody smaller than themselves, he'd hit them fast then question what he'd done afterwards.

Sometimes I understood why he felt it necessary to put someone down who was out of order, but other times I didn't and I'd say to him, 'Why do you always have to hit out?' and he'd either laugh it off or say, 'I don't know, babe – it just happens.'

It took a long time before my parents accepted that Lenny and me were a couple. At first when he picked me up from home he'd toot his horn without getting out of the car. That went to knocking on the door but standing well back, to actually getting inside, but staying in the passage. My parents acknowledged him but never got into small talk.

It was the complete opposite when I went to his place, though to be fair to my parents I'd never showered his mum with Chinese or broken her window. She was always pleased to see me and treated me like I was one of the family. I don't know if Lenny had said anything to her, but nine times out of ten the conversation came round to babies, catalogue furniture and the price of curtains. Nothing direct, but I definitely got the feeling that she saw me as a future daughter-in-law, though to be honest I don't think she had a clue what my people thought of her Lenny, who she obviously loved very much, same as he did her. I just went along with her, thinking, 'Well, that's how old people are.' That's a laugh looking back, because she could only have been in her late thirties and that's pretty young from where I'm sitting now.

Not that he mentioned nothing to me, but I wouldn't

have been against marrying Lenny – but I was only seventeen and we both had a lot of living and a lot of growing up to do before then.

You know how it is when you buy something you've never seen before then you notice it all over the place? It was the same with this marriage thing. A passing thought and next thing Lenny wants to take me for a 'special night out'. At the sound of that I expected an Italian restaurant at least, but as usual we ended up in the Standard. Lenny was quieter than usual and kept fidgeting around. After a couple of drinks he dug into his pocket and put a little velvet ring box on the table in front of me and he said, 'What d'yer think, Val?' In my head I was already ten yards in front of him but I pretended I was a bit puzzled and gave him a 'What can this be?' look. He's beaming all over his face waiting for me to open it. It couldn't be anything else but a ring, but what surprised me was how beautiful it was. Gold with a tiny claw-set diamond.

Why I say surprised is because with Lenny big was what said it all, and that never really changed, all his life. When it was his birthday any small tasteful cards were shoved to one side, but if he got one of those two-foot-high cards, that was the one that had to go on the mantelpiece, and knock everything off when he touched it – and he'd do that all day whenever somebody came in.

I should think somebody pointed him in the right direction, because no way was this his choice. He must've tried it on his own finger because I could almost get two of mine in it, but I clenched my fingers tight against it and he thought it was a perfect fit. And as I'm looking at it he's trying to make sure I know it's expensive even though the stone is small. 'It ain't a snide, Val. Tommy says it's part of a carat, and that means it's real.'

I didn't care if he'd paid half a crown for it, it was a lovely thing, but I wasn't going to let him get away with anything so I said, 'I love it – nicest ring I've seen, but it's not even my birthday.'

For five seconds his face was a picture then the penny dropped and he laughed saying, 'You know what it's for.' I said, 'What?' and he said, 'You know, our whatsername.'

I'd grown up with ideas from the pictures. A marriage proposal was white suits, violins, the bloke on one knee and roses all over the place. But this was the East End and in his own way Lenny was doing his best and I didn't really want any more than that, so I said I'd marry him.

On the Monday I took the ring to a jeweller and had it made smaller – Lenny never, ever found out.

We started our engagement off with great plans. He reckoned he could make a bit of extras looking after a pub, whatever that meant, and I intended doing a bit of overtime at the factory. That way we should be able to put away as much as ten pounds a week between us, though that would mean cutting down on the pictures, nights out, cigarettes. My mate's wedding – with the dress, reception and all the trimmings – came to about nine hundred pounds, so we knew what we had to aim for.

We never got near it. My overtime never came off and Lenny drunk his wages from the pub – and a bit more. The little bits we did manage to put away got blown every few weeks when Lenny would say, 'Fuck this. We've got to have some fun out of life.'

So my white wedding with bridesmaids and a sit-down buffet afterwards went right out the window, and I was as much to blame as him. In the end we settled it by deciding to have a quiet do. Mum and Dad and my sisters were at the registry, and on Lenny's side his nanny

Campion, Uncle Fred and his mum Rose. I wasn't a bit surprised that Jim Irwin didn't show his face. Afterwards we went back to Mum's for a sandwich and a drink, then to finish off the day we all went to Rose's for a drink.

The only reasonably sensible thing to come out of it was the week after we got engaged I put our name down on a housing association list. A month before the wedding they offered us a tiny flat in George's Square, just off Hoxton Street market. Later on we'd have a move to the other end of the same street to a flat in Persil Street, but that first one was special because it's where we started out. It badly needed decorating, but as Lenny put it, 'Piece of piss – two minutes and it'll be a palace.' It was nice to know my bloke was a handyman.

The night before he made a start he said, 'I'm doing the toilet first off. I'll slip up the market and get a bit of gear and get stuck in. Any particular colour?'

I said, 'Not really – something bright. Anything's better than that brown.'

He was waiting outside the gates when I finished work – couldn't wait to show me what he'd done. Once we got inside the flat he made me stand with my eyes closed outside the toilet door, then as he flung it open he said, 'Right, you can look now, but don't touch, it's still wet.'

The whole place was blue – dark blue – and I mean everything. Walls, ceiling, door, door handle, light switch. The only thing he hadn't painted was the pan and the floor, and they had so many drips on them he might as well have done.

He's standing all proud of himself, waiting for me to say something and my tongue wouldn't move. 'Knew it – knocked out, ain't ya?'

I was, but not in the way he thought. In the end I managed to say, 'Well, it's got rid of the brown, Len.'

'Yeah, and I've got a load of that blue left over so I'm going to do the kitchen the same.'

Lucky for me he said he couldn't do any more for a week because he couldn't get time off from work, so without saying nothing to him I went round to see his Uncle Fred.

He knew Lenny better than I did, so he understood what I was trying to say. What I asked him was if he'd let me give him a couple of pounds every week, sort of HP if you like, would he decorate the flat. He'd said no, he couldn't do that, but what he would do was give it to us as a wedding present. I argued, but not too hard, then accepted his offer.

Lenny never knew I'd been to see him and he said a couple of nights later, 'You won't believe this, babe, but Uncle Fred wants to do our place up – what a diamond he is. You know I can do it myself but I don't want to upset the old fella.' So within a fortnight our flat was turned into the little palace Lenny had promised and Fred wouldn't even take a penny for paint and wallpaper. He even redid the toilet in pale lemon, and Lenny never, ever questioned why he'd gone over what he'd done.

Our wedding, when the day came round, was so basic it left me feeling afterwards like nothing had changed. A proper white wedding is a big occasion and it leaves your head all filled up with the memory of it. A registry ceremony is all over in half an hour, and though you end up with the same bit of paper it doesn't seem the same somehow. Still, the law said it was all legal and we went back to the flat as Mr and Mrs McLean. I was happy.

— FOUR —

The morning after the wedding I just went to pieces. I vaguely remembered Lenny saying at about seven o'clock, 'Going for a run round the park, sweetheart.' When I woke up properly at half eight I looked round the bedroom and Lenny's clothes were everywhere. His suit was rolled up in a ball, his shirt was on the window-sill, and socks, shoes and pants were here and there. I just started crying and couldn't stop. Nothing to do with the mess, nothing to do with that I didn't love Lenny. In fact, if I'd been asked I doubt whether I could have put into words how I felt.

I'd looked forward to being in this situation for so long – like any girl, for years I suppose. But I'd never really thought about what it meant to leave my old life behind and start a new one with a stranger. Sounds daft to say stranger, but bottom line I didn't really know Lenny and he didn't know me, and neither of us could until we lived together – and I suppose that frightened me a bit.

When Lenny came in from his run I was still a bit tearful and he was genuinely concerned. 'Oh, babe, what's up? Missing your mum already? Give us a cuddle, 'cos I'm going to look after you from now on.'

I said, 'Don't be soft; I must've drunk too much last night, but I'll be all right in a bit.'

He just said, 'Good girl,' finished his hug with a pat on the back, and started throwing his clothes in all directions as he went for a wash at the sink. As he stuck his head under the kitchen tap water sprayed everywhere. At the same time he's saying, 'Nice bit of breakfast, Val, I'm starved,' and I couldn't help thinking that as far as he was concerned – same as most men – all he'd done was swap one mum for another. I was eighteen, little more than a baby, and I didn't know if I was ready for that sort of responsibility. Lenny was twenty-one and didn't have a care in the world.

What nobody told us, or we hadn't listened to, was how much it cost to live when your mum and dad aren't paying the bills. We'd always handed over part of our wages to our mums and thought we were paying our way. Suddenly we've got electric, gas, rent and rates bills, and I'd never even looked at one before, let alone paid them.

I was earning just over six pounds a week, and Lenny about the same plus ten bob a night down the White Hart, but you couldn't rely on that so basically we were skint most of the time. So any way we could make ends meet was welcome.

My friend Maureen lived opposite us, and same as most of the people round us she was in much the same boat. So we're talking one day about the price of food and I'm telling her feeding Lenny was like feeding the five thousand. So she said, 'You want to get yourself a freezer like I've got. Ice Star, it's called, and it's magic.'

I said, 'Well, one, I couldn't afford it and two, you've still got to buy the stuff to put in it.'

She laughed and said, 'Not if you're a bit cute, you don't.'

Seemed like when you took one of these freezers on it came full of food. No deposit, five shillings a week and you could eat for nothing for ages. The good bit came when the food was running out. A bang on the motor stopped it working, phone up the firm and they'd replace it – all filled up again.

I couldn't believe any firm could be so stupid, but more than that I couldn't believe that me – Valerie Dead Honest – was up for an idea like that. Being married was changing me in more ways than one. Once I was signed up me and Maureen worked it between us. When she got a new delivery she shared it with me, and then the same the other way round. Believe it or not this went on for a couple of years before the firm went bankrupt.

Lenny did his bit as well. He came rushing in from work one night, full of it. 'You ain't going to believe this, Val. One of the sparks on the firm showed me how to get free 'lectric.' He opened the meter cupboard by our front door and said, 'See that wheel going round in that little box? Well, that's what costs you money when you switch anything on – but I know how to stop it.'

We'd been together now long enough for me to know he couldn't even put a plug on a kettle, so I begged him to leave it alone. I said, 'Please, love, don't mess with it. You'll kill yourself stone dead.' But he was going to do it no matter what I said.

As usual he had me running around like he was a surgeon. 'Put the kettle on – get me a big needle – find them pliers Fred left here.' I said, 'Scalpel?' but he just said, 'What?' and I let it go. While he fiddled about I stood behind him without touching him, so if he went BANG I could at least ring for an ambulance.

I said he was acting like a surgeon, well, he started touching this box thing like he was doing brain surgery and I think he was shitting himself. On the bottom was a lead seal with a bit of wire going through it holding the front shut. He worked the needle up the side of the wire until he could pull it out of the lead without breaking it. He laid that carefully on the top and opened the glass flap, saying 'See that little bar? Well, if I undo that screw it should drop down. Give us a screwdriver.' I picked up the first one that I came across in the bag and handed it to him. He dropped it like it was red hot. 'Fucking hell, Val. Not one with a metal handle – Jesus. One of them insulated ones.' I gave him the right one; he turned the screw and the little wheel stopped. I said, 'What now?' and he said, 'Nothing now. That's it – free 'lectric for life.' When I pointed out the meter reader might think it a bit iffy with his box all hanging open, he said, 'That's the beauty of it. We make sure we still use a bit, but a week before he comes round I close it up, give that wire a twist and Bob's your uncle.'

Now we could afford to have the electric fire full on all day long instead of one bar for a couple of hours. I loved it. What surprised me was if I ever thought about what we were doing, I never felt one twinge of conscience that I was involved in something criminal. I knew I was being heavily influenced by Lenny when I thought, 'Fuck 'em!' instead of, 'Oh dear.' Good job Mum didn't know how I was turning out. I think I was beginning to learn early on that a conscience was OK if you could afford it, other than that you just had to blank things off.

Then Lenny got the sack.

We were having our dinner and I couldn't help noticing that the tops were off his knuckles. He'd been in two hours and hadn't mentioned it. I said, 'Been lifting pianos again?' and he knew straight away I was being sarcastic, so didn't even try and tell lies.

'I was going to tell you, babe. I panned the new foreman and they gave me the boot.'

Although my heart sank I knew him well enough to know it wouldn't have been over nothing, so I said, 'Go on, then. What happened?'

'Well, you know Billy Wright's boy works up there? Penny short of a shilling but never mind that – nice kid. He's sweeping up and he don't really know one end from the other. We all know that; that's why they pay him two bob a week. Anyway that foreman's giving him a bit of stick 'cos he's slow, and ends up telling him he's a retard and should be at home with his mum. The way I saw it was that was too near the truth to be funny. So I've chipped in and told this mug if he wants to chuck his weight around, pick on somebody his own size – like me. He threatened me with my cards if I didn't mind my own business, so I put him on his back. I swear to God, Val, I only hit him once. Fucking worth it, though.'

Every time something like this happened, I couldn't help having a flashback to a five-year-old Lenny, so could never blame him, though things would get a bit tight if he didn't get fixed up with something else pretty quick because we were on the breadline as it was – even with the fiddles.

We both lay in bed that night. We couldn't sleep but we weren't saying nothing either. This went on for ages. I'm wondering and worrying about how we're going to manage and I think Lenny knew that as well, because eventually he leaned up on one elbow and said, 'You know I love you, Val. I'll look after you,' and laid down again.

Next day he went out looking for his cousin Tony, who he hadn't seen for ages, and I knew he'd worked something out in his head the night before, because those two together meant trouble one way or another.

Tony was a lovable fella, always laughing and ready for anything. Livewire, Lenny used to call him, and he was certainly that. A bit of this and a bit of that, as he'd put it, was a way of life to him. As I was finding out more and more, Lenny didn't mind how he made a few bob. If it meant stepping over the other side of the law, he jumped at the chance and did what had to be done, as long as it didn't hurt ordinary people. On the other hand if there wasn't much about he wasn't too proud to get his hands dirty with a bit of hard graft. Though I have to say if push came to shove he much preferred the criminal way of life.

Not Tony. If he couldn't earn a shilling the criminal way he'd go without. Though that was rare because no matter what, if something wasn't fixed down he'd have it away. Put the two of them together and it stood to reason that one way or another there was going to be some sort of trouble. All that worried me was they'd both get caught doing some job or other and then get sent away again, and I told Lenny that but he laughed it off saying, 'When we got sent to Borstal that I told you about, we was grassed up. We'd never have been caught if it hadn't been for that slag that turned us in, so don't worry.'

I did all the same – every time they went out. He'd done one spell in an approved school for carrying a knife, then another in Borstal for robbery. Though these things sound serious they were only kids' stuff really, but being in his early twenties now, if he was caught for any other crime it would definitely mean proper adult prison.

The first result they got was from a warehouse just off Mile End Road. Tony had got the word that this firm distributed high-class ladies' underwear, and there was always a good market for that sort of thing. They parked Lenny's Mini up an alley, got through a window and threw out the smallest boxes they could lay their hands on. When I woke up about two o'clock, the two of them were going backwards and forwards from the car and piling boxes in the middle of my dining room. They were like a couple of kids giggling and laughing and shushing each other.

I brought a cup of tea through and Lenny was standing there grinning all over his face. 'We've hit the jackpot here, babe. Two hundred boxes of top gear.' I picked one up that had Le Chic on the lid, opened it and pulled out the biggest pair of knickers you've ever seen. Their faces were such a picture I just cracked up laughing. They open a couple of boxes each, but they were all the same. Then Lenny said, 'Tell you what, Val, you keep them – you might grow into them.'

I just said, 'Cheeky sod,' and went back to bed.

Like most times when the two of them came home all hyped up after a job, I had to lie there listening to them drinking and talking loudly about the old days, specially about the time they'd spent in Borstal. Looking back at those days they made it sound like a holiday camp, though from what Lenny had told me he'd hated being away from his family. Still, that was for my ears and not macho enough to share with Tony, no matter how close they were.

First one of them would remember something: 'What about that time you nicked all them tins of prunes from the stores, Len?'

'Don't remind me, we had the shits for a week after. An' what about you, Tone, you flash git, the only one in the place with tailored shoes and uniform?'

'That's 'cos I used me nut. Remember the time you smashed up them Welsh geezers – fuckin' hell, blood everywhere.'

'Yeah, an' you still owe me for that one. I got put on report an' it was you what started it.'

'Them fuckin' tattoos, whose idea was that, then?

Razor blade an' a biro, we must've been mad.' The tattoo on their arms was 'MUM' and years later Lenny had his taken off, but it wasn't very successful, so that explains the blue scar on his forearm you might've seen in photographs.

Their stories just went on and on and I always fell asleep long before they packed it in. I learned a lot about Lenny's teenage years, though.

By the time I woke up in the morning all the boxes of knickers were gone, and as far as I know Tony fenced the lot for about five pounds. They risked six months apiece for two pounds ten shillings.

Still, it wasn't always a waste of time. After they turned over Swans factory in Poplar everybody we knew ended up with brand-new kettles for a few pounds each. Though when you consider the size of the boxes they came in and how many they could get in that Mini, I suppose our share was about twenty quid. OK, that was like a bit more than two weeks' wages for Lenny, but then they might not have another result for a while. So they were risking time just so we could get by.

I was still working then but my money didn't go anywhere. Lenny was always saying the big one was just round the corner, and when they managed to fill our motor with car radios he thought they'd cracked it. They were expensive back then and everybody wanted one. Trouble was, the firm had what they called a silent alarm that went straight through to the police station. They were lucky the police were a bit slow off the mark or they would've been caught inside.

As it was they pulled away as a squad car came round the corner. This was about three in the morning and they were chased for twenty minutes through all the back streets of the East End. The only reason they kept in front was Lenny knew all the little turnings better than the police driver. In the end they decided to dump the car and do a runner. Tony filled his arms with radios until Len told him, 'Wouldn't look fucking suspicious, would it, with that lot?' and he dropped them.

Lenny came in on his own just as I was getting out of bed. 'Nice cup of tea, babe – I'm knackered.' Then he told me what had happened. When he got to dumping the car he said, 'I'm either going to have to lose the motor, and I can't afford that, or front it up with the law. What d'yer reckon?'

I knew the Mini was worth sixty pounds, so he was right we couldn't afford to lose it, so I said, 'What do you mean, "front it"?'

He said, 'Y'know, tell Old Bill it was nicked or something.'

You might think they would've traced him by now anyway, but fortunately he never believed in the paper-work that went with driving like most normal people. For a start he never even had a driving licence, and wouldn't get one until he was well in his forties. He didn't have insurance and I don't think the car even had a logbook, so nothing was in his name.

He sat and thought, then said, 'I know. You're better on the phone than me, you give the law a bell.' I cooked, cleaned, paid all the bills and every day I ran round behind him like a blue-arsed fly, picking up his clothes – now I had to perjure myself for him.

We went down to the phone box on the corner and I reported that we'd found the car gone when we looked over the balcony at seven o'clock that morning. First thing this person wanted to know was the registration number. I didn't have a clue, so I mouthed to Lenny: '. . . number?' He just lifted his arms up and shook his head. So I said to the copper, 'It's four something and it's red.' He must have put his hand over the mouthpiece because this muffled voice said, 'Got a right one 'ere,' then clearer, he said that he'd send somebody round that evening – madam.

I couldn't think straight all day with the worry of it. When two coppers came at half six, they'd already found the Mini. They knew we were lying, we knew they knew we were lying, and we all just went along with it.

One of them said, 'Funny thing, the keys were in it. Bit of a gift, don't you think?'

Lenny said, 'Oh, I must have been pissed.' I kicked him. 'I must've been pissed off last night – clean forgot to lock it up.' They just looked at each other. We got away with it, though somewhere in the paperwork down the station Lenny's card must have been marked in big letters.

We didn't get the car back for a fortnight – tests had to be made. When we did get it from the pound, Lenny's sunglasses were missing, and it took me all my time to stop him having a ruck with the police. He moaned about them all the way home, saying, 'Whoever took them should have their fucking hands cut off.' It didn't occur to him that the radio warehouse was probably saying the same thing about him.

I think Tony and Len both got a scare over that business. You wouldn't think so, to listen to them going over it all the time –

'What about when you took that corner on two wheels, Boy?'

'Yeah, an' I nearly tipped it over!'

'And what about you chucking radios out the window at Old Bill?'

I got fed up listening to it. In the end, laugh or not, I think they were both relieved when they agreed to knock it on the head for a bit. 'Just in case Old Bill's watching the motor.'

He still hadn't managed to get himself a proper job, but picked up a few pounds here and there with casual stuff. Like helping out on removals, unloading lorry-loads of boxes – in fact anything where a bit of muscle was needed. We got by.

Mum still didn't want to know Lenny, but that wasn't going to stop her helping out her daughter. I can't remember the number of times I went round there and she was going to 'throw away' half a joint or a packet of biscuits to make room in the cupboard. Could I use them? Mums must be all alike because it was the same with Rose. We're all sick of eating this salt bacon – could I use it before it went in the bin? There'd be four slices cut off it, so I knew what she'd said wasn't true. I loved both of them for it. They made a game of it so's I wouldn't feel Lenny and me were charity cases.

Same with Uncle Fred. After a visit he'd stop at the door and say, 'I don't like carrying a load of small change – wears holes in your pocket,' and he'd turn it all out and put it on the table by the door. The idea was I was doing him a favour by taking it off his hands, so nobody needed to feel embarrassed. Most times when I counted up the pennies, shillings and half-crowns, it added up to three or four pounds, and I know he would've made sure it was that much before he even arrived. But our life then wasn't all about scrimping and scraping and trying to manage. We were both young with no real responsibilities and up for a laugh whether we had money or not.

Sometimes when I'm talking about those days to my kids they look at me as though I've come out of the Dark Ages. Yet to me it all seems like five minutes ago.

It's a bit like when I used to talk to my nan and she'd say, 'When I was in service I got half a crown a week – pictures cost twopence and my bus fare was a halfpenny.'

I wasn't all that surprised because she was pretty ancient. Now I'm doing the same. Lenny and me used to get a Chinese takeaway on a Saturday night, a meal for two – five shillings. Another night I'd get a salt-bacon bone with loads of meat on it for sixpence. To be honest my kids and most others wouldn't even bend down and pick up that sort of money if they dropped it.

What made me think of that was back then people used to go in a garage and ask for one or two gallons of petrol. Then something or other changed and instead of gallons people asked for a pound's worth. They used to fill up your cars for you then – no self-service. And I can remember Lenny standing by the car telling the fella to 'Put in a pound, mate' like he was a millionaire. So with four gallons in the tank we could go all over the place for the week. And did we. Southend, Bournemouth, Clacton – we couldn't spend much when we got there but that didn't seem to matter. We had each other and it seemed like we didn't need much else.

I knew Lenny was a fighter and always had been, but when it came down to it I didn't know much more than that. Once we were together different people would say, 'Your Lenny – fuck me. I wouldn't like to get on the wrong side of him,' or 'Your ol' man – I reckon he could take on Cassius Clay,' but it didn't mean very much to me. I'd seen him knock those two fellas spark out in the blink of an eye, but I'd never been involved in anything like that or even been to a boxing match, so as far as I was concerned perhaps all blokes were as fast as that. Lenny never spoke about that sort of thing and at times when he had to admit he'd knocked somebody down, it was almost like he was embarrassed.

Things changed for me the day he took me to Epsom Downs. I don't think I was all that keen because I wasn't interested in horse racing, but he said, 'No, babe, it ain't the racing – we'll just go for the fair and have a good time.'

On the night before Uncle Fred had given us a handful of change so we weren't skint, but we still had to think twice about what we spent. Lenny loved that sort of thing. Hot dogs, carousel, candyfloss, dodgems, ice-cream, boat-swings – we worked our way through the fair then right at the edge we came across a boxing booth. That's something else that seems really old fashioned and even then must have been on its tail end, because I don't remember ever seeing one again. It never occurred to me that once we'd paid our money and gone inside this big tent that Lenny might consider getting into the boxing ring that was set up.

I felt a bit out of place with all these men so I clung onto Lenny's arm. We were just in time to see a man in his late thirties take a punch in the face that made blood run down his vest. He put his hands up and sort of waved them like he was saying, 'I've had enough,' and climbed out the ring. The man who had hit him was about forty and looked a right bruiser. No neck but all arms and chest, and his nose was practically flat.

A little gypsy-looking bloke jumped into the ring, held the boxer's hand up and said, 'Bad luck, friend – you nearly had my man. Who's next? Two rounds on your feet or a knockout and this bundle's yours.' And he fanned out five ten-pound notes and waved them in the air.

I said to Lenny, 'How can he afford to pay out all that money?'

He said, 'Because he thinks there ain't nobody can beat that gorilla.' Then he looked at me and I saw his chin go out.

I knew what was going through his head and I said, 'No, Len – don't even think about it, please.'

But he said, 'Look at the size of him – he can't chase me round for six minutes. I'll keep moving, he won't be able to land one on me.' While he was saying that he was pulling me down to the front. Then he shouted, 'I'll take your money.' A big cheer went up and I felt myself blushing. Don't ask me why – all those men looking, I suppose.

The little man said, 'Get yourself up 'ere. Who are you, boy?'

Lenny kissed me on the cheek, saying, 'I know what I'm doing, babe,' and jumped into the ring, shouting, 'You got it right first time, pal. It's Boy – Boy McLean from 'Oxton.'

The man's offering him gloves and Len's saying, 'I don't need fucking gloves.' But the man insisted and I found out later that these gloves, as thin as they were, made it all legal – at least in them days.

So much for Lenny telling me he was going to run round in front of this fighter – as soon as they squared up he hit him twice in the chest, so hard it sounded like chucking a brick at a wall. It didn't stop the big man but it made him screw his face up. I heard him growl, 'You c***,' and stepped forward, swinging punches one after another. Lenny just danced backwards and none of them landed on him. As his back touched the ropes he came forward again, hitting this man twice in the face and about four to the body – then the bell rang. If it had been anywhere near three minutes then pigs can fly.

Then they started again and it was the same thing, though one time Lenny dropped his hands, winked and blew a kiss at me. I thought, 'God, you are a cocky sod.' Then suddenly the other man dropped to the boards, level with my nose, and I hadn't even seen what had put him there. He got up on one elbow and the count was so slow anybody else could've counted up to thirty in the same time. So of course he got his wind back and stood up.

Looking at them both, Lenny seemed such a boy against this big lump, but no sooner was he on his feet than Lenny rushed at him, and it was that blur I spoke about with those other two fellas. He was so fast I could hardly count how many times he hit him – I never did know. But the other bloke just fell backwards and you knew he wouldn't get up for a while.

Lenny ran all round the ring with his arms up, and all the people cheering him. Then he seemed to be having an argument with the gypsy type, who was shaking his head. Then everybody's shouting, 'Give 'im the money! Give 'im the money!' Afterwards Lenny told me that the bloke had reckoned he was a ringer – like he was a professional boxer pretending he was an ordinary punter. In the end, and I think mainly because of the crowd, I saw him give Lenny the money. Lenny turned away then swung back and raised his fist, and the man ran back so fast he nearly fell over.

As we walked out everybody's trying to pat him on the back and I got the feeling he loved every minute of it. Half of me wanted to tell him off for making me worry, but in a funny way the other half of me was really proud of him.

Once we were away from the tent he got in front of me, held up the notes and said, 'How easy was that? Beats working for it.' I'd been a bit worried when he climbed in the ring – for one I didn't fancy my husband having a flat nose or be scarred up. He was handsome at that age, and I wanted him to stay like that.

But the strange thing is, from that day I never, ever

worried again. People find it hard to believe, and I think that's the first question of all that I get asked – specially now. He knew what he could do and was full of confidence, and that just rubbed off on me.

On our way home, after he told me what the gypsy had been saying, I asked him if he really would have hit him, but he just laughed, 'What, that little geezer? Course I wouldn't, but he didn't know that, did he?'

I was still torn by the way he had earned that money but it was very welcome and should've helped out on some of the bills, but typical us then we blew it on some brilliant nights out up West. I didn't need much talking round, but Lenny said, 'One day we'll be stuck indoors with loads of kids, so we gotta get out while we can.' I didn't know about loads, but one or perhaps two kids would be nice – but not for years yet.

Things turned a corner for us when Lenny managed to get fixed up with a job in a clothes place at Bow. The money was rubbish, like it always was in the rag trade, but at least it would be regular, and a bonus for me was with him out of the flat all day I didn't have to come home from work myself and spend an hour tidying up his mess.

Sometimes I used to think he was just taking advantage of me because his mum wasn't behind him to clip his ear, but Linda – his sister – told me he'd never been any different.

His brother Barry was the complete opposite, she said. Everything had to be just so with him. As he undressed whatever didn't go in the wash bin was neatly folded or hung up in the wardrobe. So what with sharing a bedroom him and Lenny had no end of fights, and the worst ones were over sharing clothes. Well, one-sided sharing, that is. When Lenny was going out he always liked to look smart, so he'd want to find something decent to wear. Only trouble was, the night before and the night before that, he'd stuffed whatever he'd been wearing under the bed or behind the cupboard. So while Barry was having a bath Lenny would nick his suit and shirt that was laid out on the bed, get dressed and shoot out, leaving his brother a pile of wrinkled gear.

Linda was a mine of information when it came to this new husband of mine. She cleared up something that had puzzled me for a long time.

Going back a bit, when we first got the flat, most of our furniture came from either Rose or my mum. We went out and chose it but between them they paid for it. One of the pieces was a solid teak G-Plan dining table with matching chairs and in its day the best you could get within our price range. This table being heavy had a couple of uses as far as Lenny was concerned. One was for what it was made for, eating off, the other was as part of his weight-training equipment. 'Legs,' he used to say. 'Legs are your most important bits. More people have lost fights because their legs gave up halfway through than anything else.'

So what he'd do was get himself under this table, lay on his back, then lift it up and down a hundred times. Probably did more than that most of the time, because I wouldn't be taking any notice, and he'd shout, 'How'm I doing, babe? What am I up to?' The first times that happened I might have said, 'Dunno, love,' from the kitchen, and he'd go, 'Fuck me, Val. What's the matter with you? Can't you count?' After that I'd just guess a number and that kept him happy.

Anyway, he crawled out this time and stood doing knee bends. I've got to say he did have some legs on him. Full of muscle and as hard as stone. Not that I would've said as such, but that didn't matter because he said it for himself often enough. He gave his thighs a slap and said to me, 'See them? You wouldn't believe I was a cripple when I was a baby.' I had to say it was hard to believe. 'Yeah, I was like that Tiny Jim in that film we saw over Christmas – leg irons, you know. What it was, I was such a big baby my little legs couldn't carry the weight, so they went all bent.' I mean he wouldn't have made up something like that, but I'd never heard anything like it before.

Me not knowing about something didn't mean that it wasn't true, but it seemed strange enough to puzzle me for some time. So when Linda and me were talking about Lenny as a kid, I came out with what he'd told me and she laughed and said, 'I remember those irons all right. If we were out shopping with Mum and we went past a cake shop, that little sod would stick his arms straight out, scream the place down and kick everything in sight with those lumps of iron. Obviously Lenny was too young to know why, but the real reason he had to wear them was because he had rickets.'

I knew half the kids in the East End suffered from that way back in the old days, but it made me think what a struggle his mum and dad must've had if one of their kids could get a vitamin deficiency at the beginning of the fifties.

I never did mention to Lenny what Linda had told me and he died never knowing the real reason he'd worn those calipers as a baby.

In the last few months of his life he had to wear a leg support. Plastic, not the metal kind – though the same thing, really. And it did cross my mind that he'd compare the beginning of his life with the end, but he never did, or at least he never said.

Other things that either Linda or Lorraine (Boo) told me made me think he'd been a very mixed-up little boy. It wouldn't take a psychiatrist to work out why. The whole family were put through all kinds of abuse from that Irwin, but for whatever reason Lenny was singled out to take kicks, punches and mental torture from day one.

Nobody could explain why he did some of the things he did. Like walking along the pavement, then stopping suddenly, going back a few yards to tap his foot on one of the slabs and saying out loud, 'One – Two,' then just carry on like nothing had happened. This wasn't just once – he did it all the time, and it breaks my heart to picture that sad little baby, who because of what he was going through, was being driven to the edge of becoming a mental case.

If he was eating his dinner and one of the others stretched across his plate, he'd go absolutely mad, screaming about germs and dirt falling into his food. Boo said sometimes he'd grab his plate and lock himself in the toilet and use the pan lid as a little table – just so it couldn't happen. Not normal, is it? But then what was normal in his early years.

That he grew up to become the hardest man in Britain says a lot about his strength of character. I never looked at him like that, he was just my Lenny and I never gave it any thought. But to people outside our home he proved over and over again that he was everything they saw in him – no weaknesses, no failings. He managed to outgrow all those strange childhood mannerisms and leave them so far behind that he probably forgot he'd ever been like it – and that's assuming he was even aware of them at the time.

There was just one thing he kept from those years and that was hating to hear people eating. Boo and Linda both told me that if they accidentally smacked their lips at the table Lenny would go right into one. Over the years we turned it into a joke indoors, and he went along with it, but underneath it still made his blood pressure go up.

There were hundreds of incidents, so I'll just give you a few for example. Being in the pictures behind somebody eating popcorn. I'd know what was going to happen because he'd start puffing and fidgeting. After about five minutes he'd lean over the seat, tap the bloke on the shoulder and say to him, 'Excuse me, pal, I'm here to see the movie, not listen to you stuffing your face, so pack it in or move well away from me.' The bloke didn't move, but he didn't eat any more either.

Another time, a year or so before Lenny died, our friend Eric was sitting in our conservatory. Eric's a proper livewire, always laughing. So he's lying back on the cane settee and, never shy, he says, ' 'Ere, Val, got any crisps? I'm starving.' What could I say? Everybody's got crisps in their cupboard. I got him a packet but I didn't dare look at Lenny. Eric lies back again and starts eating, and you've never heard nothing like it. Not his fault. How can you eat crisps quietly? I could see that every crunch was like being stabbed for Lenny. He started fidgeting and the fingers were drumming, then he burst out, 'For fuck's sake, Eric – will you suck those bastard things – you're doing my head in.' Eric just laughed – crunched the last few and never did know that Lenny was deadly serious.

Same with sweets. Lenny could eat a pound bag of toffees as quick as he could get the papers off, but never, ever in front of people. If he was offered he'd just pat his stomach and say, 'Nah – too fat already,' even though he would've loved one. Didn't want to hear noises, but equally didn't want no one to hear him. Still, we've all got our funny ways, and his could've been worse.

Going back to us, then. Like I said, Lenny got the warehouse job. This place was something to do with a clothes catalogue, and as orders came in they had to be parcelled up and posted off – and that's what he was doing. The girls would bring in the parcels they'd done, give Lenny a job number, then he had to print a label, stick it on, then when he had a load, take it round to the Post Office. Dead easy and boring.

Towards the end of his first week, on one of these deliveries the man behind the counter said, 'I can't sign your card for this one – ain't got no label. What's up, was your tongue getting dry?' And that, as Lenny was telling me the same night, is 'What got my nut turning.'

You'd have thought he was planning World War Three. 'This is what you've got to do, Val. First thing go to that printers near the market and get them to make up a rubber stamp with your name and address on it – but don't tell them who you are.'

I said, 'That's going to be a bit difficult being as they're going to make all our address details up in rubber.'

'You're right. Forget that. Go into Woolworths and buy one of those John Bull printing outfits, and sticky labels if they do them. You got that? Won't forget, will you?'

I said, 'No, Len, I think I can remember two things at the same time, but what's this all about?'

'You'll see, babe. It's a blinder and worth a few quid.'

I didn't bother to ask again because he could be a big kid sometimes. I got the stuff he wanted, and after tea he sat at the table and opened up this printing outfit. For the next half-hour all I got from him was, 'Oh, bollocks – fuck this,' before he gave up and shouted, 'Val! Give us an 'and before I chuck the bleedin' lot out the window.'

All you had to do with this set was slide little rubber blocks onto a pad. Each one was a letter or a number, and you just made up whatever you wanted to print.

Apart from having no patience Lenny's fingers were so big he couldn't pick up the little pieces. Took me about five minutes. Once it was pressed on an inkpad you could stamp it out on paper. I didn't want to spoil his secret but it didn't take Einstein to put two and two together as to what he was planning to do.

This was a Thursday. On the next Tuesday the postman delivered three parcels with our labels stuck on them. It was like Christmas and I couldn't wait to rip them open. By the time I did and spread what was in them across the table, I found there was a selection of ladies' clothes – all brand new – from a coat down to lacy underwear. Then I started to worry. If they've been ticked off in my name it wouldn't be long before the police was knocking on my door. Lenny had covered that, though. What he'd done was put our label on the parcels, but over the top a proper one that he'd only licked on two corners. It hung on long enough to be checked in, but by the time they were thrown in with a load more parcels they just fell off. I mean, Lenny used his head.

It wasn't like he did it every day, but one way and another we were making a reasonable bit on the side. It was down to me to get rid of every little piece of package or wrapping, and cut labels off some of the clothes. Then if we did get the law searching our flat there would be nothing incriminating lying about.

The selling bit was easy. Don't forget, everybody we knew, and their friends and so on, were all in the same boat, struggling to get by, so anything on the cheap was always welcome – no question of worrying about being grassed up. Some of the women, though, could be really stupid sometimes. They'd say, 'Ooo, Val, this is nice – you ain't got it in blue, have you?' And I'd have to say, 'This ain't Marks and Spencer's, and for two quid it don't matter what colour it is.'

Somehow, what we were doing didn't seem like stealing. But bottom line there was no other word for it, and that went against everything I'd been taught while I was growing up. Mum would've killed me if she knew what I was up to, but the way I saw it was at that time in my life I just couldn't afford to have morals – so I just stopped thinking about it.

Stands to reason it couldn't go on for ever and once complaints over missing goods got too much, the firm shut down Lenny's section and changed all the system. Before that, though, they did give him a right checking over, but all his paperwork was in order so they couldn't prove it was anything to do with him. I think they knew it was down to Lenny, but had to swallow it without involving the police.

As far as my own job went, that came to an end when I told my boss, Mrs Baxter, to stick it up her behind. It had been coming for a long time because I just hated being there every day. Nothing to do with laziness, just the endless boredom of running stuff through a sewing machine.

I was told off loads of times for talking when I should've been working, or making the other girls laugh so they weren't working. The crunch came when we got back in after being in the pub opposite for our lunch. I tripped over a coat that was on the floor and fell down. Didn't hurt myself but this Mrs B. flew over and started going on about being drunk. Drunk? I'd had half a light ale, and what with going out with Lenny for so long I could drink her or anybody under the table and still be sober. I thought, 'Bloody cheek,' and on top of that I thought, 'I'm a married woman, not some little school kid,' so without thinking I told her exactly where to put her job. She didn't even argue, just stormed off to the wages office and came back with my cards before I'd even collected my things.

So now we had two sets of P45s stuck behind the clock on the mantelpiece. Irresponsible or what? We didn't worry about it at all, but then we still had a few pounds that I'd managed to save from selling the knock-off clothes.

It was a different story when I had to stop answering the door to the rent man. I was telling Lenny one night that as I came back from his mum's there was a fella knocking on our door. Suit, clipboard – probably the Co-op man looking for some furniture money. I walked past him on the landing like I was a neighbour, and when I got a couple of doors down I said to him, 'No good knocking there, love, they've gone away.' He's gone, 'Oh dear. Any idea where they've moved to?' I said, 'I think Mrs McLean mentioned Australia – family out there or something,' and he went off shaking his head.

Lenny's in the bedroom and I'm washing up and I can hear him laughing and saying, 'Good girl – good girl. Perhaps they'll write it off. But listen, sweetheart. Don't worry, we'll soon be in the money – I'm doing a bank job tomorrow. How do I look?' As I've turned round he's standing in the kitchen doorway and he's got one of my stockings pulled tight over his face.

I just shrieked: 'You bloody fool, you've got to be joking.'

He pulled it off saying, 'Sort of, babe. Charlie wants me to give him a hand shifting desks round the Midland.'

I just said, 'You bugger,' and flung a soapy dishcloth right in his face. Course then it ended up down my back and the pair of us screamed about like a couple of kids. Which, thinking about it, was just what we were then.

It was a joke, I know, but as he'd said it for those few

seconds I really did get a shock of fear, because always in the back of my mind was the thought that some of the people he knocked about with would suck him into something serious. He wasn't a fool, and no way was he easily led, but he could never turn his back if somebody asked for a favour. Best of it was, nine times out of ten he never made a penny out of things he did for other people.

Even though he was nothing like as big as he'd become eventually, he always looked like somebody you wouldn't want to mess with, plus it was known pretty well all over that he could knock anybody spark out before they knew it was coming. So if any of the people he knew was owed money or had been ripped off somehow, Lenny was the first one they came to for backup.

I used to say to him, 'Len, I love you because you're always ready to help people out, but a lot of them are really taking the mickey out of you. They're making money and then buying you a pint.'

He said, 'You're right, Val. What I'll do is get one of those taxi meters and stick it on my head, then before I do a favour I'll start it ticking away.'

I just said, 'Don't get the hump and be sarcastic with me, you know I'm right.' And he did. But it was a long time before he really earned out of what he was good at.

Whether Lenny had a fight coming up or if he was having a rest for a bit, he never stopped training. It was just something he'd always done and I suppose after a while it comes a habit. So I don't know if it was that or my cooking, but he seemed to fill out a bit more every week. It was funny, more than once as he squeezed into that little Mini car he'd say, 'You know what, Val? I'm sure this fucking motor's getting smaller and smaller. Gonna have to stop washing it.' That was a joke; it never saw soapy water from the day he got it until he smashed it into the dustbin locker.

So I said, 'Len, don't it occur to you that you're getting bigger and bigger?'

He just said, 'Nah, I've had these same trousers for two years.'

'Yeah,' I said, 'and I've moved the buttons three times and you still can't breathe in them.'

When I say about people taking the mickey, that was always the builder Dougie Chapman's game, though Lenny couldn't see it at first.

Before that, though, he had a few weeks in another clothes warehouse. It wasn't cards in, so I didn't count it as a proper job, but what it came down to was Lenny being paid ten pounds a week to rob the place, not that the firm knew that. It was night work and I wasn't too keen on being on my own, but as Lenny often said you play with the hand you're dealt, so I didn't say anything.

Seven the next morning he came into the bedroom looking like Michelin Man – he was huge. And as I sat up in bed he started to *da-da da da* to 'The Stripper' tune, and with all the actions, peeling off women's clothes that were wrapped round him under a big overcoat. Dresses, jumpers, underwear – it just kept coming.

When it was all piled on the bed he flung himself down beside me saying, 'Not a bad night, eh, babe? There's got to be a better way, though. What if I got lifted? Imagine the headlines in the *Advertiser*: "Big Lenny caught wearing women's underwear." I'd never live it down.'

That's when he pulled Tony back in again. There was a nightwatchman on the main gate, so what they did was get Tony to drive up the back alley about four o'clock and flash his lights. Lenny would be at the window waiting for the signal, then he'd chuck a load of stuff down to him. I sold off the first lot Len brought home, but after that he said, 'I'm gonna fence off everything we get from now on. I don't want to risk getting you nicked, babe. Never forgive myself.'

It all came to an end when a police Panda car started to make itself busy during the small hours. Lenny got a gut feeling that he'd be pushing his luck to carry on so jacked in the job. But that was after he'd spoken to this Dougie and got all fired up about learning a trade.

When I asked him what had brought all this on he said, 'Well, you know I've always fucked about, bit of this, bit of that, jobs with no future? I've been thinking for a long time now, it's about time I settled down and got something behind me.'

Sometimes Lenny could look you straight in the eye, tell a right whopper and believe every word of it. I guessed that this career change had been in his head for about an hour – ever since this builder bloke Dougie had had a word in his ear. Lenny was a very shrewd judge of character – better than I was, and very little gets past me. Yet if he wanted something badly enough all his instincts went straight out the window. Just like it would twenty years later when a film deal was dangled under his nose.

As Lenny told it, this man had got in touch with him through a mate and suggested he took him on the firm to learn the decorating game, and as a bit of extras, mind him when he took the wages round in case somebody tried to rob him. Sounded a bit of a story to me and when this Dougie came up to our flat I was even more convinced, because he struck me as a right slimy character.

Lenny wouldn't hear a word against him, though. 'You watch, sweetheart. Might take a few weeks before

Six faces of Lenny.
(Simon Fowler)

Nanny Campion's house, where Lenny was born.

A young Lenny in the Standard.

Me at fourteen:
I'm in the middle.

Dinner with Nanny Spinks.

Left: Taking our marriage vows.

Below: Outside the registry office with, from the left, Nanny Campion, Len's mum Rose, us, and my mum Lillian.

Above: Lenny's favourite uncle, Fred.

Right: With my life-long friend Rita.

Right: Me with Jamie and Kelly.

Below: We loved our Spanish holidays. This was taken in Majorca.

Lenny and me with Ritchie Anderson and Ritchie's wife Val, seated on the right.

Lenny with Kenny Mac and, on the right, his cousin John Wall.

Lenny trained all his life.

Above: **John Nash, on the right, and Alex Steen in his usual dark glasses.**

Left: **Lenny and Craig Fairbrass.**

I'm a proper decorator – you know, wallpapering and that – but I'm not bad on the brush already.' A picture of our toilet came into my head. 'So I'll learn a few wrinkles and then take off and do jobs of me own. Might even get a van and a few cards printed.'

In his head he'd gone from nicking ladies' clothes to big firm of decorators in two hours. But it never happened.

Monday to Thursday he was 'learning the game'. Fridays he followed Dougie about as he paid his men. There were hundreds of them because he had a contract with the council doing up their flats all over. Every night he came home, except Friday, he looked like he was a chimney sweep. I used to dig him out, though not too much because I knew he'd get the hump. I'd say, 'How come Uncle Fred puts up wallpaper in a suit?' or 'When's the firm going to give you a nice pair of white overalls?' Then he'd get all serious.

'Trouble with you is you want everything yesterday. You don't understand what's involved. Dougie told me, and he's been in the game for years, that it's all about preparation. If you don't get that right you're wasting your time.'

I said, 'But, Len, you've been preparing for about three weeks now,' but he just cocked a deaf 'un.

What was happening was this Dougie had him doing every filthy job that needed doing. Scraping off old paint, rubbing down miles of woodwork and picking up wet wallpaper off the floor.

One Thursday night we were sitting watching our little black and white telly. Lenny was breathing heavy through his nose, always a sign that he was thinking, then he said, 'Would you say I'm a bully?' He wasn't and I said so. 'What about thug, then?'

I said, 'I don't know why you're asking these things, but no, you're not. We both know you can have a fight, but you don't shove people around. What's up?'

'Well, last Friday Dougie short-changed one of the painters – said he'd fucked up a room or something – and the fella said, "You wouldn't have done that without your big bully behind you." On top of that I'm getting whispers that a lot of the fellas seem to think I'm some sort of thug. Know what I mean? Like I'm against them instead of being one of them.'

The next week after he'd done his bit of minding all day he was in the same sort of mood. He was always the same when he had a problem – long silences, then he'd say something as if you'd been in on whatever he'd been thinking about. 'He thinks they're all mugs, y'know.'

'Who's that, Len?'

'Dougie – all them fellas are trying to do is earn a bit of bread – an' he says they're no-value mugs and I reckon he thinks I'm the same. He wants me up Mare Street Monday, just him and me, so I think I'll square him up then.'

I knew what that meant and though I didn't have any time for this builder or contractor or whatever he was called, I had to say, 'Lenny, be sensible. Just have a quiet word, don't go into one and get yourself in trouble.'

'Look, babe, I'm sorry if I let you down and don't become a painter, but I hate what I'm doing. I don't mind all the shit jobs and getting rotten dirty every day, but I ain't going to be used by some gutless coward to put the frighteners on ordinary working blokes.' I left it at that.

Monday, half one, he walked in with that big grin on his face. I didn't even have to look at his knuckles to know that he'd handed his notice in – effective there and then.

A bit later there was a bang on the door. I opened it

and there were two coppers, and hiding behind them was Dougie. But not hidden enough that I couldn't see he had a lump on his chin like a small orange. I called Lenny and when he came up the passage I stood so that I could stop him if he decided to give the law some of what the other fella had got.

He was so polite, though; I could've fallen over. 'Hello, officers, how can I help you?'

I don't know what they expected but it certainly wasn't that.

The taller one said, 'We want to talk to you about an allegation of an assault on Mr Chapman here.'

The other chipped in, saying, 'That's a punch on the jaw.'

Lenny said, 'Thank you, officer, I don't understand big words,' sarcastic like. 'Between you an' me I think there's been a little misunderstanding 'ere, so if me and my pal Dougie can have a private word it'll be sorted in one minute.'

By this time Dougie had moved down the balcony, but with the copper saying, 'Sensible idea – c'mon, Mr Chapman,' he came and stepped inside, though you could see he would rather have jumped over the rail.

Lenny said, 'My friend,' put his arms round his shoulders and eased him into the kitchen. I followed them. Out of the sight of the coppers Lenny changed completely. Caught him by the throat, pinned him to the wall and said, 'You gutless c*** – you dare bring the law to my home frightening my missus. Well, listen, you walk out of 'ere with a smile on your mug and tell 'em you've made a dreadful mistake – which as I see it you have anyway. If you don't I will break every bone in your body, and when they mend I'll do it again.'

I had to say, 'That's enough, babe,' because Dougie's eyes were rolling up in his head – and he let him go.

While Chapman's explaining to the law that perhaps he'd overreacted to a bit of horseplay, Lenny had his arm round him, friendly like. But I knew it was because this bloke's legs had turned to jelly and he would've fallen down otherwise. We got a nice apology from the law, and when the door was shut Lenny said, 'Can you believe that git? And I used to think he was sound as a pound. I should've listened to you, Val. Tell you what, if I ever let myself get sucked in again, just you remind me about that piece of shit.'

As it happens I did do that about a thousand times in the future, but if it suited him it didn't make a blind bit of difference.

It's funny how you can be so close to somebody and not see them as other people do. Does that mean they're keeping a side of them away from you, or a side of them away from anybody outside the door? With Lenny I think he let only me see the softer side because if he showed it outside, he thought it would be taken as a sign of weakness. I don't think that would have been necessarily so, but he did because on the streets it was all about image.

I might be a woman, but that didn't stop me understanding what men have to live up to, particularly when there's a reputation to keep up. We're too busy keeping things together to worry about that sort of thing, but men's lives are all about front, respect, being somebody and having face.

Lenny was no different, though, when it was just him and me. He relaxed and let his guard down. That's when he became the clown. He had a boyish humour that never changed in his short life. Silly stuff – made-up rhymes, little tricks, Christmas cracker jokes – and he was the one that laughed the loudest.

I'd hear his name mentioned outside when people

didn't know who I was. Like it might be in Peliccis' having a cup of tea and I'd overhear somebody saying, 'Lenny McLean – cor, he's a hard bastard,' and I'd think, 'He might be but there's more to him than you'll ever know.' As tough as he was he had his insecurities – again something he never lost completely.

If we had to go somewhere we hadn't been before, like Hastings or Windsor, he'd find his way there. Then if he was told he'd gone twenty-five miles longer the way he went, he'd take the new directions on board to be polite, ignore them completely and stick to the route he knew. If he had to get to a job by bus because the car wouldn't start, he'd ask me a hundred times before he left, was I sure it was a number 89 or 126 he had to get on. Perhaps all men are the same – I don't know.

No end of times during a day he'd tell me he loved me, or wanted to know if I loved him – looking for reassurance, same as asking, 'Am I looking after you, babe?' 'Am I a good husband?' 'Are you glad you married me?' I always answered yes because it was true, but I never failed to be touched by the way his face lit up, no matter how many times it was said.

Occasionally if we were cuddled up on the settee and not talking about anything in particular, out of the blue he might say something like, 'When we have kids I won't ever lay a finger on them,' and I knew that past of his was running through his mind.

Another giveaway was rubbing a scar above his eyes that I knew came from Jim Irwin's fist. Don't let me give the impression he was whining about what he'd gone through or using it as some sort of excuse, because it never came out like that. Listening to him relive his childhood, it struck me that with an adult mind he was trying to understand why and come to terms with it. He never did, though.

Looking at it now, I suppose he was using me as a therapist as he unloaded all that pain. Not that either of us knew it at the time, because at that age we would have thought it a bit too clever. They say a problem shared is a problem halved, and it is true enough, but I could've done without my share and the way it made me feel.

Even now, trying to make sense of it, I imagine my Jamie at six years old in the same situation. At that age he was a fat little thing, into everything and always smiling. All he asked for was two parents who loved him and looked after him, and that's what he got. But what if he had been locked outside as a tiny kid so he had to sleep in a stinking dustbin locker? I don't care what anybody might have told me, if my baby wasn't under my roof at night I'd want to know exactly where he was – and I'd check that he was safe. Or what if he had his little fingers slammed in a drawer, hot tea 'accidentally' spilt on his legs, or slapped in the ear so many times his hearing was never right again? It just fills me with disgust.

No wonder I only went round Lenny's mum's when I knew Irwin was out of the way, because I couldn't bear to look at him. Funny thing is, Rose never spoke of those times. I don't blame her, and perhaps she'd blanked out what she knew. On the other hand, according to Lenny, most of what went on was behind her back. Sometimes when I was visiting it couldn't be helped and Irwin would come in. Like I said, he never said anything out of place to me but I often wondered if he knew what I knew. If he did he never showed it, and again if he did, knowing the sort of person he was he wouldn't care anything about what this bit of a girl thought.

Only once was there ever a glimpse of what he really

was, and it backed Lenny's words up one hundred per cent.

He'd come in one night just as we were leaving. Lenny was just putting his coat on when there was a knock on the door. He went to open it and I could hear some young fellas saying something. He went outside then came back in almost carrying his brother Kruger because he was absolutely blind drunk. Irwin shot out of his armchair, ran over and practically jumped in the air as he brought his knuckles down on the top of Kruger's head, and he just fell to the floor.

My stomach turned over because by the look on Lenny's face he was going to kill Irwin right there in front of us. Rose got in between them and pushed Lenny out of the room and I followed them as quick as I could. I didn't want to be left in the same room as that pig. By the time I got to the front door Lenny was practically in tears of frustration and Rose was whispering, 'Remember what I said – it'll be all right, son. I'll deal with it.'

All the way home he kept smashing his hand on the steering wheel, swearing and cursing and saying, 'One day I'll kill him stone dead.' I never said a word; just let him get it out of his system.

Kruger came round to see Lenny the next night and as I let him in I asked him how his head was. He looked at me as though it was a strange thing to ask and said, 'Bit of a hangover, why's that?'

I just said, 'Don't matter.' If he didn't remember, and his mum hadn't said that Jim had knocked him spark out, it wasn't for me to say anything.

I sometimes wonder that if Lenny had handed out a proper straightener to his stepdad, whether it might have got rid of a lot of his aggression. Because that's what he was doing every time he got stuck into some bully, putting himself in the place of the victim and lashing out – and God help anybody that came up against him then.

He used to get all wound up if he was watching the news or reading the paper and there was a mention of a kid being abused, or some old man getting turned over. He'd do his nut – and I mean really go into one. And I'd have to say, 'Calm down, Len, that's happened a hundred miles away. You can't do nothing about it.'

Then an old lady who lived round the corner from us got mugged and Lenny went crazy. They didn't call it mugging then, it was bag snatching, though it's still the same thing. She'd been coming back from Roman Road – broad daylight, this was – when a bloke grabbed hold of her, took her bag and the rings off her fingers, then punched her in the face. Eighty-two years old.

I'm saying Len went mad over it, but so did everybody local, me included. But, end of the day, what can you do? Hope the police catch him, beat him up in the cells, then put him away for ten years where hopefully he gets knifed or scalded, and you have to leave it at that. Not Lenny. He took it as personally as if it had been his own mum.

I don't know how many times he got people to enquire round the local nick if they'd caught him yet. They never had and wouldn't have given out that sort of information anyway. So he put the word out on the streets. I've already said he was well known and well respected. And while a lot of low-lifes he had to deal with wouldn't grass anybody normally, no matter what they've done, because it was Lenny asking they made an effort. Probably selfish, thinking it can only do them a bit of good if Lenny McLean owed them one.

I suppose the bloke who robbed the old lady thought he was playing it a bit clever, because it was about six weeks before a fence got the offer of a diamond ring and a gold wedding ring. As it turned out it was a fence that Tony used whenever he had a bit of gear he wanted to shift. One ring's like another, so that didn't prove anything. But this low-life, kidding himself about that old saying 'honour among thieves', and thinking there was some truth in it, let it slip that he'd got a result from some silly old tart.

A few enquiries were made and this fence came to see Lenny, who happened to be out. I knew him vaguely so I asked him in, but he said, 'No, I won't. I'm on my own,' and I remembered this code they all had. If he'd had a wife or girlfriend with him it would've been OK, but what you never did was visit a woman when the old man wasn't around. So he gave me a piece of paper saying, 'Here's the name and address that Len wanted.'

When Len came in for his tea and I gave him the note I thought he would've reacted more than he did. He knew I knew what it was about, so he just nodded to himself and out came the jaw. He couldn't settle all night. He was up and down and he hardly watched any of *Steptoe and Son*, and usually you didn't breathe while that was on the telly. About eleven he went into the bedroom and came out putting his leather knuckle guard in his pocket. He leaned over the back of the settee, gave me a kiss on the top of the head and said, 'Gotta go to work, babe. Won't be too late,' and that was that.

I'd like to be able to tell you exactly what this fella got when Lenny got hold of him, but I was never told. All Lenny said when he climbed into bed at half one was, 'Don't ask, Val – it's all sorted,' so I didn't.

End of the week there was a piece in the *Advertiser* that said a badly injured man had been found in Homerton High Street, the victim of a hit and run, and the police were making enquiries, but nothing ever came of it. A long time later I asked Lenny why he hadn't passed on a name to the law and he gave me a look that said, 'Leave it out, Val,' and I knew it had been a waste of time asking.

What he did do was offer to buy the stolen rings, but the fence wouldn't have it and gave them to him. So the old lady got them back, but she was never the same again and died about two years after.

— FIVE —

What with Lenny being out of work, he'd started talking a lot about doing the big one, and I started to worry that if he didn't get some sort of work pretty soon he was going to get himself into trouble. The thing is, he was really a criminal at heart. Like I said, he wasn't against doing a day's work, but when his pockets were empty and he couldn't buy a round in the pub, it was only natural for him – like a lot of people in the East End – to turn his mind to getting money any way he could. Trouble was, he got so fed up chasing jobs, criminal or otherwise, that never came off, he'd started to lie about on the settee thinking it was all a waste of time.

He was drinking a lot more as well, though where the money came for that I don't know.

I was in bed waiting for him to come home and there was this almighty crash, then it went all quiet. Ten minutes later he came into the bedroom and as he's getting undressed I said, 'What's going on, Len?'

He just said, 'Nothing, sweetheart. Knocked over a dustbin with the motor, I think.' Next morning he's looked out of the window and screamed, 'Fucking hell, Val, come and see what some bastard's done to my motor.'

I shouted back, 'I can't, I'm being sick.'

He said, 'Never mind that – I don't feel too good myself. You'll have to get down and move it.'

I finished what I was doing, cleaned my teeth with him moaning, 'What you doing?' all the time, then went to see what he was on about. The back end of our Mini was sticking out of the smashed-in doors of the bin room in the flats opposite. He's still raving about 'Bastard kids' until I pointed out that it might be something to do with him being paralytic when he parked up the night before.

That made him think, then he ignored it, saying, 'Whatever – slip down and move it, sweetheart.'

I said, 'I can't drive, Len, you know that.' He gave a big sigh like it was all my fault, and started putting his shoes on, but I was on the way back to the toilet again.

He'd obviously tried to start the car and couldn't and by the time I looked out again he had a rope round the back end and was pulling it across the road, and from what I could see the front wheels weren't even turning.

By the time we were having a cup of tea he was right into one. 'Nothing's going right for me at the moment. Everything I touch goes pear-shaped.'

I said, 'Not everything.'

'Yes, babe, everything. No poxy job, no poxy money, and now my motor's bolloxed – and it ain't nothing to smile about, either. What? Why you looking like that?'

I wanted to make a big song and dance about it – say something clever, build up the moment, but three words said it all. 'Lenny, I'm pregnant.' Now it was my turn for the big grin.

It took a lot to knock Lenny speechless, but he certainly was after that. He just looked at me and said, 'You sure? Who told you? How did that happen?'

I said, 'Course I'm sure. I've had morning sickness for a week – nobody has to tell me, I'm a woman. There's ways of knowing, and what do you mean, "How did that happen?"'

He burst out laughing when I said that. 'Nah, I didn't mean ... You know ... I dunno ... Oh, bollocks, give us a cuddle, sweetheart. I'm trying to say I'm over the moon.'

For the rest of the morning everything else was forgotten and he drove me mad with questions. He didn't have a clue, really. In the end I said, 'Didn't your mother teach you anything about girls?'

He thought about that then said, 'Yeah, don't pull their hair – that was me first day at school, though,' and we both fell about.

I think what I'd just told him made him jump at the next thing I said later that afternoon. By this time we were living in Allen Road, just round the corner from Roman Road in Bethnal Green, so I'd been up the market for a bit of shopping, against his advice that I should be sitting down with my feet up. On the way past the paper shop I had a glance at the adverts in the window in case there was a cheap pram going. God knows why, I still had seven or eight months to go. There wasn't, but I noticed a local firm was looking for window cleaners, and thought it might suit Len for a couple of weeks.

Instead of going up to the flat to tell Lenny, I thought I'd save my legs and phone this firm up on the way home. They asked me a load of questions. Was he fit, did he mind heights, and did he have a clean driving licence. I said yes, yes, and completely spotless. Well, it was because he didn't even have a licence to get dirty. They said he could start on the Monday – cards in, and pick a van up from the yard at eight o'clock.

He was in the bath when I got home, so just in case he went into one at what I'd done, I told him through the door. I needn't have worried. He was well pleased. Just kept saying 'Good stuff, babe.' His way of thinking, I found out later, was he'd often heard people say kids cost a fortune – so as far as he was concerned the meter was ticking from the moment I told him. So in a way the job was a godsend to buy loads of baby stuff. I was going to explain they don't cost all that until they go to school but didn't, thinking it'd keep him keen.

Then the panic started. Not about the baby, but about the job. 'They'll be expecting a window cleaner, then?'

I said, 'Well, a plumber wouldn't be much help.'

He said, 'No, what I'm saying is I'm not, am I?'

'Len, all you've got to do is wash them down and polish up with another cloth. How hard is that?'

'I better have a little practice.' So I've got to find him some cloths, fill up the washing-up bowl, and take them onto the balcony where's he's sizing the job up.

Watching him from inside the kitchen was funny. His lips were pursed and his eyebrows were all furrowed up in concentration. What he did was wash a big circle in the glass – never touched the corners. Then when he saw me looking he winked at me and said, 'Is that your kettle I can hear, Missus?' like I was a customer. He did the kitchen and the little toilet window, and he'd had enough. 'Cracked it, babe.' I said, 'What, the glass?' He said, 'No, I mean I've got the hang of it. Fucking hard work, though.'

Once he started, though, he found it easy, what with squeegees and rubber scrapers, and he was happier than I'd seen him for a long time. The only thing he wasn't keen on was those cradle things on high-rise flats. I guessed that would happen because he'd told me ages before that ever since he thought his stepfather was going to throw him over the balcony, looking down from a height made him feel funny.

Typical Len, though, he found a way round it when he'd only been there three weeks. They didn't have those fancy aluminium ladders like they do now – they used wooden ones. So about three foot up he smashed one of the rungs, then told the guv'nor that it'd broke under him and done his knee in. Course he gets the wind up in case Lenny reports it to the safety people (which he wouldn't have because he didn't know about that sort of thing) and gave him a chargehand's job. Len put that pretend limp on for so long I began to think it would end up permanent. He even did it indoors until I told him to pack it in.

For a long time he treated me like I might break in half if he gave me a cuddle, or worried if he thought I'd been standing on a chair to clean the top part of the windows – though not worried enough to make him do them for me. Like he said, 'You can't expect me to do it all day, then come home and do it all night.' I said, 'Once a month would be nice,' but his shutters were down by then.

I was lucky, I suppose, I didn't have any problems while I was carrying. No varicose veins, no swollen ankles, no water retention – I was just me, except for that extra bump. I didn't complain about anything, so Lenny stopped treating me like I was fragile and let me get on with it. Then he worried about anything happening if he wasn't around. That's when he had the idea to teach me to drive. His thinking being that if my waters broke I could jump into a two-ton window-cleaner's van and take myself off to the hospital with eight long ladders flapping around on top.

I'm not knocking the van. We were lucky because we couldn't afford to get another car and the firm let him use it in his own time. But going up West for a night out with my feet up on a load of buckets wasn't my idea of luxury travel.

I said to him, 'Len, if you're not around it means you're at work, so the van won't be here.'

He said, 'No, I mean at night.'

'Yes, but if you're not here at night you'll be out in the van.'

He just shook his head. 'Val, I love you, but you can be fucking awkward sometimes. D'you want to learn to drive or not?'

I said, 'Yes, please.'

Never, ever do I want to go through that experience again. Having a baby was going to be a laugh compared with sitting beside Lenny as he played driving instructor. If he said, 'Fuck's sake,' once he must've said it a million times. Good job I knew he loved me to death and never doubted it for a minute, because all of a sudden I'd become the silliest cow in the world.

I think if I'd had somebody nice and calm telling me what to do I could've got the hang of it in a couple of hours. As it was, with him sitting beside me puffing, blowing and sighing, everything I did went all wrong. For a start I was perched on the front of the seat and my feet barely touched the pedals. I'd only ever been used to being a passenger in the Mini – now all of a sudden I'm behind the wheel of a tank. It was all right for him to shout and swear at me, but if anybody else had spoken to me like that he would've done his nut.

Once the van was doing a nice twenty miles an hour in third gear, it was great. I only got problems with starting and stopping. I was driving down Old Ford Road, took a left into Grove Road heading towards Mile End, and somebody braked suddenly in front of me and I stalled the motor. Every time I started it up it kangarooed forward and stalled again. A queue's built up behind me and every one of those drivers started beeping their horns. Lenny's said, 'Don't worry, babe – keep calm.' Then he climbed out, stood in the road at the back of the van and just looked down the line of cars. Apart from the traffic on the other side of the road, it went dead quiet. Not a single horn. And though I couldn't see, I could imagine all these drivers suddenly found something interesting to look at on the floor or in the glove compartment – anything but catch Lenny's eye.

He got back in the van, put his arm round me and said, 'You take your time, sweetheart, you're doing all right. Fuck 'em.' Five minutes down the road I was back to being as silly as arse'oles when I clipped the kerb taking a corner.

One time he directed me from Bethnal Green Road, all through the back streets until we came out by Vallance Road. He said, 'Go on, babe, under the arches and take a left.' As I've gone under the arch there was all this banging and scraping and the van stalled. For a minute I thought I'd run into the wall. But I hadn't, the ladders on top of the van had got wedged tight under the brickwork. Off he went again. 'Now look what you've done!' Nothing to do with him telling me to go that way. He got into the driver's seat, revved up the engine like it was an aeroplane taking off, and managed to drive out, leaving one of the firm's ladders smashed to bits all over the road.

After about three weeks of going out evenings and weekends he said one afternoon when we got home, 'You'll do.'

I said, 'What, I'm ready to take a test?'

He said, 'Don't be daft – no point in wasting money, 'cos you'd never pass. What I mean is you'll do for driving.'

And that was it for years, until I eventually got round to getting a driving licence. Passed first time.

Things seemed to be going nicely for us about that

time. I had this little football sticking out in front that was slowly getting bigger and bigger, but apart from that I didn't get all fat like I thought I would. Mum said what with the way I was carrying – all at the front, that is – I was definitely going to have a boy, but I didn't say nothing to Lenny because as far as he was concerned I couldn't have anything else.

As far as his work went, he'd got it all wrapped up one way or another. This firm had gangs all over the place and as long as the work got done they didn't really interfere with the day-to-day running. So Lenny would pick all his men up, drop them off where they had to be, then he'd be back home for about half nine. Three o'clock he'd shoot off to make his rounds, picking the blokes up. He was dead easy-going. If they wanted time off they only had to ask, and that's where Lenny started to make a bit extra.

His gang must've had the best time-keeping record ever, because the wages sheet I filled in every week never showed an hour lost. What Lenny was doing was booking the men in for a full week, then on a Friday morning, after he'd picked up all their wage packets, he'd bring them home for me to write up new envelopes I'd got from W. H. Smith's, with a lesser amount. The firm never knew and the men were happy enough because even though they'd had one or two days off, they were never deducted as much as they expected they would be. Anybody else would've kept the lot, but not Lenny.

I don't know if it was just us or whether life's much the same for everybody, but no sooner do you start to think everything's on the up, when it goes pear-shaped. A new manager took over and him and Lenny never hit it off from day one. He tried to stop the vans being used when it wasn't for work, and he started making spot checks on the gangs. I think every time he did that Lenny was at home on the settee, but the blokes covered for him because he was well liked so he never actually got found out.

Then he had a go at Lenny over something or other and came close to getting a right-hander, so it stands to reason Lenny's time was running a bit short. He reckons he was grassed up over the wages thing, but I just think this manager found out for himself.

We were in bed this Saturday morning, about half seven, when we're woke up with hammering on the front door. Lenny's jumped out the bed effing and blinding, and made for the door. I said, 'Put some pants on first, Len,' so he came back and this banging's still going on.

Next thing he's opened the door and I laid there listening to this right ruck going on. I was going to get up, but with me expecting to give birth any day now, I thought I'd better leave it to Lenny, whatever it was. He was screaming like he did when he really went into one, then people ran past the window on the balcony. I couldn't see them because the curtain was pulled, but I could hear heavy footsteps. Then I heard Len run past and I thought, 'Thank God he stuck his pants on,' because in the heat of the moment he wouldn't have given it a second's thought.

When he came back into the bedroom he was steaming. He had a yellow card in his hand and as he tore it in little pieces he said, 'See that? That's your job out the window.' He meant his own job but said that because I'd got it in the first place. He said, 'That c*** of a manager's given me my cards and he had a couple of Old Bill standing behind him, but I fucked the three of them off.' He got back into bed and said, 'Listen, babe, make me right – I've tried it your way and now I'm back where I started. So don't complain, sweetheart, but from now on I'm going to make a living for the three of us in me own way.' If he expected an argument from me, he didn't get one. He'd never let me down so far, and I didn't suppose he was going to start then.

Funny how you don't notice changes that are happening right under your nose. I mean I couldn't really miss the fact that from that first night I'd met him, he'd put on almost five stone in weight. Not fat, muscle, and he was a very impressive-looking fella. But apart from that I seemed to have missed the change from boy to man. He was still as daft as a brush when it suited him, but looking at him that morning as he was so serious about looking after me the best way he could, for the first time I saw him in a different light and never had a single worry about how the future might turn out.

Ten minutes later he was doing handstands against the wardrobe to make me laugh – but that side of him was never going to change for the rest of his life.

For the next week he didn't do very much at all. We went out a few times, but with me feeling a bit tired and frightened of having a baby in a shop like you sometimes read about, not too far. Freddie, a friend of Len's, came in and out a few times for a cup of tea and a chat, but apart from that things were very quiet. Then just as I'm thinking he's going to turn into one of those husbands a lot of my friends had – settee all day, pub at night – he says, 'Got a bit of work tomorrow, babe. Might be all day but it'll be a nice earner.' If he'd wanted to tell me more he would've done, so I didn't ask.

He went out at ten the next morning and didn't come back until nearly midnight. I'd waited up for him and the first thing he did, after a little kiss, was shower me with pound notes, saying, 'Get yourself a new nightie for going into hospital, and that pram you've been looking at.' I don't think the money meant anything to him at all. What pleased him was the fact that he was proving what he'd said he'd do. I counted it and there was well over a hundred pounds. A lot of money when wages were like twenty pounds a week. I said, 'Where—' But he cut me off, saying, 'Don't ask, babe.'

How strange is it that it wasn't until I read his book that I found out where that money had come from? Lenny, Freddie and a couple of other fellas had gone off to Hastings to hold a bank manager hostage in his house, then get him to open up the vaults when the time was right. The information Freddie had bought said the manager lived on his own, but when they got there it turned out he had a wife and kids. I don't know about the others, but I wasn't a bit surprised to read that straight away Lenny pulled the plug on the job. Where women and children were concerned there's no way he would harm them or let anybody else even as much as frighten them. The money he brought home? Typical Freddie, he couldn't bear the thought of a wasted journey so held up an off licence on the way back. Lenny and the other two are sitting in the car waiting for him to come out with crisps and fags and on the spur of the moment he's pulling a gun on the owner. Why Lenny never mentioned what he'd been up to that day I can only put down to me being close to having our baby. If he'd told me I think I would've gone into labour there and then.

As it happened, less than two weeks later I was able to give him something he wanted more than anything else in the world – a baby boy.

When the time came, 15 April 1971, I didn't end up arriving at the hospital in a window-cleaning van, though it was close because Lenny hung on to the keys until one of the under-managers practically got on his knees and begged for the van back. The manager himself never showed his face and there was no way he could involve the police after hiring two off-duty coppers to put the frighteners on Lenny. Got turned the other way a bit, though.

No, when I started to get regular pains ('No expense too much for my Val!'), Lenny called a taxi. Twenty-four hours I was in labour and afterwards, according to Len, it was the hardest day's work he'd ever done.

I'll never forget his face when he saw Jamie for the first time, though that name was only in the back of my head right then. Like I said before, big meant the best to Lenny and when he pushed through those double doors all I could see was flowers. He must've bought out the stall at the hospital gates.

I'm not knocking all the other husbands that came in that night, but I'll tell you, every one of those women looked at my Lenny as he walked up the ward. Not because of that forest of plants, but because he looked like somebody. Daft, really. I'd been with him for a long while and I still thought he was the best bloke I could ever have chosen.

He sat by the bed and kept patting my hand, and looking at me as though suddenly I was different. He said, 'Is it all right? Y'know, fingers and toes an' all that?' He laughed as he said it but I knew he'd worried – it's only natural.

I said, 'He's not an *it* any more, Len, he's a boy and as perfect as you could get.'

He leant over and touched the baby on the nose with one finger, saying, 'He's the beautifullest thing I've ever seen.' He wasn't really – with his little red screwed-up face and two tufts of gingery hair, he was a funny little thing – but I knew just what Lenny meant.

I said, 'D'you want to hold him?' and he sort of pushed his chair back.

'Er, no. I better not.'

I said, 'He's a McLean – tougher than he looks, you

won't break him,' sat up and passed him over. That was strange – this big man whose hands were almost as big as the baby, cradling him like he was made of glass. He didn't say anything, just kept shaking his head like he couldn't believe what he was holding. In a way I couldn't imagine what was going through his head right then, but knowing him the way I did I had a good idea. And I was right when he came out with, 'I wish my dad was here right now to see his grandson.'

I said, 'Don't you think he's looking down on us now, then?' and he said, 'Yeah, course he is, babe.' Then handed Jamie back to me while he dug around in his pocket for a hanky. A lovely moment to remember.

I think we both thought that once the baby arrived our lives would change overnight, but apart from what you'd expect with nappies hanging over the bath and a few sleepless nights, things carried on much as they had before.

From the first minute he set eyes on his son he was calling him Little Lenny and I let that go until I came out of hospital then told him I really wanted Jamie as his name. It's funny, my sister was expecting a baby almost the same time as me and we'd both chosen the names Jason or Jamie. No particular reason other than perhaps they were fashionable at the time. So in a way we were in a friendly race to see which one of us would have a boy first. I won, though she had a boy as well. What was strange is that without knowing, because I'd never been told, James was my real father's middle name.

I think I told Lenny that one Lenny McLean was more than enough for me to cope with, but that was only a joke. The truth is I didn't want Jamie to be a miniature version of his dad. I wanted him to grow up with his own identity and be a man in his own right without people expecting him to be another Lenny just because they had the same name. Lenny never really minded and since then Jamie's made a success of his life under his own steam, so I think I made the right choice.

Once Jamie was crawling around I used to sit and watch the two of them playing on the floor and think if those people who come up against him could see him now, they wouldn't believe it.

There was a bit of a ruck with some neighbours further along the balcony, and on one hand Lenny reacted the way he did because of his own baby, but then again he would've got himself involved no matter what.

We're indoors when we heard shouting and screaming from a few flats away. Lenny's jumped up, run to the door just as this youngster's coming towards him pushing a baby in a pushchair. She's crying and it looked like she had a slap mark on her face. I'm behind Len by now and as he's said, 'What's up, love?' a bottle came flying along the balcony, missing the baby by a fraction and smashed all over the place. She's run one way and Lenny flew the other where a front door had slammed shut. He never even stopped to knock, just shouldered the door open. Next thing he's dragging this girl's husband outside by the neck. He wasn't a little bloke but Lenny held him one-handed and he couldn't move. He's shaking the husband at the broken glass and screaming over and over again, 'Did you try and kill that baby? Did you try and kill that baby?'

This man must have been drunk minutes before but he didn't half sober up quick. Lenny gave him a couple of digs with his right fist – didn't knock him out but he knew he'd had them. Then Len said, 'Now listen, you coward, you bully – if I hear one sound from your flat in the future I'm gonna come in there and hurt you. Got it?' The bloke just shook his head and Lenny dropped him.

If that poor girl had called the police they would've

come round eventually, then said, 'Domestic – nothing we can do,' then she would've got a good hiding once they'd gone. As it was he got what he deserved and then had to live with the thought that Lenny was three doors away and keeping an eye on things.

By the time I'd looked in on Jamie and then followed Len through, he was sitting on the settee and his feet were in a pool of blood. When I've looked his soles were cut to bits. He'd only run through all that glass in his bare feet. I wanted him to go and get some stitches but he wouldn't have it. 'Leave it out, Val, just a few nicks,' so I had to pull the worst of them together with thin strips of Elastoplast. He never complained once and I don't think he even felt the pain. The only concession he made was to wear an extra pair of socks when he went out.

I said nothing really changed after the baby, but it had, though nothing to do with him. What with Lenny giving up working straight and concentrating on making a good living on the other side of the law, suddenly we had money to spare. We had a telephone put in, and that was a relief because he was wearing a groove in the stairs up and down to a callbox. I got a washing machine, a fridge, a Hoover – real luxuries, and not on the book, either. I felt quite proud of my home.

A lot of the girls near us had toddlers the same age as mine, so of course we'd be in and out of each other's places, like you do. When they came into mine you couldn't help noticing they were having a good look and wondering where the money was coming from, then the conversation would come round to 'What does your old man do for a living?' Their husbands would be up the fish market or bricklayers or lorry drivers, so when I told them Lenny was in licensed management they were really impressed. Well, it was only a white lie because by now he was looking after a few local pubs. And better than saying, 'He has a fight every now and then,' because they all would've said, 'Well, so does mine every time he goes out on the piss.' They wouldn't've understood what Lenny was all about, and I didn't think it was worth the aggravation to put them right.

As far as the criminal side of his life went, I never interfered. What could I say, anyway? He'd made his mind up how he was going to make a living and that's what he was doing. He was a very strong character so it would've been a waste of time getting all moral and asking him to get a job in a factory. The only thing I ever said was, 'Lenny, please don't hurt anybody.'

We've all read of ordinary people getting shot or smashed over the head because they wouldn't hand over their firm's money. I always thought of their wives and kids who had a hero for a husband or dad, but a dead or brain-damaged one. I know I said it to Lenny more than once, and each time he'd give me a look that said, 'Don't you know me by now?' and say, 'Val, have I ever interfered with straight-goers making a living?' And that was the end of that. It never stopped me saying it – just in case he needed reminding.

Sometimes he'd come in, throw a load of money on the table and hardly say a word. That was wages and not worth talking about.

Another time I wouldn't be able to stop him rabbiting on about what they'd done. Like when him and three others went all the way up to Nottingham one afternoon to turn over a television warehouse. All I got from Lenny when he left home was, 'Going to work, babe,' so as always I never knew what he was up to until it was all over. 'Going to work' covered so many things; to be honest I never really worried like I would've if he said he was robbing somewhere.

The information that had been paid for said this place was on an industrial estate, plenty of empty lorries and only two security guards, and that was why Lenny was on board – to take care of them. Back then things were much simpler. Now they've only got to press a button and the police are all over the place, or sneeze and it seems they can get your home telephone number from your DNA.

Once they were through the wire Lenny was sent to look after the security men. As he said, 'Val, they shit themselves when I walked into their little office.' I said, 'Who wouldn't, seeing the size of you,' but he said, 'No, I soon put them straight and they turned out to be good lads. D'you know what? It took them lazy bastards two hours to load them tellies up – thought we was going to be there all night.' When I asked him what he'd done with these two fellas he said they'd had 'A nice cup of tea, a few games of cards and a good chat. Didn't half talk funny, though,' and gave me a couple of Now Thens and Me Dook to let me know what he meant.

Two of them drove a lorry each to Exeter for unloading and Lenny and the other bloke came home in the car. Like he said, 'I don't do humping boxes.'

I can remember saying to him, 'Aren't you worried those security people are going to give a description of you to the police?'

'Nah,' he said. 'Treat 'em decent and with a bit of respect and you can bet your life whose side they'd be on. After all, they don't get a bonus if I'm nicked. On the other hand they can do themselves a bit of good if I turn into a six-foot black guy.' Months after I do know that a couple of envelopes were sent up north. Whether they were accepted or not I don't know – depends on the consciences of those fellas.

I don't want to make out Lenny was some kind of

Robin Hood, but as he said, 'We're taking from them big firms. We ain't nicking stuff off working men, so I ain't gonna start knocking them about.'

Sometimes Lenny did use a bit of violence, and that's when they did a lot of lorry hijackings, almost one after another. Probably doesn't happen today in the same way, what with mobile phones and all that. But then, after the usual tip-off, a team of blokes would follow a certain container lorry that might be loaded with cigarettes or spirits. At the right spot they'd cut across the front of the lorry and stop it. Then it was up to Lenny to approach the driver. I said he used violence, but that doesn't mean he went steaming in with a pickaxe handle. What he did was suggest to the driver that if he wanted to be a mug he could spend the next few hours tied up in a bush and if it was raining well that was just hard luck. On the other hand if he wanted to do himself a bit of good all he had to do was agree to a tap on the forehead and then get a nice little wage packet a few weeks later.

Lenny had been handing out belts for so many years by then he could raise a really impressive bruise without knocking the person out or putting them in hospital, and nine times out of ten the drivers went along with it. When the police questioned them that nasty knock on the head had given them loss of memory. Afterwards, even though it would have been the easiest thing in the world to do, not one of those drivers ever got stitched up over the money that had been promised to them.

I don't know how many times he got on about the Great Train Robbery. He'd say, 'They got a blinding result, then some mug fucked it all up by giving that old man a crack on the head – spoilt it completely.'

Though the money he was earning was good and didn't take a lot of effort to get hold of, bottom line

Lenny didn't really like what he was being paid to do. That's why he bent over backwards to get results without having to go too strong.

What he did like was a challenge when the odds were equal. Like being pulled in to take on the minders that worked for some of the big firms. People talk about honour among thieves, but the way I saw it there was never much of that flying around. No matter what the deal was, one side or the other was trying to get some advantage over the other. That's why both sides always had minders on hand, and Lenny was the best. The fact that nothing or nobody ever frightened him used to worry me a bit because I knew he'd never back down from anything that was thrown at him.

A North London firm hired him to mind them while they did a deal with a group of IRA men. I didn't know nothing about it at the time and it was years later before I knew what had gone on and only then because he accidentally let it slip in conversation. All he had to do was keep an eye on things while cash and bearer bonds were swapped over. Funny thing was Lenny didn't seem to think it was unusual that everybody involved, except him, was carrying guns. There was trouble and he had to threaten to rip somebody's face off before it quietened down. Fortunately none of those Irishmen took a shot at Lenny. No wonder he kept quiet about that 'bit of work'. That night, when I asked him what he'd been up to, he barely looked up from his paper as he said, 'Not much, babe, not much.'

One night he came home with a couple of guns. Guns. I nearly freaked out. The only guns I'd ever seen were on the telly or at the pictures, now I've got two in my living room. Just carrying those things was worth ten years. When I asked him why the hell he had them, as calm as you like he said, 'Couple of plastic gangsters got a bit leery, but they'll be scratching their arses with a big lump of plaster for the next couple of months.'

He used to say, 'Anybody who pulls a gun out and stands waving it about, like in the pictures, is never going to fire it. It's all front, at least nine times out of ten.' I'd say, 'What about the odd one, though?' and he'd laugh. 'With odds like that I never give it a thought.' Time and time again he'd say, 'They're cowards – fucking gutless cowards hiding behind a shooter. Half the time they're pissing themselves more than whoever they're pointing it at.'

That might have been true back then, but things have changed since then and I don't think he'd be so casual nowadays, because there's a lot of people around who'd murder their granny for a tenner. And that's all down to drugs. One of the things Lenny hated as much as he did paedophiles and muggers of old people. And it was because of the way he felt that the Hippodrome and other clubs he looked after became practically drug-free zones. Once he'd given out his own kind of justice to any dealers he came across, they weighed up the odds and decided to go to places where they were more easy-going. And believe me when I say 'his kind of justice'. The details of what he did to these people wouldn't make pleasant reading, so I'll leave it out, the same as he was asked to do in his own book.

Over the years he took a lot of guns off people and he was never tempted to hold onto one of them. He hated them and every one ended up in the Thames. In fact the two I just mentioned I made him get rid of then and there. He huffed and puffed and said it would wait until the morning, but no way was I going to be able to sleep with loaded guns on my sideboard.

I said he did a lot of work for firms when they were

doing business, and I mean firms in the sense of gangsters, for want of a better word. But I think the public would be amazed to know that this sort of heavy stuff wasn't just confined to the underworld. Sometimes Lenny stood in on deals that were taking place in posh boardrooms of well known companies. And the main people involved were, and a lot of them still are, household names. Politicians, even. I'd love to name names, but for me that's all in the past and I don't think I could stand the aggravation. Lenny would have said, 'Fuck you – sue me,' but that was him not me.

I'm jumping ahead quite a bit because a lot of this sort of work was over a number of years, and before that he got well into minding pubs and his bare-knuckle fighting.

— SIX —

Lenny was looking after pubs when I first met him, but in a way that was more looking in at closing time on the two or three busy nights. That's when trouble usually kicked off, so he'd be around to take care of it, and for that he got his drinks for nothing. He took it much more seriously when he was offered good money on a regular basis.

Lenny and me were in a pub down Hoxton one night. This was about half eight, and we were just having a quick drink before going up West. Must've been a Friday night because that's when my mum always looked after Jamie to give us a break.

Lenny was sitting with his back to a pillar and I was facing the bar – it wasn't too full up. Two fellas came in. Tough-looking men. 'Sovereigns', Lenny would've said. I was watching them, but I wasn't at the same time, you know how it is when you're having a drink. They must've asked the barmaid for the guv'nor because she went out the back and Bill came through. I couldn't hear what was being said but it looked like they were having an argument, though speaking quiet.

Next thing I saw the nearest one take a knife from his belt and hold it below the bar. I said to Lenny, 'Len, I think Bill's having a bit of trouble over there.'

He gave a big sigh like it was the end of the world, said, 'Fuck me,' and got up.

I said, 'Mind out, one of those fellas has got a knife.'

He looked and said, 'That ain't a knife, babe, it's a fucking bayonet.'

He went straight over to the bar, put his arms around the shoulders of these two men, said, 'All right, gents?' then grabbed both of them by the hair on the back of their heads and smashed their faces down onto the bar. Still holding their hair he banged their heads together, then dragged them across the floor and out the door. It must've taken thirty seconds from start to finish and everybody just stood looking with their mouths open. What happened outside I don't know.

The blood streaming down their faces made me feel sick and I hated being made to see something like that, but I couldn't blame Lenny. What was the alternative? The landlord handing over a big lump of money he'd worked hard for? Or lying behind the bar with a knife in his throat? Not difficult to answer.

When Lenny came back in everybody cheered and he gave them a nod. He came over to me and said, 'Sorry about that, Val. Ain't gonna spoil your night out, is it?'

I just said, 'No, Len, you had to do it.'

Bill came over and shook Lenny's hand and said, 'I owe you big time, son, come and see me tomorrow sometime,' and I saw him nod towards me as much as to say 'Not in front of the wife,' and we left to go up town.

If any ordinary bloke had done what Lenny had, he'd talk about it for months. 'I done these two great big fellas.' Though after a bit it would turn into six men and two ran off. Either that or their heart would be banging so hard they'd have to lie down for a couple of hours. As far as Lenny was concerned it was done and finished.

I started to say something about what had gone on while we were having our meal, but he just shook his head and said, 'Leave it, Val – it's all over.'

He did go and see Bill the next day, out of hours, and it seemed he'd had that trouble coming for a little while. It just happened to come to a head the night we were there. As Lenny told me, what he was offering was fifty pounds a week all the time he could put Len's name up.

I said, 'What, above the door?' and he burst out laughing.

'No, Val, sometimes I think your brain's no bigger than a walnut. No, he means put the word out that Lenny McLean's got the place under his wing – not in coloured lights over the door.'

He loved it. His name was getting respect. Some of this respect came from fear, I know. But most of it was from people who knew that if they were in trouble they only had to ask and he was there at a hundred miles an hour. I've known loads of times when the phone's rung in the middle of the night and he's got up and gone out in five minutes, just because somebody asked for help. These weren't the piss-takers I mentioned earlier, the ones that wanted Lenny's power for a pint of beer. He'd taken on board what I'd said about people like that and from then on didn't do favours – 'favours don't put steam on the table'. And he said that to everybody.

The difference was, with the ordinary people who'd got themselves into something too big to handle themselves, he'd say, once he'd sorted it out, 'Don't forget – you owe me a favour now,' and that would be the end of it. In fact I can't think of a single time when he called a favour in, or, come to think of it, ever asked anybody for help.

There was an old man I used to say hello to most mornings when he was walking his dog. I say old, but he was in his late fifties and that seemed old back then. He didn't have a lot to say for himself one day and when

I've asked him 'What's up?' I got his life story. Though what was bothering him was that he'd borrowed fifty pounds off a moneylender because nobody else would touch him.

That's OK, but somehow these street loans have a habit of getting bigger even if you were paying a bit off. I don't understand how it works, but fall behind a couple of weeks and there was no chance of catching up. This man's loan had reached two hundred pounds, and that was as far as he was going to be allowed to go. They'd threatened to beat him up if he didn't come up with a good part of what he owed.

I told Lenny. On the Thursday night when these men were due he was already in this man's maisonette having a cup of tea when they came hammering on the door. The old man answered it and one of them grabbed him by the shirtfront just as Lenny came up behind him pretending he was his son and saying, 'What's going on, Dad?'

He got in front of his 'dad' and said, 'Right, you two mugs can fuck off nice and quiet or I can knock you both spark out for threatening my old fella.' This is the old man telling me this (Lenny hardly mentioned it when he come home). 'On the other hand, I think I'll just knock the pair of you out anyway.' By this time they're at the front gate and one of them's threatening to get the law because they're being robbed of what's owed. They might have been bullies but they had some bottle to argue with Lenny when he was steamed up.

'OK, boys,' he said. 'My old man ain't no thief, how much did he borrow?'

'Fifty quid.'

'Right, and how much has he paid you back?'

'Errr . . . twenty-five, but there's interest on what's left.'

'OK, you've earned yourself a fiver.' And he gave them thirty pounds and threatened to break their backs if they showed up again.

Then he said to the old man, 'Now you owe me. Every week, without fail, I want you to give my Val two bob until we're all squared up. And if you don't you'll have me banging on your door.'

Every Friday for the next month he was waiting for me with this couple of shillings, and I felt embarrassed taking it off him – even though compared with the other one it was the loan of the year. I didn't say to Lenny that I felt guilty, and off his own back he said, 'Your mate, the old fella with the dog, still giving you cash?'

I said, 'Every week – never misses.'

'That's good, babe, I like a man who sticks to a deal. Tell him to buy a new lead and some tins of dog food with the rest. It's written off.'

That old man cried when I told him and I felt more embarrassed than I had taking his money. It wasn't enough for Lenny to shell out thirty quid, which meant nothing to him. He had to prove that he wasn't being taken for a mug.

Even though for the first time in our lives we had decent money coming in, he was still driving around in an old banger. Most people when they get a few bob together tear out and get a decent car – lets the neighbours know you're on the up and up. Lenny never gave it a second's thought and never did.

If anyone turned up to see him in a clapped-out old Capri with the wings rusted through, he didn't think, 'Hold up, they're on their uppers.' In fact he probably didn't even notice. It was the person getting out of the car he was interested in and how they performed that counted.

It wasn't until the last couple of years of his life that he gave in and treated himself to a Mercedes, and that was only because I suggested it. But back then he was driving a Maxi, I think it was, and this car would never start. I don't know why he put up with it.

Almost every day I'd watch him from the window as he was going out. Same thing every time. He'd get in, try and turn it over on the key, then get out and push it down the road until it fired up – then jump in and away. Most people, if their car won't start, get a couple of mates to give them a push. So it says something about his strength that he did what he did every morning as easy as pushing a kid's scooter.

He's already told the story about when it packed up completely and he left it in Blackwall Tunnel. What he didn't say was that it caused a ten-mile tailback and was on the radio traffic news for about three hours. That night he came home in a Ford Cortina.

Next morning I watched him bump start it all the way down the road, exactly the same as the other one. When I pointed out to him that he'd bought a pile of rubbish he said, 'No, I haven't. This motor starts up in half the distance.' But even he got fed up with it after a couple of weeks and went back to tear the head off the bloke that had sold it to him.

Before he went out that day I said to him, 'Don't go too strong, Len, just get your money back and leave it at that.' I didn't want him to get himself into trouble over a car. Even though this dealer had 'rumped him', as Lenny put it, that didn't mean he had to get a right-hander. He gave me that look that said, 'Would I ever?' and took off.

As it turned out he didn't go steaming in because he took a liking to the bloke. Kenny, as his name was, replaced the motor and offered him the chance of a bit of work.

The replacement car was a reasonably new Ford Escort, and compared with some of the old wrecks we'd been driving around in it was like a Rolls-Royce; to me, anyway. Straight away bells started ringing in my head. Nobody swaps a forty-pound banger for something like that unless 'the bit of work' is right on the other side of the fence.

I asked him, 'How dodgy is this bit of business he's talking about?'

He said, 'No, sweetheart, it ain't nothing like that. He wants to sort out a fight for cash.'

I said, 'He must be mad. How big is he?' That made him laugh.

'Beat you to it, babe. I thought that when he came out with it, but what he means is he knows a few people who arrange what they call bare-knuckles. It ain't legal but if you get a pull it's like having no tax on your motor – two quid and all forgotten.'

I had a feeling I wasn't getting the whole story but I let it go. As Lenny said, this Kenny was probably full of piss and wind, like a lot of people, and it might never happen. And it didn't. In a way I was pleased that he wouldn't be fighting for a living, as well as thinking that Len had got himself a good deal on a car that it looked like he wasn't going to have to pay for.

The neighbours thought we'd got a good deal as well. Half of them thought he'd robbed a bank – the other half that we'd come up on the pools.

Things went quiet for a bit. Lenny was drawing good wages from a few pubs so he wasn't out getting up to things to bring money in. My days were spent like any other housewife – cleaning, tidying and looking after

Jamie. For once we were like everybody else – normal. No aggravation at all.

It was well over six weeks before he got a phone call from Kenny Mac. Lenny came off the phone saying, 'He's only gone and done it.'

I said, 'What's that?'

He said, 'Sorted a fight out like he said he would, an' you ain't gonna believe this – it's worth five hundred notes – cash.'

It was hard to believe. I said to him, 'When is it and where is it?'

'Tomorrow night, babe, and it's down at Kenny's gym.' That impressed me because I'd always had a funny feeling that this sort of thing wasn't above board. But if it was in a proper gym, the set up had to be a bit half-decent. 'Tell you what, we'll shoot down there in the morning – it's only in Kingsland Road – and I can suss out the deal and you can see what it's all about.'

Next morning we parked outside these big double gates and Lenny walked me into a yard full of lorries, cars and all kinds of old scrap. That didn't surprise me because I already knew that was the man's business.

A short stocky man came over, shook hands with Lenny, introduced himself as Kenny and said, 'So you're My Val? He's told me all about you. You coming to see your old man do the business tonight?'

I said, 'I might do if you've got a bar in your gym.'

He looked at Lenny, then laughed so hard I thought he'd do himself some damage. His face went red and he coughed like it was going to be his last. 'Your missus, Len, she can have a laugh, can't she? I like that.'

I didn't really get what he found so funny, but I laughed along with him. 'So where's your gym, then, Kenny?'

'Yeah,' Lenny said, 'wouldn't mind a look myself – see where it's all happening.'

Kenny gave us a funny look and said, 'What, the old hungry gym? It's over the back behind the caravans.' No wonder we hadn't been able to see it first off.

We followed him between some lorries, right round a line of mobile homes and up to an open-fronted lean-to. At the back was a bit of a fence and two horses looked over it, getting all excited thinking we were bringing their dinner.

There was a bag hanging from the roof, and big square lumps of straw lying around with sacks over them. Kenny waved his arms, saying, 'That's it – all the training facilities you'll ever want. Toilets round the back – up the wall.' I wanted to scream out laughing, but Kenny seemed so serious I didn't dare.

I'm still thinking it can't all be as rough as this so I said, 'Where's the ring?'

He said, 'You're standing in it.' This was a muddy patch just outside the lean-to.

'What about all the crowd? Doesn't seem a lot of room, really.'

He looked at me as if he was wondering whether I was taking the piss, decided I wasn't, so spoke like I was some silly woman who didn't understand these things. 'Crowds? No, darling, this ain't the Albert Hall.' I thought to myself, 'That's come as a big surprise.' 'Some nights we have two or three high-rollers and some nights we might have forty travelling people – that's it. Nice and private.'

Lenny wasn't taking any notice. I saw him out the corner of my eye going up to the horses. He went to pat one on the head and it took a snap at him. He didn't half jump back quick. He looked round to see if we'd noticed and I looked away pretending I hadn't. He was frightened of nothing or nobody, but he was only human.

Next thing he's taken a swing at this big sandbag. The rope broke and the bag flew about ten feet across the lean-to. 'Fucking 'ell, boy,' Kenny said, 'do you know how long that's been hanging up there? Fifteen years an' you've gone and broke it first time you show your face.'

Len just laughed, came over, patted him on the head and said, 'Yeah, but it never come up against Lenny McLean before. See you tonight – be lucky.'

On the way home we picked Jamie up from Rose's. We didn't have to worry about Jim Irwin because he'd got some sort of business going on up north so he was hardly ever there.

Rose didn't seem well at all, and hadn't done for a while, but all you ever got out of her was 'Just a bit tired,' or if Lenny asked what was up with her she'd say, 'Women's things, son,' and of course he wouldn't take it any further. We never mentioned where we'd been because even though she knew her boy could be a bit of a handful, she didn't know half of what he got up to or was capable of. We left her reading and rereading a letter that had come from Barry in Australia that morning.

At five o'clock I gave Len a dinner that would've fed half the street. Six o'clock he's opening and closing cupboards in the kitchen looking for biscuits. 'Starving, babe, how d'you expect me to show Kenny what I can do if I don't keep my strength up?' He ate two packets of custard creams and he was 'off to work'.

He was back indoors by half eight and I said, 'What's up? Cancelled, was it?'

He did what he loved doing and showered me with five-, ten- and twenty-pound notes. 'Yeah, I cancelled their bloke in two minutes. He was a pikey – big bastard.

An' I reckon I was giving him more than a stone – but he was a piece of piss.' As I scrambled about picking all this money up I thought, 'One of these times he's just going to hand me a bundle with an elastic band round it.' But I never said anything because I knew that in his head was the thought that the big gesture was his way of proving – like he'd promised – that he was a money-getter.

While I'm on my hands and knees he's hovering above me saying, 'You should've bin there, Val. Fuck me, I thought I was going to have to work a bit hard for five hundred notes, but on my mother's life I only hit 'im once.' And he's shadow-boxing and showing me how he threw the punch that put the bloke down; as if I needed telling.

I said, 'Don't swear on people's lives, Len, you know I don't like it, specially your mum's.' I could've bitten my tongue off because that remark took the wind right out of his sails. He wasn't daft, he knew there was more wrong with her than she let on, but what worried him the most was the thought that Jim Irwin was giving her a real hard time. He often asked me that, as if I'd know, but I just said she'd soon let us know if he was, because I didn't want him going off on one and seriously hurting Jim. Strange as it might seem, Rose didn't hate Jim. Perhaps when they were on their own he was a different person – it can happen.

After that first fight Kenny couldn't wait to get Len lined up against a few others, and the end result was always the same. Lenny made a big thing about doing it for the money, but really it was nothing to do with that. Not even when he brought home a thousand or fifteen hundred. We'd go through him chucking it all over the place, then he'd forget about it. As long as he had a bit of cash in his pocket as far as he was concerned I could blow the rest. Not that I did. You don't grow up with nothing, then overnight get into the habit of spending too much.

After a while I had a box in the back of the cupboard that was so full of notes I had to put three elastic bands round it to keep it closed. Lenny didn't believe in banks. He reckoned there was too many toe-rags out there and they weren't safe, no matter how many times I tried to tell him they wouldn't be robbing his money when they turned the bank over.

It's funny really, we had all that cash and I still went up the market at the end of the day to take advantage of the meat and fruit being cheaper. I was still pleased if I got a couple of pounds knocked off the price of baby clothes, and if one of the neighbours had something off the back of a lorry I was in the queue, same as everybody else.

It never crossed my mind at first, but as our savings grew it suddenly didn't seem so far out of reach to think of buying a house. Now that was a dream worth looking forward to, but we had a long way to go yet.

We were sitting watching the telly one night and Lenny said, 'I've been thinking, Val.' Then I'd be thinking, 'Here we go – another scheme on its way.' 'Now the boy's off your hands how about you come down Kenny's gym and have a little bit of light training with me, 'cos you're getting a little bit er . . . er . . . chubby.'

I said, 'You're asking for a smack in the eye. Jamie's a year old and he won't be off my hands until he's twelve or fifteen.'

'No, what I meant is you ain't carrying him around all the time.'

'And the other thing, you cheeky sod, being over eight months pregnant wouldn't have nothing to do with me looking like the side of a house?'

He gave me that puzzled look. 'Oh yeah, I forgot.'

Then he burst out laughing. 'Cor, you don't half rise to a wind-up.'

Two weeks later he's pushing open the ward doors behind a bunch of flowers as big as the one before. We'd already chosen the name Kelly if it turned out to be a girl. At least I had. Lenny's choice was Lenora, and he was serious. I said to him, 'Where did you get a name like that?'

He said, 'Out of that film on telly where the bird married a bloke from some planet.'

I said, 'That was Leonora, and how long would a kid last round here with a name like that? You'd only end up calling her Lenny anyway.' So Kelly it was.

He took one look at her lying in my arms and stepped back pretending he was shocked. 'Not another carrot top, babe?' Then he put a frown on. 'Old one-legged Ginger from down the market ain't been visiting while I've been out, has he?'

All I could say was, 'Don't make me laugh, Len, I'm too sore.'

This time he couldn't wait to pick his baby up. He held her out in front of him and she screwed her face up and clenched her little fists. 'Look at that, Val, she's going to be a fighter – bet yer life.' I hoped not, but as it happens she turned out to be like her dad in more ways than one.

Everything was going well for us but I couldn't help thinking, 'There's got to be something waiting round the corner to give us a knock-back.' But it never happened, though.

Lenny was taking on fights every now and then – paid fights, that is. I'm not talking about fights in the boxing ring but bare knuckles at fairgrounds, Kenny's yard and the back yards of pubs. On top of that it looked like he was having a tear-up almost every night because he was looking after about half a dozen pubs by then and between the lot of them there was always something going on. Every morning it was the same. 'Quiet night, love?' 'Yeah, not bad. Had to hand out a couple of slaps – soon sorted.' When I say looking after these pubs, I don't mean he was stood on the doors all night. What he'd do was sort of have a tour round these places during the evening making sure everybody was behaving themselves, but as you can imagine, six pubs and there's always going to be something going off.

I only ever found out what his nights were really like from other people, and it turned out that his 'little slaps' had been full-scale fights with sometimes half a dozen young likely lads.

I was getting some veg one Saturday morning and the fella on the stall said, 'How's the old man's arm?'

I said, 'What d'you mean? Nothing wrong with Lenny's arm.'

He looked like he wished he hadn't said anything, but went on, 'I see him having a ruck with a few geezers last night and one of them stuck a knife in 'im.'

I've said, 'No, you must have it wrong, he would've said.'

Well, you would've thought it was worth mentioning but he hadn't said a word when he'd come home. I know it was about three in the morning, but we'd had a little chat like we always did before I went to sleep again.

He was sitting with his feet up on the table when I got back. I said, 'All right, babe?'

He said, 'Top of the world – couldn't be better.'

I leant over to give him a kiss and as I did I put a hand on each of his arms and gave a little squeeze. He went, 'Fuck me, Val – steady.'

So I lifted his T-shirt arm up and there was an inch-long cut pulled together with a piece of plaster. 'Top of the world, eh? What's this?' He looked at the cut like he'd never seen it before.

'Oh, that, it's nothing.'

'Nothing? You've been knifed.'

'Not really, babe, it was only a penknife,' as though that made all the difference.

'Len, you should have had it seen to properly, you could get blood poisoning.'

'Nah, I put on a load of that Germolene ointment.'

I gave up.

Though I knew nobody could hurt him with fists or boots, it did worry me that too many people were carrying weapons. I just prayed to God that none of them pulled a gun on him and then used it. As far as his bare-knuckle fights that Kenny arranged, I never gave them a second's thought. They were one-to-one and I knew he could handle it.

I don't think there was a fight where he didn't say, 'Why don't you park the kids at your mum's and come and see your old man giving it some?' I always made some excuse or other because watching two blokes knocking lumps out of each other wasn't my idea of a good night out, even though one of them was my husband. The other thing was though I had every faith in what he could do, it would be just my luck to show myself the time he come up against somebody bigger and tougher than he was. Then I'd have to stand by and watch him get hurt.

Years down the line it's laughable that I could have thought like that, but by then he'd proved himself a thousand times. At that time, though, there was always the thought that things could go wrong. I mean, Henry Cooper put Cassius Clay flat on his back, and who could've imagined that?

Eventually I gave in, in case he thought I wasn't there

to support him, but I said to him I wasn't going to stand on my own in the middle of a crowd of rough blokes like a lemon, so he arranged for his cousin Johnny Wall to come along.

It's painful to think of the run-up to that and a lot of other fights. Lenny's gone and the kids are both grown up now – adults leading their own lives – and I'm thinking of how it was back then. He'd say to little chubby Jamie, 'Gonna help me work out, boy? And you, Tiddler,' he'd say to Kelly. Course they start punching him and he's going, 'Hold up – hold up – what have I told you? You gotta warm up first.' Then the three of them would lie on the floor doing press-ups. Jamie always managed half a dozen but Kelly never got the hang of what she was supposed to be doing, and all you could see was this little bum going up and down – never even used her arms.

Then he'd say, 'Right all, aboard,' and they'd get on his back while he did about thirty of these press-ups. They're screaming and shouting and Lenny was as bad as them. After that it was, 'OK, Kell, you're the ref. Jamie, get in your corner and wait for the bell.' Kelly would go, 'Ring ring,' and he'd say, 'No, it's *ding*, you soppy date.' Then with Lenny on his knees Jamie would fly in punching for all he's worth until Lenny's flat on his back shouting, 'He's too tough for me – stop the fight, ref,' and Kelly would go, '*Ring, ring.*'

That was lovely seeing them all playing like that – only trouble was it was sending out the wrong message. I'd hear a carry-on just outside the front door and when I'd look Jamie and some boy would be pushing and shoving each other, and one, the other or both would be crying, 'He took my ball' – 'No I didn't.' I'd tell them off, pull Jamie inside and tell him that he should keep his hands to himself and that fighting wasn't nice. Then I'd get, 'But Daddy does.' Talk about put you on the spot. All I could think of to say was, 'Well, he's a grown-up – that makes it different.' Pretty lame answer really but he was too young for me to go into all the ins and outs.

So this fight came round and after dropping the kids off we set off for Romford. I don't know what I expected but it certainly wasn't ending up in a gypsy camp. We picked Kenny up on the way and the four of us got there about seven.

As we pulled into a field and parked up beside a line of caravans, it opened up into a big circle of all different kinds of living quarters. There was chrome trailers, old camper vans, and lots of round-top caravans, all painted with flowers and horses.

Lenny and Johnny had disappeared behind a lorry for, as they put it, a leak. I pointed out these old-fashioned painted caravans to Kenny and he said, 'Don't call 'em that, Val, not in front of these people, say *vardo* – they'll love you.' We're still on our own and getting funny looks from all these gypsies, and some old man who looked about a hundred looked at me and said something that sounded like 'Koshto divus chi.'

I said to Kenny, 'Whatever he just said to me, wasn't rude, was it?'

He said, 'No. He was just saying, "Good day, daughter."'

I thought that was nice, so I turned round and gave him a smile and a little wave.

Lenny came back saying, 'All right, sweetheart? Ain't scared, are you?'

How could I be and I said so. 'What, with you here? Course not.'

As far as supporters went it was all a bit one-sided. Three of us and about fifty of them, not counting the faces peering out of these caravans (sorry, Kenny – vardos) and bare-arsed kids running around. I don't think I've ever felt so out of place anywhere in my life. I've got my best blue coat on, a handbag and my high heels kept sticking in the ground. No wonder they were all looking.

When I saw the man Lenny was going to fight my heart went in my mouth. He was huge. Not as tall as Len, but ever so broad-shouldered and muscular. He'd got no hair and his eyes practically met in the middle of his head. I hadn't seen anything like him outside a horror film.

Lenny pulled his shirt off and gave it to me. Then as he gave me a kiss on the cheek he whispered, 'Make me right – have I ever lost?' I shook my head. 'Well, don't look so worried, then – love you,' and he pushed through this circle of men, flexing his arms. Sounds a bit girlie now, but as I looked at this handsome powerful man, my stomach gave a little flip as I thought, 'That's my husband out there.'

I wasn't the only one he was impressing. Once we'd pushed up to the front I noticed more than one of the gypsy women eyeing him up and down. As one of the men shouted, 'Goo on. Goo on,' like he was talking to a horse, Lenny and the other bloke sort of ran up to each other. I had my eyes half closed and my fingers crossed, but as the gypsy hit Len hard on the arm muscle I thought, 'You bastard,' and next minute I'm giving it the same as everybody else.

I wished I'd had a camera. As he took the punch on the left arm, Len swung his right and caught this fella right on the side of the head. His face went like it was made of rubber, but he didn't go down. It was interesting to see how Lenny never got a mark on his face, and I suppose that was the same as every fight. Every part of him was moving forward, but somehow he managed to keep his head well back.

They went round and round swapping punches, and it looked to me like the other fighter was getting tired. He took a couple of hard belts, then he managed to get his arms round Lenny and next thing he's biting his shoulder – really biting. I said to Kenny and Johnny, 'Why don't the ref stop him? That can't be allowed.' They didn't even look at me. One said, 'Ain't no ref,' and the other one, 'Ain't no rules.' I saw Lenny screw his face up, then quick as you like nutted this fella who was hanging off his shoulder. He just dropped to his knees and the same man as before shouted, 'Whoa – Whoa.'

Lenny came over to us, grinning. 'Enjoying yourself, babe?' While I'm looking at the bleeding teeth marks on his shoulder Kenny said, 'Mind out, Val,' and poured some stuff out of a little bottle onto the wound. It would take ten lines to put down the effs Len came out with and he only stopped when the man shouted, 'Goo on!' again.

Kenny saw me looking at this bottle and said, 'Peroxide – kills the germs. Same stuff you dye your hair with,' then jumped back laughing as I went to slap him.

I think the sting of the peroxide had given Lenny the hump because no sooner had the two of them met in the middle than Lenny hit him full force on the forehead. If you think somebody flying through the air with their feet off the ground is only in films, you should've been there. He must've gone about six feet and laid there spark out. It was all over.

As Len was giving me a cuddle John John said, 'Hold up, Len, you're dripping claret down the back of Val's coat,' and when we looked the knuckles on his right hand were split wide open – and I mean gaping open like little mouths. I wrapped my scarf round his hand and Kenny said, 'I'll pick up the dough, then we'll slip into the Royal Free on the way back for a couple of stitches.'

Len's saying, 'Fuck off, you tart, it ain't nothing,' but Kenny was gone.

We must have been fiddling about for five or six minutes before we left, and the gypsy man was still lying where Len had dropped him. It was like all of a sudden he's 'no value' because none of his mates or family, if they were there, went anywhere near him. I said to Lenny, 'You sure he's not dead?' and he just laughed.

'Course he ain't dead – he was lucky he took it on the head.'

In bed that night I was holding his bandaged hand and I said, 'Don't you ever get scared when you're up against some of these fighting men?'

He said, 'Babe, you know I don't have to pretend with you, if I was a bit nervous I'd tell you. But the honest truth is no, I'm not scared – not even a little bit. I don't want to drag all that past up again, but when you're about four or five stone and you're looking up at a bloke who weighs twenty stone and he's going to punch your lights out, you learn to take it. Yeah, I was frightened then, but I promised myself it'd never happen again.' Silly question, really.

He'd been out for a run round Victoria Park before me and the kids got up. I lay in bed listening to him singing 'Tea for Two' and 'I Like a Nice Cup of Tea in the Morning', so I took the hint. When I walked into the sitting room with a cup of tea he was in the armchair taking the bandage off his hand and carefully biting off the stitches one by one. I shouted, 'God's sake, Len, what are you doing?'

He carried on, saying, 'Just getting rid of this lot.'

I said, 'I can see that, but why?'

He said, 'If any of those mugs round the pub see a bandage or a fistful of stitches they're gonna think I'm out of action – try and take me on, then I'll have to hurt them. Make sense?'

No, it didn't, and later as I'm trying to pull the edges of the deep splits together with plasters, I tried to work out the strange logic in his head. It didn't get me any-where, though – I mean how can a neat bandage be any different from a row of plasters on his hand? But that's what he wanted and he did the same time and time again – and that's why he ended up with horribly scarred hands for the rest of his life.

Years after this I remember being in one of the smaller clubs he minded – not the Hippodrome, a place round Old Street. He didn't usually want me in places when he was working, so there must've been a reason for me being there. Perhaps it was his night off and we'd just popped in so he could show his face. Doesn't matter.

I was sitting to one side and Lenny was talking to one of the doormen. All of a sudden some man came up behind him and hit him full across the back of the head with an iron bar. It all happened so quickly I never even had time to be worried. Lenny put his hand to the back of his head, spun round and punched him about half a dozen times until about five blokes pulled him off. Hit-ting him like he did was a waste of time because after the first punch I don't suppose the man felt a thing.

Lenny came over to me saying, 'Sorry, babe – that's why I don't want you around places like this.' He's rubbed the back of his neck and when he saw the blood on his hand said, 'I feel fucking sick, Val.'

I said, 'Oh, Len, that's probably concussion, we better go up the hospital.'

He gave me the look that meant I was back to being silly as arse'oles again. 'Not that kind of sick – I mean I'm fucking sick about me shirt. It's brand new – now it's ruined.' What could I say? We went out the back and one of the girls put a pad over the cut, but that was all the treatment he'd have.

I'm not being funny but his skull must've been about an inch thick to take a blow like that, and according to Rose's mum, Nanny Campion, it ran in the family. Her brother Jimmy Spinks, who was the guv'nor of Hoxton in his day, took exactly the same thing, sorted out the people who'd attacked him then took a walk up to the hospital for a few stitches.

I don't think Lenny deliberately tried to be like his Uncle Jimmy, but I got told often enough that he was a dead ringer for him. Even Reggie Kray told me that. It's funny how hereditary stuff can slip a generation. Obviously I never knew Lenny's real dad, but looking at photographs of him it's hard to think that they're father and son. Raymond, or Kruger as he was always called, looks a lot like his dad judging by photographs, but when you compare him against Len they're like chalk and cheese.

It wasn't only looks and build that Lenny inherited from his great-uncle, but from what I heard, temper as well. Not temper like a lot of men where they kick up a ruck because their dinner's not ready, or you've talked over the football results on telly. I mean flaring up when somebody gets out of order with either me or people who couldn't stand up for themselves.

We were just going to walk in a pub when we noticed a man and a woman arguing. She shoved him and he gave her a backhander. Lenny said, 'See that, Val? I'm gonna give him a tug.'

I said, 'Leave it, Len, it's just a husband and wife having a row – probably do it every night.'

'Yeah, but not in front of me.' He went over and

literally picked this man off the ground by the back of his coat. He said, 'Listen, pal, if you're busting to put one on somebody, let's you and me 'ave some.'

Next thing this woman's screaming, 'Leave him alone, you fucking bully,' and trying to give Lenny a slap. He's still got this man kicking his feet in the air. He looked over to me and shook his head as much as to say 'What do you do?', put him down, patted him on the head and said, 'Be nice,' and walked away.

More than once I saved different people from getting a good hiding. I came back from shopping one day, parked the car up and started getting my stuff out of the boot. Next thing this man's beside me, all aggressive, saying, 'Move your fucking motor, you're in my place.'

I said, 'Do what?'

He said, 'Move it, I ain't gonna argue.'

I couldn't believe anybody could be so rude, so I've given him as good as I got.

Then the screaming from the balcony above started. 'Oi, you c*** – get away from my missus.' This fella's mouth dropped. 'Stay there, you mug, I'm coming down.'

I said to this man, 'You've got about five seconds to get in your car or they'll be taking you away in an ambulance.' He did it in three. He took off so quick he left his shoe lying in the road. As he's tore off with all this smoke coming out the back, Lenny came flying out of the main doors going, 'The bastard, why didn't you stop him, Val? I know him – he's that lairy git from over the corner, I'll break his neck when he comes back.'

I said, 'It was nothing, Len, he was just saying about the vandalism round here – just got excited.'

Down came the eyebrows. 'You sure? Looked like he was digging you out.'

I laughed it off. 'Don't be silly, you'll have to get new glasses.' And he accepted it. That man deserved a straightener for talking to a woman like that – but not from Lenny.

Much the same as that time when we were teenagers and he belted those fellas for talking to me in the street. If we were in a club and he left me on my own for five minutes, half a minute after he'd gone some man would come over to see if I was on my own or offering to buy me a drink. It's the name of the game when you're in a club or pub and it never bothered me. A polite, 'No, thank you, I'm with somebody,' to their offer and that was the end of it. But if Lenny spotted anybody talking to me he'd be over like a shot, wanting to know if I was being chatted up. I always said, 'No, Len, he wanted to know where the toilets were,' or 'He was asking if I knew whether the club sold cigarettes.' Any silly answer except the truth, otherwise there'd be murders. Not so much from jealousy – more because he'd take it as a sign of disrespect towards me. I can't say he was any better or any worse than most men were when it came to possessiveness.

Even then, like today, young people weren't too worried about what each other got up to – within reason. But as has often been said, Lenny was born out of time. His way of thinking belonged to the era that his Uncle Jimmy came from, so I suppose, like that generation, there was always that hint of 'This is my woman – keep well away.'

That reminds me of a time when he was doing a radio interview. The interviewer, thinking he was going to get a cracking answer that would point the finger at gangsters from the man himself, asked, 'Mr McLean, in your opinion who are the most dangerous people you know of?'

I know it was on the radio but you could hear Lenny thinking before coming out with: 'I reckon it's jealous people.' Sounded a strange answer until you thought about it. Jealous people don't think straight – they dive in without weighing up the pros and cons and would knife somebody in the back without a second's thought.

Nothing to do with jealousy, but flying off the handle without thinking happened when we were living in a house instead of flats. I said to Len that I was thinking of either getting Uncle Fred over or a carpenter in to make me up some window boxes to brighten the front up. He said, 'Why d'you want to do that? Few bits of wood nailed together? Leave it out, I'll have a go myself – piece of piss.'

Everything was a piece of piss to him until he found out different, but it was no good arguing with him. 'Right, babe,' he said, 'slip down to Tommy's, lively, and get him to borrow me a saw and hammer and a measuring thing.'

I said, 'You don't want him to come and do it while he's at it, do you?'

'Now don't be sarky, Val. While you're at it ask him if he's got some planks and nails.' Old Tommy never turned a hair when I asked him for that lot, he knew Lenny of old.

By the time I struggled back up the road carrying the tools and wood, Len was stripped for action in shorts and a T-shirt. I've made a cup of tea and as I've noticed the dustmen up the road, taken the bin out and told Len his tea was indoors. 'Measured it all up, babe – raring to go.' He's come in, got his tea and taken it out to the front door then all of a sudden I heard him shouting. I've gone to see what's going on and found him having a go at the dustmen. 'One of you lot 'ave done a wrong 'un – somebody's nicked me tape measure.'

The three fellas are shitting themselves because standing at the top of our step Lenny looked like the side of a house. They're going, 'Not us, Len. We wouldn't do that.' I felt sorry for them all because we'd known them for years and they were good lads.

Len's still giving it some. Then he said, 'I'm going indoors for one minute and when I come out I wanna see that measurer on the windowsill where it was – or look out.'

We went inside and as I walked into the kitchen I said to Lenny, 'Is this what you've been looking for?' and picked up Tommy's tape measure.

He went, 'Oh, fuckin' 'ell.'

I said, 'You've made a right show of yourself, now go and tell those, boys you made a mistake and you're sorry.' By this time they're a good bit down the road, so Lenny's jumped down the steps and run after them shouting, 'Oi! Oi!' They've looked up, thought he was going to have them, so taken to their heels and run round the corner. The lorry took off like a racing car as well. So a quarter of Strahan Road and all of Medway Road never got their bins emptied that week.

The next time they came I gave them a drink from Lenny as an apology and they had a good laugh, but as one of them said, 'It wasn't funny at the time.' They really thought he was going to hammer them all. They needn't have worried either way because even if one of them had been silly enough to pick up his tape, he wouldn't really have laid a hand on them. Mind you, one of his bollockings wouldn't be something you wanted too often.

I'm jumping ahead with this house because we hadn't reached that point then, but it wasn't far off.

He said to me, 'Val, that bit of wedge you keep nicking off me?'

I said, 'Well, if you want to carry it in your pocket all rolled up like a lot of silly idiots do – you keep it.'

He said, 'Hold up, don't go all humpy. What I'm saying is, can I cream a bit off the top?'

I said, 'It's not my money, it's ours, and you can do what you like with it.' Though as I'm speaking I'm hoping he hasn't got some scheme in mind that might blow our house money.

He said, 'Good stuff, babe. I've just been offered four Beamers' – BMWs – 'from Scotch Jack – top of the range and so cheap it'll be like I'm stealing 'em.'

I said, 'That'll be like the bloke you're getting them from, then.' I got the look.

A week later these cars have been sent down from Scotland and they're sitting out the front in a line like we were going to a wedding. Lenny spent more time up and down shouting over the balcony, 'Get away from my motors, you little bleeders,' at the local kids than sitting in his armchair.

'Right, Val, bang an advert in the *Advertiser*, you know what to say.'

'What's that, Len, "Black BMW"?'

'No – bit more'n that.'

I said, 'I don't know any more than that.'

He got all exasperated. 'Well, copy something out of last week's paper.'

I dug out the paper from under the cushion, looked through the motoring section and said to him: 'How does this sound – "Red Wolseley – 40,000 miles – one owner."'

He said, 'What's that got to do with anything?'

I said, 'You said copy one of the adverts.'

He tried to keep a straight face but couldn't help laughing. 'No time for taking the piss – this is serious. There's a lot of dough sitting out in the road. Copy the style. "Black BMW – wheels – last owner a nun" – all that cobblers.'

I'm not daft. I knew what he meant; I just loved to wind him up when he went all serious.

This was the weekend. I put the advert in on the Monday and by Tuesday he'd asked me a hundred times if anybody had rung up – no matter how many times I told him the paper wasn't even out yet. By the following Monday and we'd had no calls he had the complete arse-ache with the whole business. I think the main problem was they were just too upmarket for the area the *Advertiser* covered.

I told him he should give it a couple of weeks, but he just said, 'No. Fuck it. I'm sending 'em back,' and he got on the phone to this Scotch Jack. He wasn't happy about forgetting the deal they had until Lenny told him, 'Plod have been sniffing around them.' Within the hour four men turned up to take them away. Well, three of them because I'd talked Len into keeping the only convertible amongst them for me. It was a beautiful car. Black like the rest, but with a white soft-top.

For the rest of the week I was like the Queen, driving around with the top down. Then one morning I looked out and said to Lenny, 'Has it been raining?'

He said, 'What, in this heatwave? Why's that?'

I said, 'Well, there's a big puddle of water on top of my car.' I never thought much more of it until I went down later on and saw the top had been slashed to bits. I could have cried. In fact thinking about it – I probably did. I was completely gutted, specially as it wasn't even insured. It must have been local kids or somebody with a grudge against Lenny, and with a list that long there was no way he'd find out who did it, no matter how much he raved and swore.

Once he'd calmed down he said, 'Val, this street's turned into a hole.'

I said, 'It's not the street, Len, the world's changing. It's the same everywhere.'

'S'pose you're right, babe, but I think we should have a move. Rent a place right out in the country – all that grass and stuff, kids would love it.'

It was something he often came out with, the old dream of some little cottage with roses round the porch, but that's all it was in reality – a dream. Lenny could no more move out of the smoke than fly in the air, and though it sounded lovely, neither could I. But once Len got an idea in his head you just had to go along with it until he ran out of steam.

Of course I'm straight in there. 'We don't have to rent, you know, we could buy our own house if you wanted.'

'Nah, cost a bomb, and I don't want one of them mortgage things round my neck.'

I went into the bedroom and came back with the box. Then, for once in my life, it was my turn and I tipped all the money in it right over his head. I told you he had no interest in money – it was like he'd never seen it before. 'Fucking hell, sweetheart, what have you been up to? Where d'you get hold of this sort of folding?'

I said, 'What did you think I was doing with all your fight money?'

He went, 'Oh yeah – course – how much we got?'

To be honest, I didn't have a clue. I knew it was a lot but never counted it in case there wasn't as much as I thought. So the two of us sat there and counted and counted until we went cross-eyed.

Lenny would insist on counting out loud and I couldn't concentrate myself. 'Five hundred and twenty. Five hundred and – oh, fuck it. Twenty – forty – sixty.' In the end I said, 'Please, Lenny, don't count out loud, you're doing my head in. Count up to a hundred then lay it to one side and start again.'

It made me dizzy by the time we'd finished. But what a lovely way to get dizzy. Twenty-seven thousand pounds and a few odd tens and fives. I couldn't believe it. It only seemed like yesterday when I was scratching around for twenty-seven pennies to get a loaf of bread, and now, because of that big man's fists and courage, we were sitting on a fortune. I just cuddled him to death.

Now Lenny wants to move the next day. Obviously there were no country properties in the estate agents' up the Roman, so we had to wait a couple of days for brochures from their other branches. Once they turned up we scanned through them like a couple of excited kids, then planned out a route so that we could look at half a dozen in one go.

Talking about it the night before I think we both got carried away. 'See this, babe, we could get a little pony for Kell – loads of room,' or 'What about this one, it's got a vegetable garden; we could grow all our own spuds and stuff. What d'yer think?' What did I think? I could buy a shopping bag full of veg for a couple of pounds up the market, and the thought of Lenny turning into Percy Thrower made me smile, but I didn't say anything.

We set off at eight in the morning and headed for Hatfield as the first stop. From there we went to Stevenage, Harlow, Stansted, and Chelmsford and finished at Brentwood on our way back into town.

When we turned out of Allen Road and headed off towards the countryside Lenny sang all the way and the kids joined in. By the time we viewed the fourth house Jamie and Kelly were zonked out in the back – didn't even get out of the car, and Lenny had gone all quiet.

At the sixth house we didn't even knock on the door, just sat in a lay-by up the road and looked round. All we could see were miles of fields, dotted with trees, and it was so quiet we could hear each other breathing. All day long we'd gee'd each other along. 'Oh, that's nice – blinding garden. Yeah, this'll do – mark that one down, Val. Did you like that one?' and so on and so on. But sitting in that country lane we didn't even have to speak. We'd been together long enough to know what the other one was thinking. He looked at me and I looked at him, then he started the engine and said, 'Fuck the country,' and drove off.

Next day, on the way to see a friend of mine who lived in Arbery Road, just off the Roman, I missed my turn and took the next, which was Strahan Road. As I drove up to it a For Sale sign caught my eye, and thinking, 'Why not?' I pulled over and knocked on the door. I spoke to the nice old couple and arranged to call back that evening with Lenny.

For the rest of the day I wondered what he'd say when he came home. The night before I think we were so tired and flattened at how things had turned out we hadn't discussed what the next step was. As it turned out he was well up for it, and once we'd been shown all through the house he just raised his eyebrows to me and I nodded. We were going for it.

That same night Lenny said, 'That country place – perhaps when we're older, eh?' and it was never mentioned again.

Five weeks later we got the keys and moved in. With the kids at school and Len out on some business, I couldn't stop myself wandering through the house just looking. It was only a Victorian terrace but after the flat it was like a mansion, and going upstairs to the bathroom and bedrooms was a novelty I didn't get over for a long time.

There was still an atmosphere between my family and Lenny, and I used to think: 'Why don't they accept he was just a silly boy when he got up to all sorts in his early days, and not bear a grudge for ever?' They loved the kids, though, and no matter what they thought about Lenny they never let that spoil what they had with Jamie and Kelly. Couldn't they see that I was happy? I had two of the best kids you could ever wish for, Lenny treated me well – as he used to put it, 'You can have the moon if you want it, Val.' Now we were houseowners, and back then it set you apart a bit and showed everybody you were on the up.

Family aside, as far as I was concerned life couldn't get any better. Then Lenny's mum died.

I'll never forget that night. She hadn't been a well woman for a long time. Nothing what you might call life-threatening, but she did have asthma and used to breathe into one of those things if she had a turn. Funnily enough she used to get attacks if she was upset or stressed, and the poor woman had enough of that in her life. What none of us knew, though, was she used that inhaler too much and it caused her heart to enlarge. Eventually it just gave out on her.

She was of the old school. No matter how many times we said she should see a doctor, it was always, 'No need for that,' or 'Yes, I'll make an appointment next week,' and of course next week never comes. In hindsight me or Lenny or one of the others should have insisted she got herself proper treatment, but she was a young woman, not some frail old lady in her eighties who would let herself be told what to do.

Jim Irwin seemed to be around less and less as time went on, and I think all of us breathed a sigh of relief. But not Rose. Like everything else she kept what she was feeling to herself, though once when we were on our own she said, 'He's having an affair, y'know.' Rumours had been flying around for ages that he was up to something on all the trips he took up north, but I didn't know that she knew. Silly really, she was his wife, God help her – and wives don't have to be told.

I acted dumb. 'Who's that, Mum?'

'Jim,' she said. 'He's got another woman, and who can blame him, look at me?'

I did and I saw this prematurely old woman with a lined face and greying hair, and I wanted to stab Jim Irwin for what he was doing.

Lenny took a phone call, and while I'm looking at him to see who it was, like you do, the blood just drained completely out of his face. All he said was, 'On me way,' and dropped the phone. 'Get your coat on, Val, Mum's been taken bad and she's up Bart's.'

I said, 'Oh, Len – wait a minute while I get Marie to look after the kids,' but he said, 'Sorry, babe – no time for that. Follow me up as quick as you can,' and he flew out of the door without even putting his jacket on.

Always the way, Marie was out. Another woman further down was out and by the time I'd got hold of somebody else and got myself to Bart's Hospital, it was all over. Well, I didn't realize it was all over. But as I walked into the waiting room outside the ward, my eyes went straight to Lenny who, obviously angry, was pushing Jim away with both hands. Jim was crying. I thought, 'Please, Len, don't cause a ruck with your mum laying ill next door.' Then he saw me, came over and put his arms round me in a tight hug. I felt my stomach turn over. I looked up and there were tears in his eyes. He said something but it was all choked up, and all I heard was, 'Gone, babe.' I couldn't speak myself, just squeezed him. After a bit he said, 'C'mon, Val, they said there's nothing we can do here for now – let's go home.'

I looked back and saw Lorraine comforting Jim, who

was still sobbing. She didn't bear a grudge about the past, or else saw him different from Len.

When we got in the kids were asleep in bed, and the babysitter, seeing we were upset, didn't hang about. This was about eleven at night by then. I made a cup of tea and we just sat there while Lenny just talked and talked his pain away. There was nothing I could say – all I could do was listen. He talked about what life was like when his dad was alive. Probably sunnier than it really was, but you do that looking back. His mum and dad sounded like two kids who were very much in love. Silly, laughing, having fun. I could relate to that. His dad singing 'Yellow Rose of Texas', and making them laugh. His dad giving him a piggyback across the park with the kids running behind screaming. He just went on and on.

Then he started on Jim Irwin and I listened to a lot of those horrible stories all over again. He said, 'D'you know what, Val? In her dying breath she asked me not to hurt him for what he done. How could she say that? He ruined her life and he ruined all our lives. We're all ravin' fucking lunatics because of what he done – well, I am, anyway. How could she?'

I said, 'Len, none of us will ever know what she really felt for Jim.'

'Val,' he said, 'she made me promise an' I did, but all I want to do is kill him stone dead. Make me right?'

I said, 'Try and put it behind you, babe. Wherever she is she'll know you've kept your promise because you loved her.'

He said, 'Yeah – I did.' Then he put his head in his hands and cried. I put my arms round him and cried as well because it tore me apart to see this big tough man hurting so badly.

In a way I was relieved that he felt he could let

himself go like that. Most men, full of that macho stuff, never let their emotions show and bottle everything up. The way I see it is, it's got to come out one way or another.

I remember when Lenny was working on his book with Peter, I took tea and sandwiches into them both and he was talking about what I've just said. In fact he was saying how him and his mum both cried at the end. Then he thought for a bit and said to Peter, 'No, take that bit out. Just say I got a bit upset.' He just couldn't admit publicly that the hardest fighter in Britain was man enough to shed tears.

Between Rose dying and being cremated at Finchley Crematorium, Len was very quiet. Night-times were the worst because he'd sit and think. The kids would be in bed, and when you've been together a while you don't have to make conversation for the sake of it.

I don't think we put the telly on at all, so there'd be these long silences, then every now and then he'd say what he was thinking. 'Was I a good son, Val?'

I said, 'You loved her and you always let her know you did – that's nice for a mum.'

'Gave her a hard time when I was a kid. You know I got sent away, don't you?'

I said, 'Yes, but that was over nothing.'

He said, 'I know, but before they took me away in the bus I told her to fucking well pack in crying – well I might not have swore, but you know what I mean.'

I said, 'Lenny, you were both upset – that was your way of handling it.'

'Bad, though. She had enough on her plate and I was giving it the big 'un. If there's one thing in my life I could change it would be that. I'd like to go back, tell her I'm sorry and just cuddle her to death.'

Funny how one thing can stick in your mind all your

life. Rose probably never thought about it again after it was said; yet he even put it in his book so it was right up the front of his mind.

They say the good die young. She was forty-two, so that proves something. And my Lenny only seven years older when his time came – so that's saying something as well.

The kids missed their nan but they soon forgot, and in its own way that wasn't a bad thing. You don't really want babies dwelling on death and all that. It took a lot longer for Lenny and me.

— SEVEN —

Lenny came bursting into the house one night stinking of drink and with blood all down his shirt and trousers. Straight away I thought he'd been stabbed again, so I'm going, 'Where are you hurt? Where are you hurt?'

He was shaking his head. 'You remember Jimmy Briggs?'

I said, 'Vaguely.'

He said, 'Me and him was on the piss all day, then he got out of his pram and I hurt him.'

'Well, if he was as drunk as you must've been I don't suppose he'll even remember.'

'No, Val, I mean I hurt him – bad. Lucky I didn't kill him. I better get this gear off in case Old Bill takes an interest.'

He stripped off there and then and went out into the yard in his underpants, to put his clothes in the bin, I supposed. A waste but by the look of him when he came in none of it was going to be fit to wear again anyway. He had a bath and from then until about ten, when he went down one of his clubs, he paced up and down. A couple of times he picked the phone up then changed his mind.

All I knew was that him and Jimmy had a fall-out over something, and then got into a fight. Nothing unusual in that, except it wasn't like him to have a ruck with his friends – and even more unusual to worry about the consequences afterwards.

He crawled into bed about three, and as I woke up he said, 'Anything happen, babe?'

I said, 'My sister rang, that's all.'

'Thank fuck for that – goodnight, love.'

Next thing I knew was being woken up by a smashing sound from downstairs. Why I didn't have a heart attack I'll never know. Lenny's out of the bedroom door before I had my eyes open properly. Then I heard shouting from him and lots of raised voices. I grabbed my dressing gown and went to the top of the stairs, and looking down I saw Lenny with his hands up in a 'don't you touch me' sort of way, and he was facing about four or five policemen – all dressed up in helmets and padded waistcoats. I noticed the edge of the front door was broken.

Lenny shouted up to me, 'Val, sling my gear down. I ain't letting these mugs come up there when you ain't got no clothes on.'

I collected up what he'd been wearing the night before and took them down. The policemen were holding long truncheons, but they didn't go near Lenny while he was getting dressed. I'm saying, 'What's going on?' and not one of them would answer me.

Lenny gave me a kiss and said, 'Don't worry, babe, they've made some mistake,' and gave a little wink. Then they took him away.

As soon as he was gone an inspector came up the steps saying, 'Mrs McLean, your husband has been arrested for attempted murder and will be held at Shepherdess Walk station, if you want to pass that information to his solicitor.'

I said, 'You're joking,' and he said, 'Yes, we do this for amusement when things are quiet.' I told him straight: 'Don't be clever with me because you're wearing that uniform – you know what I meant, and what about this door? When will you mend it?'

He laughed – nasty bastard. 'Oh, that's your problem. My officers had to use force when your husband refused to open the door.'

I said to him, 'But they never even knocked.'

I was wasting my breath because he came back with: 'I can assure you they did – for some considerable time.' How can you argue? Before he left he said a team would be round later on – 'Don't touch anything until they have completed their enquiries.' No wonder people lose respect for the law when arrogant sods like that treat you like dirt.

It must've been a Saturday or school holidays because the kids were at home that day. Can you believe they slept right through all that carry-on? About eleven a couple of forensic people turned up. First thing they wanted was the clothes Lenny had been wearing the day before. I told them that's what he'd put on when they took him away, but I don't think they believed me because they looked in the washing machine, in the bathroom and dug about in the wash bin and cupboards.

Jamie was playing out the front but Kelly was under my feet the whole time. She wanted a drink, a biscuit, drawing paper. In the end I dug a carrot out of the veg rack and told her to go and feed the rabbit. I locked the kitchen door behind her because I couldn't be dealing with these men and her at the same time.

It was all very one-sided. They asked me questions but wouldn't answer anything when I asked them. Then Kelly started banging on the door, 'Mummy, come and see this.' I ignored her. Then the little madam's kicking the door, 'Come and see what I've found,' and getting wound up like her dad would. Even those men got fed up in the end, what with the noise she was making, and started packing up their clipboards and stuff. As they're going one of them said, 'We might be back later on.' I didn't even answer, just wedged the front door shut behind them.

When I opened the back door Kelly was standing there saying, 'Look what silly Daddy's put in with my rabbit,' and she was holding Lenny's bloodstained clothes. I just thought, 'Jesus, that was close.' I parcelled them up, rang a good friend of ours and he came round and took them away within ten minutes.

It was a terrible worry at the time but luckily it all got sorted out. Specially when Jimmy Briggs stood up to the law and denied Lenny had been the one that had hurt him. And he had been hurt, because apart from everything else Lenny had bitten his throat and, as we found out after, he had actually died before he was taken to hospital.

Once we got over the relief of no charges being brought we had time to think about it, and to be honest I was totally disgusted, and I said that to him. He said, 'I've got to make you right. But remember no matter how you feel about what I did, I feel a hundred times worse. The drink done it and I'll tell you what – it's lemonade for me from now on. I promise you.' And he never broke that promise for the rest of his life.

The police never did pay for the front door, even though, technically, as far as they were concerned Lenny had been innocent. We asked often enough, but as they knew we would, we gave up in the end.

I've often heard different people saying Lenny must've hated the law. Yet even though he spent a lot of his life on the edge or over the other side, though it might sound strange, he had respect for most policemen. I know he stuck his finger up to them most of the time, by what he did – not literally. But he wasn't stupid, he knew like we all do that without things kept under control life wouldn't be worth living. He used to say, 'It's a game, Val. They got their job to do and we've got our job to do. Sometimes they win, sometimes we do.'

Most local coppers, and a lot of them up West, liked and respected him as well. That's why he got away with never getting a pull over not having a driving licence. Stands to reason that over more than twenty-five years' driving around he was stopped some time or other. But he got away every time without producing.

I remember coming back from shopping one day and not too far from our house I got pulled over by a police van. About half a dozen coppers got out and went all over my car. Whether I got mixed up in somebody else's business I don't know, but they kept me there for about half an hour while they checked this and that. One of them asked me for my papers and I said they were indoors. Talk about the cavalry coming over the hill. This policeman was digging in his pocket for a notebook when Lenny starts shouting from up the road. He's got fed up waiting for me to come home and make him a cup of tea; he's stuck his head out of the door and seen what's going on. God, he was giving it some. 'Oi, what the fuck's going on?' As he's got closer one of the coppers said, 'OK, that'll do,' and they all got in the van and took off quick as you like.

Lenny asked me what that had all been about and my honest answer was that I didn't have a clue. I wouldn't go so far as to say they were frightened of him, because there were six of them and they were the law, but it's funny how they tidied up their business before he reached them.

So when it came to Old Bill, no way did Len hate them, but certain individuals seriously gave him the hump because they didn't just do the job they were paid for – they carried it out either stupidly or nastily.

Like the time he helped a woman who was being frightened by a load of drunks. He came out of Cairo's one night and saw four drunks shouting abuse and trying to get at a woman who'd managed to lock herself inside her car. There were three little kids with her and they were all screaming with fright. Talk about red rag to a bull. Lenny never even stopped to think, just smashed every one of them to bits. I've said often enough I'm not a lover of violence, but sometimes that's all some people understand and if I'd been there I would've cheered him on. Somebody phoned the law and told them a lunatic was beating up four men and Lenny was arrested at the scene. Cut a long story short, he ended up with a fine and a suspended sentence.

What's the matter with the law in this country? He did the right thing, the woman was eternally grateful because she'd been saved from God knows what, yet the judge who knew nothing of real life nearly sent him to prison. It was a close one and even closer when he called that judge a silly old bastard. Lenny took it all in his stride, though. When it was over all he said was, 'If they think that's some sort of warning they better think again, 'cos I'd do the same every day if I had to.'

When a similar thing happened another time it went all the other way. What happened should've been filmed for *World's Unluckiest Thieves*, except there were no CCTV cameras around then.

Lenny pulled up outside a shop to get some tobacco. He walked in and there were two fellas threatening the Pakistani shopkeeper. They weren't hitting him or anything, but as Lenny stepped in the man's said, 'These boys are robbing me.' They must've shit themselves.

There was no way they could get past Len so they both jumped over the counter to escape out of the back door – only it was locked. Lenny's followed them out the back and given them both a good hammering. Rightly or wrongly he never considered involving the police. 'What happens, babe? They go to court, pay a fine, then walk out laughing their bollocks off to go and terrify some other poor sod. But those two won't try it again for a while.'

The day after two very apologetic policemen turned up to arrest Lenny. Yet he didn't react the way anybody might have expected him to. He didn't go off on one, because these two young constables had already said if it was down to them he deserved a pat on the back. But they had their orders and Lenny went off with them laughing and joking like they were going for a night out.

I couldn't believe the neck of those robbers. They got what they deserved and should have left it at that. Instead they were saying they were buying some cigarettes when this big fella came in and knocked them about for nothing. I can only imagine that some pub lawyer, pointing out that there might be an earner in it for them somewhere down the line, must've put them up to it. What a waste of taxpayers' money. Lenny had to go through all the aggravation that went with it, like being arrested and questioned no end of times, even though the shopkeeper told them over and over that he was a hero as far as he was concerned. Somebody got a bee in their bonnet because it was Lenny and just didn't want to let it go. In the end it didn't come to anything.

Those two scrotes walked away without getting charged with attempted robbery or wasting police time and that says something about the state of the law. Lenny made a lot of enquiries afterwards because he wanted to get his hands on them and finish off what he'd started. But word must've reached them about what they were up against and almost straight away they disappeared from the addresses that a copper gave him on the quiet. If they were waiting for the fuss to die down before creeping back into the East End, then they would've had a long wait, because Lenny had a memory like an elephant over something like that. And I know that even a couple of years later he would still be asking people every now and then if they'd caught sight of those two.

It wasn't too long after that that I first heard the name Roy Shaw mentioned. It didn't mean anything to me at the time; it was just one of hundreds of names Lenny used to throw at me. Trouble was he expected me to remember them all like I was some kind of filing cabinet. He might be on the phone to somebody and he'd put his hand over the mouthpiece and say to me, 'That bald fella that had the car lot in Old Ford Road, what was his name?'

I wouldn't have a clue. 'Don't know, Len.'

'Course you do – about fifty, got done for clocking motors?'

I'd say, 'That was ten years ago.'

'You got it. What was his name?'

'Don't know, Len.'

'Oh, fucking 'ell, Val, wake up.'

But that wouldn't be the end of it. The rest of the day, every now and then I'd get: 'Thought of it yet, babe?' 'No, Len.' 'Fucking hell.' Half an hour later: 'Got it yet?' 'Still thinking, love.' This name wouldn't be one bit important but once something like that was in his head he couldn't leave it alone. And I was the silly one. Never mind that he couldn't remember it himself, I was supposed to have it on the tip of my tongue.

Some times were worse than others, and if it got too

bad I'd ring round a few people to see if they had any idea about whichever particular person he was on about. If I was lucky I'd get a name and then I'd say to him, 'That fella you were asking about, it was John Smith,' or whatever. 'Oh, right, babe,' and that was him satisfied – until the next time.

Half the trouble was Lenny lived his life at a hundred miles an hour. He didn't have time for the little ordinary things in life. If his shoelace broke as he was rushing to go out he'd sit there holding it effing and blinding, as much as to say, 'What do I do now?' Simplest thing would be to get another one out of the drawer or another pair of shoes, but no – he'd sit there huffing and puffing because I wasn't getting one for him and putting it on fast enough.

Same if he lost something. If he was careless enough to lose his lighter indoors, then he'd turn it all around so it was my fault that I couldn't put my hand on it straight away. It wasn't just me; he did it with whoever happened to be with him at the time.

It was even worse later in life when we all got mobile phones. I might be out shopping with Kelly and he'd ring with some question. After answering it the first time I'd let Kelly take all the calls after, just so as I could get some peace. She'd say, 'Mum's in the shop next door,' then he'd ring five minutes later. 'Ain't she there yet?' 'No, Dad – long queue.' Sometimes I'd hear her say, 'You're breaking up – can't hear you,' and I could imagine he's doing his nut at the other end. He wasn't nasty or aggressive with it, but his 'fuck me's' and persistence drove us all crazy.

When it came to doing business with straight-goers, as he called anybody who wasn't in the same game as him, he'd get so frustrated at the time everything took that sometimes I thought he'd do himself an injury the way he got wound up. We all know how it is. No matter who you get in touch with, whether it's a bank, the electric board or the telephone company – whatever your query is the answer will be next week, this one's on holiday, that one's off sick.

Nothing Lenny ever did took more than a few hours to get on with. I've seen him too many times get a phone call at three in the morning and go straight out to deal with something that's urgent. Everything had to be now as far as he was concerned. That's why no sooner had he heard about this fighter who was supposed to be the toughest around, he wanted to fight him the next day.

He came in from the Green Man one night and the first thing he said to me was, 'Got any spare folding in the box?' If I'd said no he would've just shrugged his shoulders. As it happened there must've been six or seven thousand in cash. What he did with our money was entirely up to him. I knew he didn't drink or gamble and wasn't up to throwing money away on stupid things, but it's only natural to ask what he wanted it for and he said, 'There's a bloke who sounds a bit tasty on the cobbles, and I'm thinking about taking him on. Only I need to put a lump of wedge up front.'

I said, 'Len, take what you want, you know what you're doing.'

He said, 'I don't need the lot – three should be enough to get me in the door.' Nothing came of it.

A lot of people have in their minds that Lenny was desperate to become the Guv'nor and worked towards that. And in a lot of ways that's what Len put down in his book. Perhaps when he was working with Peter, hindsight and reality got a bit mixed up, because thinking back I really don't remember him saying too much about being the Guv'nor. I'm not saying it might not have been in his head, just that if it was he never said it out loud, and to be honest there weren't many things he thought about that he didn't eventually tell me.

What did drive him on was the thought that there was somebody out there who everybody reckoned was unbeatable. It was the old 'I've got to be the best' inside his head that made him so desperate to climb into the ring with this person. I say 'in the ring', but in my mind at the time I thought he was talking about one of those fights in a gypsy camp, or somewhere out of sight. So when he told me ages later that somebody called Joey Pyle had arranged a fight between the two of them at Sinatra's Club I was really surprised.

When the night came he wanted me to go with him, but I made some excuse about a headache or something. Really, I didn't feel up to all that bow tie and cigar crowd that went to these sort of fights. By now I was complacent about how Lenny earned some of his money. I was like any other woman seeing her husband off to night work in a factory.

The kids and me sat and watched a bit of telly, then they went to bed and I did some ironing. I didn't sit around biting my nails; I just went on with normal things. I stayed up for him because I knew of old that he'd be buzzing after a fight and if I went to bed he'd only wake me up to tell me about it.

He showed about one o'clock and as always I scanned his face to see if he'd been marked up. Like I said before, I never wanted him to turn into one of those fighters with a flat nose and lumpy ears. He was fine. He said, 'Sorry, babe, I've blown your bit of scratch. Went against me, didn't it?' He pulled his jacket and shirt off, like he always did when he came in, and his chest and upper arms were covered in red patches.

I said, 'Wasn't a knockout, then?'

He pulled his mouth down. 'Val, please – no, I let myself down, the old wind went. On top of that his corner pulled a flanker and gave me funny gloves.' I took it that he was looking for excuses to justify losing, but he said, 'That Shawey – good strong fighter, but I wasn't fit. All my own fault.'

He looked so annoyed with himself that I had to say, 'Len, I think I know what the problem was.' He looked at me as though I'd come up with some sort of answer. 'You're over the hill – past it.'

For a second he looked at me like I was gone out, then he burst out laughing, shouting, 'Got me going there, I thought you meant it.'

That changed his mood and straight away, like always, he was looking ahead. 'Don't worry about the money, babe – I've already put my name down for another crack at him, and I promise you I won't lose. Tomorrow – diet.'

It still makes me laugh when I think of his face next dinnertime. As always he was 'fucking starving, babe'. When I brought his dinner through he was miles away. He picked up his knife and fork, then looked down at his plate. I'd laid out three lettuce leaves and a tomato. If only I'd had a camera. His face was a picture because he couldn't believe what he was seeing. I brought his proper dinner through then, but every time we looked at each other after that we couldn't help laughing.

I think losing that fight, even if it was only on points, gave him a real knock-back and that made him want to get as fit as he possibly could. Something, I've got to say, he never worried about before. It wasn't enough that he trained up on his own, we all had to be involved. 'C'mon, kids – c'mon, Val – over the park, we've got work to do.' The kids loved it – running on the spot beside their dad, skipping and running all over the place – but when he wanted me to pace him right round the park I had to draw the line. I said to him, 'I don't know if you've noticed or not but I've had two kids and the last time I ran anywhere was for a bus and that was so long ago I've forgotten when.'

'Who's past it, then?' he said, but I let that go and ended up minding coats and jumpers while the three of them tore round the park, waving to me every time they came out of the trees.

Then he pulled his cousin Johnny Wall in. He was a professional boxer and I think he gave Lenny a load of tips. I remember one time Lenny borrowed a video camera, might have been a cine back then but I didn't notice. His idea was that if he could watch himself training he might be able to see anything he might be doing wrong. It was an idea he'd picked up from somewhere – probably boxing or snooker on the telly.

The truth was he just wanted to watch himself giving it the big 'un. So I'm filming him and Johnny running past me and Lady, our dog, who wasn't very old then, was running with them. Lenny was in front and Johnny, behind, kept tripping over Lady. As they came past the camera I saw Johnny tap the dog on the bum with his foot. It wasn't hard but she yelped anyway. Lenny stopped and said, 'You kick my dog up the arse?'

Johnny said, 'Course I didn't, Len. Would I do something like that?' and they carried on.

A while later when we were watching this bit of film Lenny said, 'Hold up, Val. Did you see that? That lying bastard John John did give Lady a kick in the behind. I'll do 'im.' He didn't mean it, though.

Eventually this other fight came round and off he went to Croydon. Again I stayed at home, but if I was a betting person I would've put everything on Lenny because whether he was a hundred per cent fit or not, there was no way he'd let himself lose that fight. And he didn't. He was shouting, 'Done him, babe – done him!' as he was letting himself in the front door.

I got a blow-by-blow account – a bit different from the time before when he didn't really want to talk about it. When he came to knocking Roy Shaw clean out of the ring, he not only acted out the punch that put him there, but then changed sides in the room and demonstrated Shaw going backwards.

I said, 'You satisfied now?'

He said, 'With the wages, yes – but not the result.'

That was a puzzle. 'But you won, Len. What more do you want?'

He said, 'Er ... yeah, but that was only because he couldn't climb back in the ring quick enough. Got counted out and that proves nothing. I want to put him down and out.' Sometimes I wondered where he was coming from.

Course now both sides want a rematch, Lenny to prove this point in his head and Roy Shaw to prove that it had been a technical loss, and he was the toughest fighter around. What I'd never considered was what went on in the background of these fights. I'm not completely stupid about boxing in general, and like most people have a good idea there's a bit of shady dealing going on behind the scenes – at least it was back then – but in my naivety I thought that was mainly about a bit of dodgy betting, not the fact that enough people with guns to start a war were flying about. I don't even know why Lenny told me. He said, 'I don't want to worry you, but it seems like this next fight's attracting some heavy people.'

I said, 'Thanks for that, now I'm going to worry. What exactly is going on? Surely this is just between you and this Roy Shaw?'

'Val,' he said, 'I don't know all the ins and outs, but that shooting in the paper last week – that's all part of it.'

'So what you're telling me is that between now and when you get in the ring, somebody's going to shoot at you?'

'No, babe, it's complicated. There's all this Mob grudge going on and somehow this fight's ended up in the middle. It doesn't make any sense to me at all.'

'Well, can't you sort somebody out? That's what you're good at.'

'C'mon, sweetheart,' he said, 'I'm tops on the cobbles but I can't take on half South London at the same time. I'll have a word with Ritchie.'

He meant Ritchie Anderson, a really tough Scotsman but the nicest man you could wish to meet. Though I suppose that would depend on which side you were on. Why he was living in England I don't know, but I do know he'd been down south for years and never lost his broad accent. Lenny first met him at Epsom Downs when Ritchie had watched him fight and they were friends until the end after that. He was typical of old-style Glaswegians who've grown up in the Gorbals. Quiet spoken, not too tall, but he had a very quick temper and was always ready with a knife at the first sign of trouble. Ritchie had respect from most of the well-known villains who were around at the time, whether they were from the north or the south of London. Lenny had enormous respect for him and he didn't give that to too many people unless they deserved it.

We were both devastated when he died of throat cancer two years before Lenny passed away. Though him and Len were like chalk and cheese to look at, they both faced the end of their lives with equal toughness and courage. I remember his wife Val telling me that there was a bit of trouble in the last week of Ritchie's life, and by then that horrible disease was really well advanced and his voice was gone completely. I won't go into what it was all about, but basically he found out a friend of his had been forcibly taken to a local pub by two heavies from a South London firm. When he heard about it he was resting in his garden – remember this was shortly before he died – he did no more but jump up, grab a knife and go flying round to sort it out. He stabbed both those blokes. With him it wasn't a case of he knew he didn't have long to live so never mind the consequences – he'd never worried about consequences all his life – he just did what he felt he had to do. So that's the man Lenny turned to when he wanted his back watching.

I didn't get all the ins and outs. All I know is Ritchie got in touch with Arthur Thompson, who was like the Krays, only in Scotland. He sent people down and one way or another everything got sorted out.

I never actually met Arthur, though I often spoke to him on the phone when he rang Lenny. I always found it difficult to compare the polite, quietly speaking man on the telephone with the stories Len told me about him. He sounded a really tough man and I suppose that's why him and Lenny hit it off. All the papers called him the most dangerous gangster in Scotland and the Godfather of Glasgow, but none of that would've impressed Lenny, he liked and respected him as a man and I think the same went for Arthur the other way round.

I've often found that behind very strong men there are equally strong women and from what I heard about Arthur's wife she was as tough as they come. So not having met her either, I had this mental picture of a very large lady, who was aggressive like in the way they portray Glasgow women from those days in films. I couldn't have been more wrong if I'd tried.

What I thought was really respectful towards me and

my Lenny was that she travelled all the way down from Scotland with her daughter so as she could be at his funeral – and she wasn't a young woman by any means. She turned out to be the tiniest, loveliest person you'd want to meet. I mean it in the nicest way but she was like a little bird. I was mourning my husband, but every time I looked at her I was reminded that not only had she gone through the same thing not too long before, but that she'd had to bury her eldest son while Lenny was in prison. He was shot dead in the street and then later on her other son Billy was stabbed and nearly died. One of the family died of a drug overdose and another one was blown up by mistake. Yet she'd come through all that and a lot more and you'd never know what she'd suffered by looking at her.

I'd like to think I could be as strong as her in the same situations. Yet looking back all I can remember before that third fight against Shaw is of being frightened out of my wits and hating every minute of thinking my Lenny could get caught in the middle of something that wasn't his business and end up getting himself shot.

So the fight booked for the Rainbow Theatre in Tottenham came round and Lenny said, 'I know you ain't a big fight fan, babe, but I wouldn't mind knowing you was sitting ringside for me – how about it?' He was right; I wasn't a fight fan, and people think that's a bit strange considering I was married to the toughest fighter around. I know his fists gave us a good living but I never was, or ever could be, one of those women who get something out of two men beating each other up. But as he'd asked me and as this fight seemed to mean a lot to him, I agreed to go along with him.

This place used to be the Tottenham Royal dance hall, but now it was all different. There was a ring set up and table and chairs all round it so people could have a drink and a meal before or during the fights. As it happens I didn't sit ringside but a good bit back, and it was a long time after before I found out that all the seats round the ring were taken up with Ritchie's friends carrying guns. I was glad I didn't know it at the time, though to be honest I don't think there was any serious threat of trouble or else Lenny wouldn't have let me be there.

This was the first time I'd set eyes on Roy Shaw and he really did think he was something as he gave it the big 'un walking down to the ring. Right then he was known as the Guv'nor but he wasn't going to hang on to that title for long. There's no getting away from it, he was a very tough man. Like Lenny he'd had a rough start to his life. He'd done his share of prison time and eventually ended up in Broadmoor hospital. When he came out he did what he was good at and that was fighting, but on 11 September 1978 he found out he wasn't good enough to beat my Len.

I won't even try and describe this fight – I probably missed some of the best action because when it got too rough I closed my eyes. Apart from what was going on in the ring I had something else to think about.

About twenty-five minutes before it was going to start, while everybody was getting settled, somebody said, 'Hello, Val, is that you?' I looked round and there was Jim Irwin. I hadn't seen anything of him since Rose died, and he looked like he'd aged about twenty years.

Once his mum was gone Lenny didn't want anything to do with him at all. Not that he had before, but what with calling round to see Rose he hadn't been able to avoid bumping into him every now and then. Not many months after the funeral Jim had moved away from the East End and in with Rose's sister. Lenny didn't like the idea of that at all and wanted to kick up a ruck, but as I told him, what his aunt did was her business and at least he was well away from us.

I couldn't ignore him and I'm not that rude that I would, so I said, 'Hello, Jim. What are you doing here?'

He looked a bit embarrassed. 'I was up this way and I thought I'd try and have a word with Len. You know, clear the air a bit.'

I couldn't believe he could even consider trying to make things right after all this time, specially after the way Lenny had spoken to him at the hospital. But it wasn't for me to stop him trying so I just said, 'I'm not sure if they'll let you in the dressing rooms, but all you can do is try.'

It was hard looking at that old man and thinking about how he'd treated Lenny and his family all those years ago. Was he even aware of the damage he'd caused? Was he thinking that if he said he was sorry Lenny would forgive him? I knew that wouldn't happen in a million years, so as the fight was going on I couldn't help wondering if Jim had seen Lenny. And if he had, what had been said? If it had upset Len in any way it certainly didn't show by the way he was knocking Shaw around the ring. He really did look very good, and as usual I got that proud feeling in the pit of my stomach.

When the end came it was all over in thirty seconds. I started to think, 'If Shaw doesn't fall down soon he'll end up with brain damage,' because Lenny just didn't stop hitting him around the head. Eventually Shaw couldn't take any more, fell to one side and the crowd went mad. Lenny put his arms in the air and shouted, 'Who's the Guv'nor?' and they all shouted back at him. Then he did it again only louder, and you couldn't hear yourself think with the whole place shouting, 'LENNY, LENNY, LENNY!'

It wasn't me to stand up and join in but inside I was thinking, 'You've always been the Guv'nor, anyway. You didn't have to win a fight to prove that.' But he had, and though it was an unofficial title it meant something to the crowd, and would mean something to everybody from then on.

There's been talk ever since of Shaw wanting a rematch and Lenny turning him down. But that's all it ever was – talk, because to suggest that Lenny could ever refuse a challenge is so ridiculous it's hardly worth thinking about.

The same as I heard recently that he wouldn't turn up for a fight with Charles Bronson, suggesting that Lenny didn't have the bottle to take him on, and that's a laugh. I'm not talking about the actor, but the other one who makes a living out of being the maddest and most dangerous prisoner the system's ever had to handle. Personally I think his so-called madness is about as much the same talk as Lenny and his 'Fuckin' ravin' lunatic' – about as far from the truth as you could possibly get – but if it helps to earn him a living then good luck to him. For a start I doubt whether the prison authorities would've let Lenny inside for a bare-knuckle fight, while if any challenge was put out at all by Charlie, or whoever looks after his interests, it would've only ever have been a publicity stunt and not to be taken too seriously. Much in the same way that Frank Warren used to put Lenny's name up against whoever happened to be in the news at the moment. Like some SAS man or that Mr T from the television series. No one really expected anything to come from these offers but it kept Lenny's name up front.

No, when it came down to it Lenny could never refuse a fight – want it or not. It was the way he was. If somebody had turned up at our house the week before he died, he would've taken them on. After Irwin, nothing could hurt him and nobody could put him down.

I've read some sneering comments in the paper almost – well, not even almost, *definitely* – saying he was lying about having three thousand fights. If the truth is known, that's even on the low side, when you consider he started fighting properly around the age of seventeen. Doesn't take much working out over twenty-five years. Perhaps there was some confusion over fights in the ring and fights in general, though in his book he made it clear enough. It's pretty obvious to anybody that he wasn't referring to that many proper bouts – not even professional boxers have anything near that in their career. But add those proper set-up fights to night after night of coming up against trouble in his job, and sometimes that could be three or four from starting work until he came home, and his estimate starts to look a bit slim.

There are always people ready to jump on what they reckon is the slightest sign of weakness. Like they often come out with, 'Why didn't he admit in his book to being beaten by Cliff Field?' Give Lenny some human nature. Yes, Cliff beat him. He never put him down or hurt him, but Len was so out-pointed by the fifth there was no sense in carrying on. I'd like to make some excuse as to why it happened but then why should I? The simple truth was Cliff was a very strong fighter and a very skilled one at that. Perhaps Lenny expected a pushover and never got himself seriously ready for that fight. Perhaps he felt under the weather; who knows? Whatever – he lost the fight, though not in his own mind. If he'd been knocked spark out I think he would've put his hand up to it afterwards, but he never had a lot of time for a win by points.

That's why he never really counted the win he got over Shaw in that second fight, and by the same account didn't think he'd been beaten in the first. Beaten, in Lenny's mind, meant being down and out for the count. Nobody ever put him on his back apart from Irwin, and I don't even have to go there again.

Some fights were harder than others, and he came up against some of the toughest men the other side could put together. Without exception every one of them he took on was well matched in height and weight. To say they were anything but some of the best would make less of what he achieved. They all had the stamina and muscle, but what they didn't have was Lenny's particular brand of aggression that came from deep inside him, and that made him absolutely unbeatable.

In his book he says that gaining the title of Guv'nor was something he'd aimed for for years and years, and perhaps that's how it was in his mind while he was doing the book. But really he never mentioned that particular fight ever again after the first night.

On the way home I asked him what Jim Irwin had wanted and he just shook his head and said, 'I dunno really – getting old, trying to turn the clock back – who knows?'

I said, 'You didn't hit him or nothing, did you?'

He said, 'No, course I didn't – just fucked him off,' and he wouldn't say any more, or there was nothing else to say.

Jim himself died of cancer a year or so before Lenny and I suppose somebody must've been sad about that, but I have to say Lenny wasn't one of them. He didn't make a fuss like 'good riddance' or anything nasty, he just nodded his head when he was told, and that was that.

Apart from picking up the large end of five figures after beating Shaw, what it did for him was make his name even more sought after. Offers of fights came in from all directions and a lot of them were to raise money for charity. I don't mean big official charities; I mean the kind where ordinary people are trying their damnedest to raise money for special cases, usually children. They only had to mention kids and they didn't have to say any more to get Lenny to agree. Some of them were 'on the cobbles', as he would have said, but most were on the unlicensed circuit.

One of them makes me smile when I think about it. It was at the Rainbow Theatre and he was taking on the boxer Johnny Clarke. Lenny beat him, as you'd expect, and enough money was raised to buy an electric wheel-chair for a little boy, but the funny bit is what happened before the fight.

I don't know where Lenny was, but I was sitting on my own. A good-looking fella came up to me and asked if it would be all right if he sat beside me. Well, I couldn't stop him so I said yes. He made a bit of small talk – 'nice place, haven't seen you before' sort of thing. I'm a woman, I know when I'm getting chatted up, but I didn't say anything. I could see the wheels turning in his head and he said, 'Did you know I was on the card tonight?'

I said, 'No, I didn't. What's your name?'

He told me it was John Clarke then he said, 'When it's all over d'you fancy a drink or something?'

I couldn't help laughing. I said, 'You don't know who I am, do you?'

He said, 'Should I?'

I said, 'I'm Lenny McLean's wife, Val.'

I think if he could've jumped up and run out at a hundred miles an hour he would've. He said, 'Oh, Christ – I'm sorry – no offence.'

I said, 'Don't worry, these things happen,' and he looked relieved. Of course he wasn't so keen to sit with me any more, and as he's off he said, 'Ah . . . you won't mention this to Len, will you?' I just said no, thinking if I did Lenny wouldn't see the funny side and would've done him before the bell even went, and that would be unfair because the man didn't know who I was. Sometimes Lenny could be just that bit too old fashioned.

It was about this time that he had one of his trips to Scotland. I think the idea was that Ritchie and a few others thought it was about time he made some good money for them and himself out of the Guv'nor title. He said to me, 'C'mon, Val, you've never been over the border. Why don't we go and make a bit of a holiday out of it?' But I knew what would happen. The people he'd be mixing with didn't have a lot of time for women, at least where business is concerned, and being Scotch people they'd be even worse. So me and the kids would spend a week on our own, and we could do that just as easy in our own home so I said, 'Perhaps next time.'

I can still see him limping in the door about four days later. Both hands were plastered up and he could barely put one of his feet on the ground. It turned out both his hands were broken and a couple of toes. When I asked him why they hadn't splinted his toes up or whatever they do, he said, 'I didn't have time, I wanted to get home.' I pointed out that if he didn't get these things sorted out properly, by the time he was old he'd be crippled with arthritis.

Well, that was something he didn't have to suffer.

After a good result he was usually buzzing for ages, but he didn't have a lot to say for himself and that was unusual in itself. After putting up with his silence for a couple of hours I said, 'Something wrong, babe? Going down with something?'

He said, 'Going down might be a bit too near the truth for comfort. I don't want to worry you, babe, but

I'm not a hundred per cent sure I didn't kill that Scotch fella.' Why did he always say, 'I don't want to worry you,' then do the exact opposite?

I said, 'Tell me you're not serious, Len?'

He said, 'I just don't know. I really did give him some stick, then Ritchie pulled me in the motor and here I am.'

To convince myself more than him I said, 'I'm sure one of them would've told you to keep your head down if that was the case. You're tired, that's all. Just forget it for tonight.' He got a phone call from Arthur Thompson in the morning and Lenny repeated it exactly as Arthur had said it. 'Don't give it another thought, son, the whole matter is closed.' But to my mind as far as any answer went, it was left wide open. Nothing ever came of it and it wasn't ever mentioned again.

According to a headline in the *Scottish Daily Record* after Len died, it had 'I killed a man in Scotland', but I think that was just a journalist stretching things to make a good story. In my heart I don't think it happened. At least I hope not.

We took a proper holiday after that. Not because Lenny wanted to hide up, but the same as with his stitches, he didn't want to be seen limping or plastered up. We went to Spain and those air stewardesses fussed around him like he'd been in a road accident – and he loved it. If only they knew what he'd really been up to.

It was lovely to get away from the phone for a couple of weeks. At home I'd get calls from my mum, my sisters and a few other friends. But nine times out of ten it would be a man's voice asking if he was about, and seven times out of ten it would mean Lenny throwing his jacket on and flying out 'For a bit of work, babe.'

I think he was as pleased as me to get away from the constant aggravation as well. But like all holidays they go too quickly. We'd hardly got the suitcases in the door when Len took a call from one of his clubs. I heard him say, 'I've just got off the fucking plane – no, see you Monday,' and banged it down. He looked at me and I looked at him. Yes, we were home again.

— EIGHT —

He hadn't been working long at the Barbican Club up in Smithfield, and it seemed like there was nothing but trouble night after night. Lenny had calmed a lot of it down once he took over the door, but that didn't happen overnight, so no wonder they were panicking with him out of the way for two weeks.

Typical Lenny, he didn't leave it until the Monday but showed his face on the Sunday night. 'Can't let Dennis down, babe, he's paying good dough to depend on me.' Yes, he was, but after a certain bit of trouble in the club I got the impression that loyalty was a bit one-sided.

I got a telephone call from Snow Hill police station one night and it was Lenny telling me he wouldn't be home that night because he'd beaten up eighteen men and they were holding him. It was a very quick call and it was only after I'd made myself a cup of tea and was thinking about what he'd said that I thought, 'Eighteen men?' He couldn't have said that. Eight I could believe because I knew what he was capable of. I must have misheard.

I rang Ritchie Anderson and told him Len had been arrested over some fight but it hadn't made sense. He told me not to worry and that he'd go to the station right away and get some details. About half one he turned up at the house with his wife Val and he couldn't stop laughing. I'm all worried about what's happening to Lenny and he's choking on what he's trying to tell me. It turned out they'd actually let Ritchie have a word with Len, which showed he got a bit of respect even on the other side of the fence. And true enough, Lenny had had a ruck with eighteen drunk young fellas. All right, we all know that individually kids in their twenties couldn't even push Lenny out of the way, but put them all together and they can make up a real handful.

When Lenny got home about eleven the next morning he was fuming. 'Can you believe it, babe, they're definitely thinking about charging me for going up against that mob. Still, fuck 'em. I ain't even going to think about it.' That's what he said, though I think he gave what might happen a lot more thought than he let on over the next month. He'd known too many people go down for something they hadn't done to take it lightly.

When the letter came saying no further proceedings would be taken I've got to say it was a relief to me. Lenny just shrugged as much as to say, 'Never thought it would go any other way,' but I noticed he sang a lot that morning.

It sounds like we constantly lived our lives under a cloud of worry and aggravation, and compared with the average family I suppose we did. But when that's been a way of life for years and years you get used to it. I'd listen to people saying about they'd got some motoring offence coming up in court and they'd be wringing their hands wondering how it was all going to end. The very worst that could happen would be a twenty-pound fine, so how would they react if, regular as clockwork, they were facing prison time?

I was always sympathetic but inside I was thinking, 'You haven't got a clue what life's all about.' And that was Lenny rubbing off on me, because he thought like that all the time. Since he died I've heard a few comments from people who've read his book saying that they got the impression he didn't like ordinary people very much. And if that's how they saw it, somehow or other that's how he must have put it across, but it's not true. I suppose what he was saying was outside the circle he moved in – which let's face it, was basically criminal, violent and dangerous – nobody really understood what real life was all about.

Because of the nature of what he got involved in, most of the deals were done with the shake of a hand and God help anybody who thought they could back out once a deal was set up. At the same time most things were done, or attempted to be done straight away. If anybody got a name for letting people down or taking their time when it came to business, then they might as well find some other line of work because nobody would touch them.

The times I heard Lenny complain, 'Fucking straight-goers, I can't deal with them.' What he meant was everything took ten times longer than it should have to get done, or people were evasive – you know, 'Cheque's in the post,' sort of thing. He hated that, so blamed, like I said, everybody outside this inner circle.

But when it came down to individuals he had all the time in the world for them, no matter who they were. Whether it was hearing all those stories about his Uncle Jimmy Spinks when he was growing up, what with him being the Hoxton Guv'nor and looking out for people, I don't know. But I would think it had quite an influence on him.

It was like inside he felt he had to live up to being the Guv'nor. And though it seems strange to me and lots of others now, over the years that term has been used to describe all kinds of people. Mike Reid's an example. I saw something in a magazine only months ago. There was a picture of Mike and above it 'The Guv'nor' – might have been a video cover – perhaps he's sometimes called the Guv'nor of Comedy, I don't know. But since Lenny's book took the charts by storm and people learned all about him and the things he got up to, just say Guv'nor anywhere and, doesn't matter who you're talking to, they'll know you mean Lenny McLean.

That's today and has been for years, but honestly I don't think it'll ever be any different. He made that title his own and took it with him when he died.

Going back to the Barbican, I think the publicity that came from taking on that many people quietened any trouble right down. I don't mean it was headlines in the papers, but something like that soon got about by word of mouth. If he could take on and beat eighteen fellas, what chance did two, three or five stand? So no matter how hard the troublemakers thought they were, they went elsewhere and became somebody else's problem.

That suited Len because though he never shied away from doing what he was paid to do, he preferred sitting in a little back office with a lemonade or cup of tea, just showing his face every now and then. And that's what he was doing when a couple of men tried to kill him.

As usual the first I heard was when one of the other doormen at the club, Bill Sullivan, called me on the telephone. Do you know, I used to dread the sound of that phone when Lenny was at work, because half the time it meant some sort of trouble. When the other half didn't, I'd still be worried before picking the receiver up. This one, though, was the one I'd been waiting for, for years.

The first thing Bill said was, 'Don't worry, Val.' That was guaranteed to send my stomach flying up into my chest. 'Lenny's been shot.'

I could hardly bring myself to ask, 'Is he dead?'

He said, 'No, no, definitely not, but I took a bump on the head when it happened and all I know is he was still on his feet and he's gone off to Bart's on his own.' I couldn't speak so I just put the phone down so as I could call a cab.

While I was waiting I kept turning over in my head, 'Still on his feet.' That was a good sign, but on the other hand knowing Lenny he could have a big hole in his chest and still wouldn't give anybody the satisfaction of falling down.

When they let me into the side ward to see him, he was lying face down with a cage thing over his bottom half. I crept round in case he was asleep, and he looked like he was, but he opened one eye and said, 'Sorry, babe, I told them not to phone you.' I let that go because I was really concerned about the extent of his injuries and with that thing over him I was frightened his spine might be damaged, because that would be the end of him.

In that position I couldn't even cuddle him, so I held his hand and gave his forehead a kiss. He said, 'Don't laugh, Val.' Funny how people say things that don't fit the occasion. I was fighting back tears and he said that. 'Don't laugh, Val – they shot me in the bum,' and I did laugh. It was bad enough, I know, but I was so relieved that it wasn't any vital organs, if you know what I mean, that I couldn't help myself. He said, 'Good girl, that's the stuff,' meaning 'pleased you're not taking it too bad'. I said, 'Does it hurt?' and all he said was, 'Yeah, smarts a little bit.' Why didn't he ever feel pain like other people?

A nurse came in and gave him an injection and he just drifted off, so I stayed ten minutes then left. Before I did, though, I had a word with the doctor. And though the words 'shot in the bum' make people smile when they first hear it, from what he told me it was a very serious wound. Not too much higher and Lenny might never have walked again. As it was the shotgun had torn such a big hole in the muscle he'd have the most horrible scarring for the rest of his life.

I was only indoors five minutes when I got a call from another one of the doormen to tell me what had happened. He'd been standing to one side so never got hurt himself. Seemed that Lenny was just outside the door of the club with his back to the road and talking to Bill who was inside the club. Two fellas came riding down the pavement on a motorbike and the passenger fired a shotgun at Lenny hitting him in the back. Bill got knocked down the stairs with the shock of all the glass in the doors exploding, but Lenny instead of diving for cover went after the men as they turned round to come back and shoot him again. All he could do was kick the bike wheel and they got away. Nobody could give a description because they were wearing those crash helmets that have a black shield over the face.

I couldn't believe Lenny had gone up against a shotgun when he'd already been shot once, but that was the man he was and there wouldn't be any point in me having a go at him for taking the risk.

After a couple of days he was ready for coming home and he got in a right strop when he was told there was no chance of that. He said he was missing me and the kids, but the real reason was that he was starving. Because he hadn't said nothing to me, and none of the staff had bothered to point it out, there was no way I could've known that he wouldn't eat the hospital food. You'd think a man the size he was would eat anything put in front of him, but he could be really fussy. Not that you had to be particularly fussy not to want the food they dished up, but it couldn't be easy to please every-body yet no one else complained. So being days before he finally told me, like I said he was absolutely starving.

It was no good the nurses trying to tell him he had to eat what they put in front of him, because in the end he would've slung it at them. So I had to start taking in food for him. That meant cooking something right at the last minute so it would stay hot until I got to the hospital. Usually he asked for bacon sandwiches, but the first time I took in a big bag of chicken legs. I gave them to him, then said I'd have a quick word with Sister. She walked back to his bed with me just in time to catch him passing a leg to the man beside him who had a notice above his head saying NIL BY MOUTH. She told them both off, and unlike Lenny, he took it like a little lamb. Either he was too sore to argue or she had something I didn't have.

There must've been a dozen chicken legs in that bag and he ate them one after another. With the result that, hours later when I was at home, the Sister called me and said that Lenny had indigestion, but nothing she could say would convince him that he wasn't having a heart attack. Would I call in and reassure him. By the time I got back to the hospital and into the ward he was asleep, but he woke up as I spoke to him and his first words were, 'Thank Christ you're here, I've had a heart attack.'

Now because of the way he'd been laying his face was all distorted and creased up, so I said, 'Don't know about that, you look like you've had a stroke.'

Next thing he's out of bed and crawling up to the Sister's desk on his hands and knees calling out, 'You'd better do something, my Val reckons I've had a stroke.' I bet that Sister thought I'd been a big help.

I think Lenny must be one of very few people to get himself chucked out of hospital for messing about. Any ordinary man would've been creased with pain for weeks, but not him. And once he could move himself without too much discomfort he didn't know what to get up to next.

He'd already had another telling off from the Sister for smoking his roll-ups when the man in the next bed was gasping for breath and on an oxygen mask. And give him his due he did pack it in. But then the same Sister warned him that he had to stop joking around because the man in the bed opposite had just had a serious stomach operation and wasn't even allowed to smile. They should have known better and put one of them at least into a private room, but I suppose the nurses thought there wasn't too much to laugh about in the men's ward, so they didn't.

So what does Len do? He pulled the curtain around his bed, put his knees into his shoes, called out, 'Oi, Bill, seen this?' and pulled the curtain back. The old man's looking anyway, so he can't avoid seeing Lenny looking like that French painter with the little stumpy legs. He's burst out laughing and his stitches have all burst open. After that they couldn't get Len out quick enough, because he was a liability.

Anybody else, rightly or wrongly, might have been a little bit ashamed of showing off a disfigurement like that. Not Lenny. Whenever the subject of his past came up, down went the trousers, and you could see people wince when they looked because it did look a mess.

I went to visit him one night and he had a right face on. I asked him if the pain was bad but he said, 'Not in the cheek of my bum you mean, babe. I've got another one on the other side.'

I said, 'How can that be?'

He made a face. 'From that pain in the arse Dennis – he's only sacked me,' and he grumbled and moaned for ages about being taken for a mug by the firm.

That's what really upset him. That he'd put up with a lot of personal aggravation to get the club straightened out and nice and quiet – then been given the elbow. Most people when they get the sack are upset and worried because that's their career – their only way of paying the mortgage and everything else. Not with Lenny, though. I know he called it his job but really it was just something to do. Show himself off in front of loads of people, or sit around talking. He didn't need it at all because he could earn fortunes by having a fight every month or two.

End of the day, I don't think Dennis had any choice about getting rid of Lenny, because as it looked like Len was attracting trouble instead of keeping it out of the club it stands to reason the police would've leant heavily on the owners. Didn't stop Len moaning about him, though. But he soon got over it once he came out of hospital and started to think seriously about who had shot him, or paid those two men to shoot him. I was convinced it was over that eighteen men business, but Lenny said, 'No way, they were straight-goers, babe. Bank clerks, City finance people – kids. Big kids, mind you, but still kids pissed out of their brains. No, there's more to it than that.'

That's when we got onto 'Val, who was that geezer in the White Hart that time?' and I've got to rack my brains for a name. Half the time I didn't even know what particular incident he was talking about because he'd never told me. But that didn't matter to Lenny. By the time he'd rounded his list down to about a hundred possibles, he gave up – or at least that's what he told me.

I won't say Lenny was secretive, in fact most of the time you couldn't stop him talking about what he'd been up to even if you tried. But over that shooting, I had to wait and read his book before I found out that he'd been tearing about all over the place to put a name to those two men. It used to amaze me how he could take on board things that would frighten ordinary people to death without turning a hair.

For instance, the average person, and I include myself in that, might have a bit of aggravation at the traffic lights – road rage, they call it now. They might have accidentally cut somebody up and next minute they're being sworn at and threatened. It can be quite frightening and they're upset about it for weeks after. I know that particular sort of incident could never happen to Lenny, but I'm just trying to put forward an example that a minor thing can be a worry for ages if you're not used to it, while something a hundred times worse could be forgotten in minutes by Len.

I'd been out shopping – seems like every time I tell a story that's how it starts, but living just off the Roman, one minute and I was at the shops, so it was like a daily habit to break the day up – I went straight into the kitchen and Lenny was sitting at the table waiting for a 'nice cup of tea' and reading the *Sun*. I busied around putting stuff in the fridge and while I'm doing that he's asking me who I saw up the shops, was it warm out, did I remember to get custard cream biscuits – just like every other day.

I went to go upstairs for something and as I got to the bottom of the stairs I couldn't help noticing bits of wood and splinters and dust all over the carpet. I shouted to Lenny, 'What's been going on here?'

He came up the passage and went, 'Oh that,' like it was the biggest surprise in the world. 'Er, somebody had a bit of a shoot up.'

I said, 'No, Len, seriously, did you drop something down the stairs?' thinking he'd brought down the old chest of drawers out of Kelly's room.

'I'm serious, babe, some mug let a few go at me but it's OK, he missed.'

I just sat on the stairs and put my head in my hands. I couldn't take it in. Lenny was concerned that I was upset, but just as concerned because I hadn't made the tea yet. He was so calm it made me angry so I ended up shouting at him even though it wasn't really his fault. 'What if I'd been at home? What if the kids had been around – would he have tried to shoot them as well?'

He gave me a cuddle, then, 'No, babe. I don't think it would've happened. I reckon he'd been waiting till you all went out.'

In a way it was fortunate that I left the front door on the latch when I went shopping, because if I hadn't Lenny would've had to open the door when the person knocked and then might've got shot at point blank. As it was Len stood at the top of the stairs and told whoever it was to come in. We didn't know it then, but the only reason Lenny wasn't hit was because the gunman was drugged up at the time and probably seeing double. Lucky as well that he used a handgun. If it had been a shotgun the man could've been blind and still hit Len.

None of it seemed real to me as I hoovered up the mess. I felt sick about what could've happened. It seems so long ago now, and hard to think something like that took place in my home. But if you dug around the Polyfilla on those stairs today, you'd come across some bullets that we never got out.

Strangely enough not one of the neighbours ever mentioned what must've sounded like a war starting. Specially as Lenny said this person had fired his handgun about five times. What can you do? You can't live in fear hour after hour; your brain won't let you. So I let it go and carried on like before – or tried to, but I always had that constant niggle at the back of my mind every time there was a knock on the door or a car stopped outside.

I was pleased in a way that the police never got involved, because after the first shooting they drove us mad coming round the house week after week. And the way they acted you'd have thought Lenny was the villain instead of the victim. Sometimes I thought this code Lenny and all the rest lived by was crazy, after all what are the police there for? But no, Lenny was no grass, as he put it, and that's what he told the police every time they showed up and tried to make him give them all the details. I'd have thought they'd be pleased there was one more crime they didn't have to spend time on, but it wasn't like that.

Long before he should've, Lenny told me he'd put the word out that he was going to take on challengers as long as the purse was big enough. His scars were still red and angry-looking, and I begged him to leave the fighting out for another couple of months until he was completely healed, but I might as well have been talking to the wall. He'd already agreed to fight some scrap dealer, and as he said, 'The chance of him smacking my arse don't even need thinking about.' Sometimes I wished he'd never had that fight.

Almost all the time, whatever damage he did to his opponent was behind closed doors – or if not behind doors exactly, behind caravans or some barn way out in the countryside. The only people that knew exactly what went on were those involved, and to them nothing was too shocking or too violent. But suddenly my Lenny is on every television set in the country and being called a homicidal maniac – a man so dangerous and so violent he should be locked up.

Afterwards I used to wonder how ever Lenny had let

himself be talked into doing what he did in front of the cameras, but I could answer that for myself. He loved the idea of showing off in front of millions. No – showing off's not the right words, more like showing what he was capable of to the biggest audience he'd ever had in his whole life. Filming the fight, or arranging to have it filmed by the BBC, was Kenny Mac's idea, I think. Bit of publicity I suppose, but I doubt whether he could've imagined how it would turn out.

In the end Lenny got branded a complete nutcase because this Bradshaw lost his bottle even before the bell went and nutted him in the face to try and gain an advantage, because he knew he couldn't beat him any other way. Lenny did what you'd expect him to do in a situation like that and the media made out he was a violent psychopath. Even the police looked at a copy of the film, hoping they could charge him with something, but luckily they couldn't. Imagine how me and the kids felt reading and seeing those comments in the news – gutted is the word. We knew what the real Lenny was like, but through no fault of his own overnight the whole country thought of him as some monster.

I didn't go to the fight, but what I saw on the *Today* programme backed up everything Len had told me afterwards. He climbed in the ring expecting a 'straightener'. And like he explained in his book, that's more of a conventional fight – a proper boxing match with rules and gloves – than an 'all in', where anything goes. Bradshaw brought what he got completely on himself. Lenny went forward to touch gloves, and that's something he wasn't normally used to. Once a bell or shout started things off, his way was to steam straight in.

So in this case he was holding back and sticking to the rules. As he took that head in the face I just held my breath, even though I'd been told what happened next.

But telling's not like seeing something in the flesh – I just knew Lenny couldn't take something like that and not react in his usual way. People said afterwards that he went right off his head, but knowing him and watching him, he battered, stamped and kicked Bradshaw almost calmly. If he had lost his head the five or six men who eventually managed to pull him off wouldn't have stood a chance, and I really do think the damage he did would've been far worse.

It goes without saying that the description of the fight I'd got from Lenny a few hours after, was nothing like what I'd just seen, but as usual to him it was just another tear-up. He'd said he'd been nutted, and he did have a red mark on his forehead, and yet again I wondered about his capacity to take pain. More than once I've banged my head on the kitchen cabinet doors, and every time it brought tears to my eyes and made me want to sit down, so what must it be like to take the full force of someone's head? I couldn't and I can't imagine.

The name-calling in the papers and on the box ran off his back like water off a duck's. It meant nothing at all to him apart from the publicity it generated. 'Babe,' he said, 'that's money in the bank,' and in a way he was right because not too long after he got a trip abroad, a terrific purse and a chance to spread his name halfway across the world.

Before that, though, we hadn't finished with guns and shootings. It's not me at all, but if there was one time in my life when I wished I had a gun myself, it was about seven months after the club shooting, when I started to get funny phone calls and strange people knocking on my door. When Lenny was indoors I wouldn't have cared if half the villains in the East End were camped out the front because I knew no harm could come to the kids or me. But Lenny wasn't one of those people who could stay cooped up indoors, he had to be out, not only working but out mixing with people – it was a way of life to him.

He was concerned and he did spend a lot more time at home, but as he said, 'I can't stay home for twenty-fours a day over something that probably won't ever happen. But what we'll do is get Big Tommy to sit in when I'm not about.'

Now Tommy was a lovely man but I wasn't having that, I'm too much of a private person. So I just said, 'You're right, Len, it was a one-off – I'm being silly.' Even when the phone calls started he tried to reassure me by saying, 'People who do that are cowards – no value. If they were going to do something they'd do it, not fuck about on the phone.'

We had one of those spyhole things fitted to the front door. Not that I would've opened the door anyway, but at least when I got a knock about half eleven at night I did see two men. One of them stood right to the side, thinking he was out of sight, but the spyhole glass gave a sort of fish-eye view, otherwise I wouldn't have spotted him. I called through the door and asked what they wanted and one said, 'I'm a mate of Lenny's, is he in?' If he was a friend he would've known Lenny was down one of the clubs working, so quick thinking I said, 'You've got the wrong house – don't know who you're after,' and they went away. But looking out of the front bedroom window I could see them further down the road sitting in a car for ages.

I rang Lenny and though he got home in twenty minutes they were gone. I couldn't get the car number and didn't even know what type of car it had been, so there wasn't much could be done about it.

What I took to be the final straw that had me scream-ing that we should take up Barry's offer and emigrate to

Australia came when one of Lenny's mates got shot in the legs. He borrowed Lenny's car for ten minutes and ended up walking with sticks for the rest of his life.

I said to Len, 'You know that was meant for you, don't you?'

But he tried to shift it away from himself saying, 'Not necessarily, Val. You know Johnny – he's into all sorts. Stands to reason he's upset somebody along the way.'

I said, 'Please don't insult my intelligence, Len, it's too much of a coincidence, what with all the rest.'

He wouldn't have it, or at least wouldn't admit it because he knew I'd had about as much as I could take. If he really believed it was down to John himself, why did he spend so much time going up to St Leonard's hospital to visit him, and why did he feel the need to give the man ten thousand pounds? Of course he was cut up about it, so was I. Whatever the reason, nobody wants to see somebody turned into a cripple, but at the end of the day, whatever he said, Lenny knew that shotgun was meant for him.

I said 'final straw' – I was wrong. That came when he sat in his armchair, all careful like an old man who'd been digging all day. I never even noticed he was wearing a tracksuit he carried in the boot, instead of the grey suit he'd gone out in.

I said, 'Tired, babe?'

He said, 'Not really, I got shot again tonight – in the back, this time.'

Do you know what it's like to go beyond reaction? I felt my stomach go over, but apart from that all I could do was stare at him in disbelief. If I'd been told over the phone like before, I think I would've collapsed or had hysterics or something. As it was I couldn't get any words out. It helped that he was sitting in front of me larger than life, so he wasn't going to die, but I suppose some sort of numbness came over me. 'Nice cup of tea, babe,' and I made one on automatic.

When he told me what happened, and there wasn't much to tell, the shooting was bad enough, but the fact that it happened fifty yards from our front door was terrifying. Something else – I actually heard the shot but as anybody would've done I put it down to a car backfiring. That's what froze my insides. The thought that he could've been dead or dying a short walk away and I was half dozing in an armchair.

As often happened he couldn't get a space outside our house so parked the car down the road. He got out, locked up and somebody shot him once in the back. At a time like that, only Lenny could think, 'I won't worry my Val,' so he got back in the car and drove himself to hospital with his bottom half soaked in blood.

As he'd got to the actual shooting he was all for ripping off the bandages to show me the wounds in his side, but I stopped him saying the hospital would go mad if they saw they'd been messed about with. He went, 'Ah, didn't tell you that bit—' and he didn't tell me he knew who'd shot him either. 'I did a runner before Old Bill came, so I won't be going back.'

I said, 'Lenny, you've got a hole right through you, you'll get blood poisoning without proper attention.'

'Thought of that, Val. Get the old fella who does the football matches – he's one of your own, he'll have a look.'

He meant Mr Gregson from down the road who belonged to the St John's Ambulance volunteers. I can put a name to him because him and his wife have been dead for years. He was a proper old East Ender and we didn't even have to explain the situation. He came in every day to dress the wounds and we never worried that it might go any further. It used to make me feel sick watching him pack stuff into these holes so they would drain properly, yet though Lenny's face would be dripping with sweat, he never once groaned or said a word. Well, never said a word about the pain he must've been in. Didn't stop him rabbiting on about his life, though – he never could miss the opportunity of a captive audience.

I don't mean this was the final straw just for me. Lenny had had enough of this hanging over our heads for so long. He wasn't frightened; he just had the complete hump over being a target. A lot of people got pulled in after that so it could be sorted out one way or another. By people I mean those that often get called 'faces', meaning they're from well-known families in the business. Bottom line, I suppose the papers would call them gangsters, though I've got to say that's not a word I ever heard used. 'What do you do for a living?' 'I'm a gangster.' 'Oh, right.' No, they were most of the time very respectable men who just happened to run organizations that happened to be criminal.

Lenny hated it when he saw that term against his name. Like after he'd appeared in *The Knock* and the papers wrote him up as 'a real-life gangster'. He'd say, 'See this shit, Val? They're making me look a mug. Gangster, for fuck's sake – that's somebody who goes ten handed to shoot one man. Is that me, babe? Make me right, is that me?' He knew the answer without me saying a word.

Why all this shooting business happened at the same time, or should I say over a certain period, I don't know. Lenny had been doing what he did for years and years and nothing like it had ever happened before. Guns had been pulled on him more than once and a few times been fired in the air, but never at him. Well, that's what I thought at the time. Since then I've found out that he'd had some near escapes – but obviously Lenny didn't think those incidents important enough to worry me by mentioning them.

It was like different people got together and made up their minds to do away with Lenny, though it wasn't like that at all.

Through Ritchie Anderson and others who I won't name, the Barbican shooting was sorted out. I can remember Lenny arguing with Ritchie after a name had been put up – that he was going to smash somebody's head off, he was going to kill them with his bare hands, and so on. But Ritchie, always the diplomat, managed to calm him down. If it had been anyone else, Len wouldn't have listened, and gone off and done whatever he wanted, but he had too much respect for Ritchie to go against him.

Somebody called Quinn did the shooting in the house and then another time paid somebody to shoot Lenny in the back. The thing was, his reason for trying to kill my husband was so stupid it would've been laughable if it weren't so serious. Lenny had straightened him out down the gym. Given this fella a slap for being out of order towards him in front of people. That was it and that was the end of it so far as Lenny was concerned. But Quinn couldn't let it go. Him being showed up festered in his head until, high on drugs and with that little disagree-ment blown right out of proportion, he was willing to commit murder. By the time Lenny found him – and it took a long time – he was in such a mental and physical state, what with worrying about Lenny coming after him as well as being a drug addict, Lenny could've snapped him in two with one hand. So he didn't lay a finger on him.

The puzzling thing was that Lenny's friend getting shot in the legs was nothing to do with either the South

London firm or Quinn. It was a few years before we found out who was responsible, and I've got to say we were both shocked. For his own reason Lenny didn't say who it was in his book and now, for my own reasons, I can't name him either.

The strange thing is Lenny didn't follow it up. I wasn't one for revenge and I certainly didn't want any more trouble, but I couldn't help saying, 'Now you know who tried to kill you, what are you going to do about it?'

But all he said was, 'If I'd been in his shoes I might've done the same myself.'

I said, 'What? You're saying you would've shot somebody?'

He said, 'No, you know I won't touch guns. What I'm saying is if I had the serious hump with him, like he did with me, I'd have got sorted, but in my own way.' And he left it there.

There was a time when he called himself an effing raving lunatic, and seemed to be proud of it – but it was a long way from the truth. That reminds me of the time his cousin Andrew brought a friend of his to meet Lenny. He loved all that because it gave him a chance to tell all his stories over again; and nobody could tell a tale like he could.

These boys had been training down at Charlie Magri's gym, so after they'd had a cup of tea and had their ears worn out, Lenny walked down the passage with them and he said to the friend, 'How's Charlie, then?'

So he answered, 'Good – he's good.'

'What did he say about me, then?'

So the boy thought for a second and said, 'Er, he said you was a good bloke.'

Lenny pulled a face. 'No, what did he say about Big Lenny?'

Same thing again: 'Nice fella and all that.'

Lenny gave a big sigh like he was talking to an imbecile and repeated the question ... only very slow and pausing after every word. This boy looked like he wanted to burst into tears then I saw Andrew wink at him. They must've had a conversation about this before. Suddenly the boy said, 'Oh yeah. He said you were a lunatic nutcase.'

That's all Lenny wanted to hear. He patted him on the shoulder, said, 'Good boy,' and came back up the passage singing.

Later Andrew told me his friend had been shitting himself because, with the face he was pulling, he thought Lenny had the hump with him.

Anybody who knew Lenny got used to telling him what he wanted to hear. I saw Peter doing it so many times. Lenny had a habit of talking to somebody on the phone then handing it over saying, 'Go on, Peter my son – 'ave a word with so and so.' He'd do it then as soon as that phone went down Lenny would be asking, 'What did they say about me?' and straight away Peter would say, 'Fucking raving lunatic,' and I'd laugh to myself, thinking, 'You liar, they never said that at all.' But it kept Len happy.

Going back to the shootings before I leave it alone, Lenny mentioned a friend of his in his book, Tommy Hole. I'd never met him but according to Lenny 'he'd suffered' and that was enough for him to take Tommy under his wing. His life is too complicated to go into, but I do know he was acquitted on a charge of murdering someone involved with Ronnie Knight. After that it seems the police had it in for him, and they eventually managed to get him an eighteen-year sentence over something to do with drugs. Always a favourite, I'm told, because a charge like that means everything you stand up in can be confiscated. He always swore he was innocent, on both charges, and as Lenny said, 'Why would he need to lie to me?' Not that it would've made any difference to him either way. If Len took to somebody, that was it, he never judged them.

A group that call themselves Justice took up his case and even though it took years to get there, eventually his sentence was quashed and he was released to go back to the East End and the wife who'd stood by him all that time. Nice happy ending, or so you'd think. Not too long after Lenny died, Tommy and some friend that happened to be with him were shot in the head while they were watching Sky Football in the Beckton, in Canning Town. From what I was told somebody had waited twenty years to finally catch up with him.

Frightening, really. That's what I meant earlier about the separate world that's going alongside the one ordinary people live in. Gangster films with loads of gunfire and killing are one of the most popular things on TV, but most people take it on board as complete fiction. When you know people who've been executed, and there's no other word for it, believe me there's nothing very exciting about it.

Lenny said to me one day, 'Remember I told you about an Eyetie geezer I met after one of the fights?'

I did as it happens, though I was pleased he wasn't asking me to remember his name. I said, 'Yes. You said he was pleased with the fight and might be able to put some work your way.'

'Blimey, babe, don't you ever forget nothing? You're right, though, that's him. Well, I think he's come up with something 'cos he wants me to shoot down to Canterbury for a bit of business.' That's all he told me and I think that's all he knew himself.

Days later, when he came back from Canterbury, he said, 'You won't believe this, babe, the geezer only wants me to go and have a fight in New York – blinding purse and all exes.' I said, 'And?' and he said, 'And nothing, he's going to sort the details and pop in next time he's up West. Don't mind, do you?' How could I mind? When it came to fights and business, whatever I thought didn't come into it. 'Something else,' he said, 'this geezer's connected – so Alex Steen reckons.'

I said, 'You make him sound like a phone. What do you mean, "connected"?'

He did that 'let's talk very slow and very clear' thing of his. 'Y' know – New York? America? All that *Godfather* stuff?'

Of course I knew all about the Mafia, or as much as anybody who'd seen the film, and to be honest it was so outside anything I'd ever come across I couldn't really take it seriously. I didn't get all shocked and ask him what he was getting himself into – I just accepted these people couldn't be any worse than most he'd been involved with over the years.

Alex Steen who I just mentioned was always a good friend to Lenny. He was a director on the British Boxing Board, but when it came to helping people he was a lot more than that. I don't think there was anybody he didn't know. Behind his back he was known as the Godfather because he wore dark glasses all the time, though that was down to an eye problem and not an affectation. In his own way I suppose he was a sort of Godfather, because he could get things done and if anybody was in trouble he'd do his best to try and sort it. And that on its own was enough for Lenny to give him a lot of respect.

Weeks afterwards Lenny rang me up from the Camden Palais, where he was working, saying, 'Just had a call from Alex. The Eyetie wants to have a meet so he's going to call in home in about an hour or so. I can get back but I might be half-hour late, 'cos I'm a bit tied up right now. Can you look after him?' I said I would and put the phone down. Two seconds later it rang again. 'He'll be on his own, but don't worry, he must be about a hundred years old.' I doubted that but whatever, I wasn't worried. I understood he was referring to that code of not visiting a woman on her own and a lot of the time it made sense, but usually it meant when somebody was away for years.

About nine o'clock this man arrived and the first thing he did was give me a bunch of flowers. I didn't get too many visitors who did that, specially from the ones in Lenny's business, so that was a good start. If I was expecting Marlon Brando, with that funny voice and puffed-out cheeks, I got a bit of a surprise. He was slightly built, no taller than me, and though he must've been in his seventies had a full head of hair, a pencil moustache and the skin on his face was like a thirty-year-old's. Don't know about being a gangster – he reminded me of an Italian ice-cream man who used to come up our street when I was a kid.

He introduced himself as Roberto and if he gave me his surname I can't remember it now. I do remember him saying he was something to do with a Gambino family, but to be honest that meant absolutely nothing to me then. Small world. It turned out he was distantly related to a friend of Lenny's who had a club in the West End – Jack Lavinsky, who I already knew was a great-nephew of Myer Lansky, who was very well known in America.

We made a lot of small talk about English weather and that sort of thing, though from what I gathered he'd lived in Canterbury for at least twenty years. After a couple of cups of tea he seemed to make himself right at home and started talking about what it was like growing up in New York in the twenties. I've always been interested in the old East End and how my grandparents and

theirs lived in the old days, and to be honest his childhood seemed much the same. He never actually used the
words Mafia, and from what I've learned since, none of
those people do. They just use the term 'family', and I
suppose if you know what they're about, it means the
same thing.

He'd spent time in what he called reformatory, so at
least that gave him and Lenny something in common.
Like a lot of things in life, it's not until afterwards that
certain incidents are more important looking back than
they were at the time. While we were chatting he was
just a nice old man, but as I thought about it later,
particularly after Lenny gave me more details about him,
it seemed unreal. I'd been passing the time of day with
someone who was, or had been, high up in an organiz-
ation of people who you only ever read about or see in
films. People who kill to get what they want – and from
things he hinted at I don't think he was any exception.

Once Lenny came home I excused myself and went
to bed, so what they talked about I don't know. What
I do know is that next morning Len was raring to take
off to the States the next week.

It actually took a couple of months before everything
was organized, and in that time he drove me mad – as
though anything I could do would make the time pass
quicker. With everything he ever did, once something
was set up or suggested, he wanted to get on with it
there and then.

When he did eventually set off it was with a very
good friend of his. Like in his own book, I can't mention
who he was because now he's a household name. And
I'm sure he wouldn't thank me for letting the world know
that at one point in his life he was involved with the
Mafia and the other sort of people Lenny mixed with.

Once he was in New York he must've cost somebody
a fortune on their phone bill because he called me every
few hours. He never got the hang of the time lapse, or
even gave it a thought, so regularly I got woken up in
the small hours to listen to the latest thing he'd got up to.
Sometimes he talked for an hour and I got every detail of
what he'd seen.

As far as the fight went, I wasn't a bit concerned. That
must seem a bit strange, what with my husband being
off in a different world and thousands of miles away, but
I knew that he'd never been beaten or hurt before so I
never imagined that this time could be any different.

I was going to say I just got on with my life as normal,
and in a way I tried to, but really I daren't go too far
from the phone because he expected me to be there
whenever he decided to call home. If I wasn't he'd want
to know why I wasn't. Nothing to do with not trusting
me or anything like that. It was just if he wanted to talk,
that was it. So if I'd gone shopping or round my mum's
for a couple of hours, as I walked back in the door the
phone would be ringing off the hook. After I'd answer it,
if I asked him if he'd rung before he'd say, 'No, this is
the first time,' but you can bet your life he'd been dialling
and redialling nonstop all the time I was out.

He rang me just before him and his friend were
picked up to go to the fight and then I didn't hear any
more. I thought that was a bit strange, because I expected
him to be full of what he'd done and how he'd beaten
the other fighter. See what I mean? I was already presum-
ing it was a foregone conclusion.

In fact the next time I spoke to him was when he
walked in the house the following morning. I can't say I
hadn't worried overnight, because it wasn't like him not
to get in touch. Not so much that he might've been hurt

in the fight, but he was dealing with people that were an unknown quantity – to me anyway, so anything could've happened.

As it turned out he'd been of the same opinion. Once he'd done what he went there to do, the two of them had gone straight to the airport and kept their heads down in case these people decided to take back the big bundle of cash he was carrying. It never happened, and was probably never going to, but that was Lenny – look ahead and weigh up the possibilities, and prepare to meet whatever it was head on.

The first thing I noticed were the bandages on his hands, but they'd been broken, cracked and fractured so many times over the years I'd almost come to expect to see him like that after a hard fight. At least his face wasn't marked and that was always so important to me. I really don't know why he wasted his time calling in to the hospital on his way home, because those bandages came off before he even went for a lie down.

I don't think the kids really understood what it meant for their dad to be a fighter. Kelly told him he was naughty while she was sitting on his lap, and when he asked why she said, ''Cos you've been fighting,' but other than that they both just accepted that it was something he did – but they couldn't.

It was just after this that we bought a caravan near Clacton. Thinking about it now, with the money he won from that fight we could've bought a nice villa in Spain, but back then people didn't think like that. Nowadays half the people I know have got some sort of place out in the sun, but then, for some reason, you didn't consider it. Lovely for holidays, but no more than that.

Lenny loved that caravan, and though we bought better ones as time went on, they were always in the same place, so we went there weekend after weekend right up until a year or so before he died. If I'm honest I've got to say that in later years I got fed up with going down there. Not because there is anything wrong with the area, in fact Clacton and the area around is a very nice place, but I found it all too quiet for my liking.

Lenny lived a different lifestyle from me. Every minute of his day was taken up with phone calls, business for other people, meetings – you name it. Then at night, from about eight o'clock until two or three in the morning, he'd be working at the clubs and all the aggravation that came with it. So to disappear off to the coast, where nobody could phone him or get in touch, was something he looked forward to all week.

Apart from long runs he did nothing at all except sit inside or outside the caravan, while I was up and down making cups of tea. Mind you, even down there he could attract trouble like a magnet.

There was a middle-aged man and his wife a couple of caravans away, and one day Lenny happened to drive on the grass so he could unload a few boxes with our bits and pieces in them. This man came storming over doing his nut and shouting and bawling at Lenny that he'd bent the grass. We couldn't believe what was going on and I'm praying Lenny doesn't go into one and give him a slap, but he just looked at him and said, 'Bent the grass? Bent the fucking grass? So what? It'll stand up on its own in five minutes. Go indoors and have a lie down before you give yourself a heart attack.' And that was that.

Later on we could see this couple had set up a table and chairs, like we all did, and had a load of friends with them having a barbecue and drinks. What set this man off again I don't know, perhaps he thought we were laughing at him, but next thing he's grabbed a garden spade and come flying over towards me. I really did think I was going to have my head smashed in.

Having explained the way Lenny has been all his life, you must be thinking I'm going to say he beat this man half to death, but he didn't, because, as always, he had different levels for sorting out different people. If they were equally matched to himself God help them because he gave them the full works. At the other end, if there was nothing of them and they gave him a lot of verbal, he wouldn't even consider using what he was capable of, but look for some other way of quietening them down. And that's what he did with this man.

As he's swinging the spade at me Lenny came up behind him, grabbed it and threw it to one side, then picked him off the ground. Of course he gave it plenty of 'I oughta kill you stone dead' and all that, but that was just to scare him. What he did do though was sit on the bench we had, pull the man over his knee and smacking his arse. And I mean smack. What a humiliation, and in front of his wife and his friends as well. But really he was lucky to get away so lightly, because he wasn't just threatening me – he really meant to hurt me. You'd think after something like that he would've found another caravan somewhere else, but they stayed where they were and for years after Lenny always called him 'Smacked Arse'.

Another time we went down on the Friday intending to stay for the week. Something happened at work so he went back to London on the Monday, saying he'd pick me and the kids up the following Friday at seven o'clock. Seven came, eight, nine, ten, and I was starting to get worried. He'd either forgotten all about us or he'd got into a fight somewhere. Half eleven he banged on the door, because I'd locked up by then, and when I opened up there he was and sure enough he had blood running down his face. But I was wrong. He hadn't been fighting; he'd driven into a tree somewhere near Clacton, then spent three hours looking for the caravan park.

We laughed about it at the time but in hindsight I think he probably had mild concussion.

NINE

As far as fighting went, by now Lenny had slowed down quite a bit. I know he wasn't too far off reaching forty, but I don't mean the speed of his reactions, because he never did lose that even when he was ill, I mean he didn't put himself out on offer like he used to do. At the same time he'd made himself such a reputation for being unbeatable, he wasn't getting too many offers anyway.

Like anything else the fight game is a business, whether it's licensed, unlicensed or bare-knuckle behind a door somewhere. So if there's a ninety-nine per cent chance that your man is going to get a good hiding, then what's the point? Every now and then an individual or a firm would weigh up the odds and think it was worth taking the risk, just to get their hands on that title, the Guv'nor. Whether he wanted to or not, Lenny never had it in him to turn down a fight, so off he'd go and prove that there was no one capable of taking away what he'd fought for all his life.

I'd stopped going to these fights by now, and I think the last one he talked me into going to was against a man called York. Lenny always called him the 'Yorkie Bar Kid', but he wasn't some little blond boy with big glasses like in the advert – he was huge. I've seen more big men in my life with Lenny than I've had hot dinners, but this one was massive. Certainly half a head taller than Len and probably two stone heavier. But really I could see he didn't have what Len had. It was in the eyes, I think. You can tell if somebody's got what they call that killer instinct. It's not something I could put my finger on, but I knew it was all over before the fight even started.

Apart from size he was a lot younger than Len, but he didn't stand a chance. The bell went, they swapped punches and this Yorkie drove Lenny into a corner. Then the only way I can describe it is that the other bloke folded up like a penknife after he took a punch in the midriff. An uppercut from Lenny straightened him right up and he fell on his back, with his arms above his head. From the minute the bell went until he was knocked spark out took about three minutes. As Lenny said, 'It was hardly worth taking his coat off.'

On the way back from Woodford he said, 'You know what, babe? I'm thinking about knocking all this on the head.'

That surprised me because I couldn't remember him ever saying anything like that before. I said, 'What's brought this on? One way or another you've been doing this since you was about eight years old. Why would you give it all up now? Feeling your age?'

He gave me such a look. 'Nah, I'll still be putting them on their backs when I'm seventy. No, what it is, the dairy's gone off it all. It's like there ain't no challenge in it any more. I mean the scratch is good, but it's like I'm doing it for the sake of it – know what I mean?' I did. He wasn't putting it in words but what he was saying was he had nothing else to prove. He was the Guv'nor and there was nowhere else to go, or anything to aim for – in the fight game, anyway.

He said, 'It's time I stepped back a bit. I've made a name for myself. I've got respect, and what with this and that we ain't ever going to go short. On top of that the club keeps my hand in, so what d'you think?'

Silly question really, because if it had been down to me he'd never have got into the fight game at all. But end of the day Lenny did what Lenny did, and I would never have tried to change him. So all I said was, 'It's up to you, babe. You're right, you don't have to prove anything to anybody.'

The club he was talking about was the London Hippodrome, one of the best in the city. And being number one on the security side was about as high as you could go in the line Len was in. For a lot of his life he was what people thought of him as – a doorman, a bouncer. But later on in life he left all that behind, and if you ever saw him walking round the club it was like he owned the whole place. It was his manor and he went out of his way to keep everything nice for the customers, who were mostly just kids out to enjoy themselves.

You'd be amazed by what I didn't know until he was doing his book, or I read it afterwards. Things that any normal person would have classed as really important never struck him like that. He didn't think it worth telling me he'd come across the man who arranged to have him shot. Once that shooting business was all over he never mentioned it again, though I couldn't help being reminded of it every time he took his shirt off. I suppose in his mind he wanted me to forget it ever happened, because he knew it had upset me a lot at the time. So when he caught up with this Quinn man he did what he had to do and left it at that.

Before he went all quiet on the subject, he had spoken a lot about what he'd do once he found him, because he did know who he was. He was going to kill him stone dead and all that, but then he said that about a lot of people – it was only a figure of speech, like when your mum used to threaten to kill you if you came in late one more time. So you can imagine how I felt when two detectives turned up one afternoon to question Lenny over the murder of Quinn. This was about eighteen months after Lenny was shot and now this man had been found shot dead in Epping Forest. And what with people never knowing when to keep their mouths shut, the finger got pointed at Lenny because it had been an open secret that he'd been after him for a long time.

I never doubted Len for a minute. If this man had been found smashed to bits it might've given me pause for thought, but I knew Lenny wasn't capable of using a gun. Well, he was more than capable, but to his way of thinking anybody who was a tough guy behind a gun was, as he put it, 'a gutless coward'. I'm not so sure that the police ever did think they had a case against him, or even that he'd done it, but for a long time we'd both thought that the law would like to put him away.

Because there wasn't enough evidence to pin down exactly when Quinn had died, it wasn't as simple as asking Lenny where he was between seven and eight on such and such a night. Today they could work it out to the minute because science has come on in leaps and bounds since then. On top of that it was quite a while before their enquiries actually brought them to our door, and by then, particularly with Len's lifestyle, it was very hard to think back to what he'd been doing at that moment in time.

It wasn't a case either of one visit, thank you very much you're in the clear. It dragged on for weeks while Lenny was backwards and forwards to Vine Street. In the end Ralph Haeems, our solicitor, more or less said, 'Charge him or forget it' – and with nothing to go on anyway they dropped it. No apology for the time wasted – nothing. And as Lenny said, 'They might have stuck it on the shelf, but bet your life they've left my name in the frame.'

The other thing he didn't tell me until days later was that somebody had approached him about making a film of his life. But then that wasn't surprising because he was always getting offers or suggestions about writing a book and all other kinds of schemes and invariably nothing ever came of any of them, so he'd never really taken them seriously.

We were sitting at the kitchen table, like we always did in the mornings, reading the papers and drinking tea, and he came out with, 'How d'you fancy being married to a film star?'

I was used to Lenny throwing out a line of whatever he was thinking about, so I didn't even stop reading, just said, 'Mmm, Paul Newman would be nice.'

He said, 'Oi, behave – no, I mean me?'

That was a new one and there wasn't much I could say to that other than, 'You? How come?'

Then he went on to tell me about somebody who'd asked him if he would consider letting this man write a film script based on his life. I just laughed, and that gave him a face. What it was, he'd had a couple of days to think about the idea of it, while I'd only just had it dropped in my lap. 'What, you think it's a stupid idea, then?'

I said, 'No, of course not. I was just thinking of you being an actor – seems funny, really.'

He said, 'Oh yeah? Who's this, then?' and I got the 'Get on your horse and drink your milk' line, with him swaggering across the kitchen. He'd been doing that John Wayne impersonation from the day I met him, so I could've been stone deaf and still known who it was.

Funny thing is no matter how many times I'd seen it,

Right: This is how others saw Lenny.

Below: A happy memory – me and Lenny in Spain.

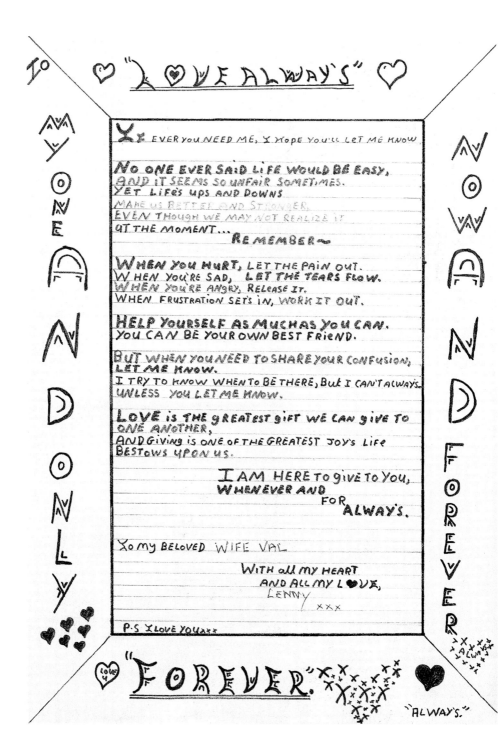

A token for me of Len's feelings while he was in prison.

Lenny McLean	Height 6'3/1.91 Chest 56/1.42 Waist 38/97 Inside leg 33/84 Collar 20/51 Shoes 11/46 Hair: Brown/Braun Eyes: Brown/Braun BOXER/LIFTS HEAVY WEIGHTS	UGLY Tel. 01·402 5564

Above: Lenny's agency card.

Right: 'How do I look?'
was one of Len's
favourite questions.

Left: Karen, me and Kelly at the Hippodrome.

Below: Lenny with his sister Boo.

Above: Lenny with Peter Gerrard, as they started to work on *The Guv'nor*.

Right: Me with Peter's wife Shirley.

Lenny and Guy Ritchie.

Taken while filming *Lock, Stock and Two Smoking Barrels*. From the left, Jason Statham, Lenny, Tony McMahon and Vinnie Jones.

A close moment
towards the end of
my husband's life.
(*Sun*)

Kelly and Jamie,
all grown up.

I gave Lenny the send-off I knew he wanted.

Lenny's book was the first 'hard man' autobiography and was even mentioned in this *Sunday Times* cartoon. (Kipper Williams)

My handsome husband. (Hugh White)

it still made me laugh – probably because he took it so seriously. I said, 'All right, you've proved your point, who is this man? A big film director?'

He said, 'Not exactly. He either owns or he's the manager of a video shop. Don't know which.'

I didn't laugh this time but I felt like it. I just thought, 'Here we go again. Another scheme that will come to nothing.' But Lenny seemed so full of the idea I didn't want to say anything to spoil whatever was going on in his head.

Like a lot of things in life, if I'd known then what I know now, I would have done anything in my power to have squashed the idea. Because the whole film thing would kill him and leave me a widow at forty-seven. You're thinking, 'No, he died of cancer,' but in my mind, and I don't know if there's any medical evidence to back this up, I'm convinced some cancers are brought on by stress. Time and time again I've heard of people getting this horrible disease, then finding out they'd had some big worry in their lives. His biggest stress came from having a twenty-five-year prison sentence hanging over his head for a year. But once that was out of the way his obsession with the film took over.

Perhaps, like they say, we've all got this thing inside us, it just needs something to make it flare up. Not very scientific, I know, but that's how I think. I don't know what was in Lenny's head at first when the idea was put to him. I know he thought he was expected to write his own story, then that he would have to act himself in the film, but obviously none of that was ever on the cards.

Once he'd decided that it was worth putting some effort into, that's when this writer turned up at our house with a tape recorder under his arm. I don't know about Lenny telling him all about his life. Half the time I was in and out of our lounge answering his, 'Val, what was that geezer's name? When was the fight with the gypsy? How many stitches did I have in my bum?'

I'm not being fair. If there was nothing else he could do, he did know how to tell a good story – it was the dates and places that tripped him up. When you live a certain way of life, you accept all the ups and downs as they come, then you sort of forget about them. But when you hear it all strung together at one time it certainly makes you think that your life has been anything but ordinary.

And that's how it must've struck the writer because day after day he sat there with his eyes popping out of his head, because Lenny couldn't just tell a story, he had to show the action that went with it. I walked in with some tea just as he was talking about how he'd had a go at some bloke. He spoke quite normal at first, then he jumped out of the chair like a madman as he demonstrated what he'd done. I'd seen it a hundred times before so I didn't even rattle the cups, but looking at this bloke sitting well back in the armchair, I could imagine he was wondering what he'd got himself into.

Lenny loved every minute of it. A fresh set of ears hanging onto his every word, what more could he ask for? Laying back in his armchair, cup of tea on his knee, roll-up in one hand dropping ash at his feet, talking about a life that to the ordinary person was way outside their experience. He wasn't being flash or making himself out to be a tough guy, but by now he'd realized his stories got a reaction from whoever he was talking to and he played up to it for all it was worth. Some of the things I heard while I was in and out with cups of tea were new to me and I'd give him a look that was saying, 'You never mentioned that bit of work when it happened,' but he wouldn't look up – just carried on talking.

Right then all this film talk was sort of exciting for both of us. Yet looking back I can't believe we were naive enough to think that once a script was written it would appear on the screen in a couple of months. That's why Lenny put his heart and soul into it.

At night, after the script bloke had gone, Lenny would sit and run through lists of actors he wanted in his film. Most of them were the biggest names in the business and most again were Americans. I did point out they'd look a bit out of place in a film about the East End, but Lenny's answer was, 'Babe, they're paid to be people they're not, they'll just have to learn the way we talk.' He threw in actors like John Wayne and Stallone, because as far as he was concerned they'd be queueing up for the chance to be in this movie. I had my doubts but I wasn't going to spoil what was going on in his head. That was Len – hundred miles an hour – he's got the film playing in cinemas all over the world and not even a word of the script written yet.

This was back in 1984, I think, and here I am nearly twenty years later and not one inch of film has been shot. Good job neither of us knew we'd just taken the first steps down the 'happy road' or we'd have both gone round the bend.

Day and night for months on end all I heard was talk about this blockbuster film that was going to earn millions. Then the talk dried up and the whole thing seemed to just die a natural death. The fella took off to do whatever scriptwriters do, and though at first Len phoned him every five minutes to see if it was done yet, when it wasn't he lost interest and got on with other things. If he was disappointed that his film wasn't up and running he never showed it, but that was him.

After all his talk about not taking on any more fights, he couldn't turn one down when it was for charity.

Somebody he used to train with down the gym years before came round looking for a donation from Lenny, because everybody knew you only had to ask and he would empty his wallet without a second's thought. This man said there was a little girl local to him in Walthamstow, who needed an operation that could only be done in America. As soon as he laid a photograph of this big-eyed, dark-haired girl of about four on the table, Lenny said, 'Get me wallet out of me jacket, babe.' By the time I came back he was asking how much was needed altogether. When the man said twenty thousand Lenny looked thoughtful, then said, 'Forget the pound notes. Gimme a call tonight and I'll have something for you.'

I knew what was in his mind before he told me just after the man left. He got on the phone and within the hour he'd got a fight arranged and enough people interested so that more than enough money could be raised than would be needed. I said, 'Who's the unlucky fella that's going to get a good hiding from you to help this little girl?'

He said, 'You don't have to worry about that, nor does he. You remember Mick Green? Well, when I put it to him he said, "Only a straightener, Len, I'm getting on a bit now." But I told him to forget the straightener, we'll get our heads together.' And that's what they did. They'd both been in the game long enough to know how to put on a good show even though they were pulling their punches.

No disrespect to Mick but the punters were there to see Lenny do his usual, and that's what they got. Lenny won, of course, but as far as all the spectators went, Mick put up a really good fight so didn't lose any face by losing. In fact he probably gained a lot by having the bottle to take on the Guv'nor.

As Lenny said, it wasn't a con really. It wasn't even

like the people laying bets down were taken for a ride because quite honestly all the money would've been on Len anyway.

On top of the money raised on the fight a box was passed around with a picture of the little girl on it, and that in itself brought in something like three thousand. It just amazed me when I thought about the generosity of these people. Most of them spent their lives on the wrong side of the law, and if they were known at all the general public would've looked down on them as thieves and villains. But when it came to a good cause I doubt whether a single one of them didn't put at least something into that box.

I don't know what the final figures were when the money was all in, but I do know the operation was paid for and fares and accommodation for the parents to go to America with their daughter. It never got a mention in the papers, not even the local ones, and it didn't make big news. But that's how Lenny wanted it. He said, 'If it gets spread about you'll always get mugs saying I did it to make myself look like a bit of a hero, and I don't want that. The way I see it, that little girl could be my Kelly, so as far as I'm concerned all the thanks I want are that she's going to live,' and he never wanted it mentioned again.

Another time when he was asked to help out a child he said, 'No problem. I'll set something up.' Only trouble was he got stabbed in the leg before he could and he had to call it off. Usual thing. Bunch of drunks in the club making a nuisance of themselves so Lenny stepped in. One of them pulled a knife and got belted unconscious for trying it on. But another one picked it up and stuck it deep into Lenny's thigh, and knowing him he would've squared the fella off before pulling the knife out.

He didn't just forget about the baby just because he

wasn't fit enough to fight. He sent a thousand pounds in cash to the people who were trying to raise money, then got on the phone to some good friends and they got something up and running. He even asked Reg Kray to chip in, and at that time he was as keen as Len to help out children.

He sent us a drawing he'd done, and I don't want to knock the man but when I saw it I thought a four-year-old had done it. It was in crayon and of a boxer in the ring – very brightly coloured. Still, with his autograph on it, it fetched good money at an auction.

It's strange when I think about it; Len got shot by a bullet that went in one side and out the other. After the initial hospital treatment the only attention this wound got was from a first-aider, yet it healed up beautifully. When he got stabbed in the thigh he got proper medical care, yet nearly died from it. That was a nightmare. Not the stabbing, because as far as he was concerned that was just part of a working night, but the nightmare came later.

The trouble with Lenny was that no matter what was wrong with him he tried to pretend it wasn't there because he never had enough time in a day to slow down. And because he didn't make a fuss like most men would, you couldn't help him because you didn't know he was suffering.

I thought he was well on the mend until he was off to do a bit of work and I noticed he looked very uncomfortable. I said, 'Your leg playing up?' and he said, 'Nah, just a bit hot, that's all. It'll be fine, don't fuss.' I told him if everything was all right then it wouldn't make any difference if I had a quick look. So with him huffing and puffing over my shoulder, I took the bandage off to see if everything was as it should be. The wound was really angry-looking and inflamed, so I said I'd drive him round to casualty. No, he didn't have time for none of that. 'Stick some Germolene on it.' If he stuck his foot down there was nothing else to say, so I couldn't argue.

What it was, he'd arranged to do a bit of minding for Alex Steen, and one thing he'd never do was let somebody down. I may have said before but some of these jobs he did would surprise the average person. Saying he's minding somebody makes you think it's for villains in a back room somewhere, but this particular job was in a bank or someplace equally as posh. Again ordinary people might think that grey little people in suits and horn-rimmed glasses carry out this sort of business. Perhaps half of them did look like that, but bank or not they must've been into some heavy stuff to need minders on either side, and I know for a fact that often guns were taken into these meetings.

As Len said, 'If I don't show up for the Godfather –' that's what they called Alex for a joke – 'there might be fucking murders, and what's that going to do for my rep?'

I can only think that if he'd gone to casualty like I suggested in the morning, perhaps he wouldn't have been fighting for his life the next day. Whether he went to work or not was neither here nor there. The poison was already starting to work, so no matter what he did other than get proper medical attention wasn't going to make any difference.

I'm not the first person to have seen it, but it really knocks you back when you see how life can change in a matter of hours. I know he had a sore leg, but apart from that, the day before he was all suited up in a nice grey two-piece, white shirt, tie and looking a million dollars. Next thing he's been rushed into hospital. I'm sitting beside his bed and he's grey faced and looking as weak and vulnerable as anybody.

At that moment I didn't realize just how serious his

condition was, though I'm not an idiot. All those tubes and everything else meant it was more than a local infection. It wasn't what was going on in his leg that had knocked him out – a nurse told me they had him on morphine so he couldn't feel the pain. Every couple of hours he'd wake up but he didn't know where he was and all he'd manage to say was, 'What's up, babe? Why you crying?' then he'd go off again.

Some things you don't ever want to hear. And when the doctor took me into a side room and said Lenny's leg had turned gangrenous and there was a possibility he might have to lose his leg, I don't think I could ever have heard such bad news in my life. Years later I'd find out that there could be something much worse to hear. He told me everything hung on what happened over the next two or three days. After that there would be no time to mess about and the leg would have to come off. And right at that moment things weren't looking good at all.

Imagine how I felt going back to the ward. I'd nothing else to do but hold Len's hand and think, and in a way it was the worst thing to do. I imagined this big strong man of mine swinging along on crutches like an old man I used to see up the market. The hardest man in Britain – the Guv'nor – reduced to a cripple. A less upsetting thought was that knowing the sort of man he was, a month after the operation he'd be bawling for a false leg so he could get back to work – 'lively'. And he wouldn't be the first.

I'd read about Douglas Bader – he'd carried on flying planes in the war after he lost both legs. And the more I thought, different people came to mind who'd got over the same thing. Only difference was, their lives didn't revolve around being a fighter.

I asked the nurse if Lenny was going to lie unconscious right up until the possibility of his life being devastated, but she told me no, they'd soon cut back on the drug and he'd wake up, though he'd still be a bit dazed. This wasn't going to happen for a while, so as much as I wanted to stay with him I knew it was sensible to go home and get some sleep, and let the kids know what was happening without going into too much detail.

Before I left I told somebody or other who was on duty that if he should come round before I got back, under no circumstances mention amputation to him, because sick as he was I could imagine him going into one if I wasn't there to calm things down. This was about ten at night – proper visiting hours got ignored in those sort of circumstances.

I suppose with the build-up of stress, I just died that night. I closed my eyes and didn't open them until late morning, so it was more like midday before I walked up that ward again. I could see Lenny was awake and by the look on his face I knew straight away that what I'd said the night before hadn't been passed on. We had a cuddle and a kiss. He asked how I was and how the kids were; was it raining; was it sunny, and I didn't want to stop all this small talk because I knew he was deliberately holding back.

This time it was him that held my hand. He said, 'I've got some bad news for you.' I made out I didn't know what it was. 'They want to take my leg off and I've told them no.' One minute I'm pretending I don't know what his bad news is and the next I'm explaining what they told me, but he didn't pick up on it. I said, 'You've heard wrong somehow, love, what they're saying is there's a faint possibility it might come to that.' – Little white lie.

He gave me that look where you felt he was looking right inside your head and said, 'If they knock me out again and I can't speak for myself, promise me you won't let them do it.'

I didn't want to do that, so said, 'If it came to that, babe, it would be for your own good, you know, to save your life.'

He said, 'Promise me and I'll tell you why.' I knew why and it nearly choked me to say I wouldn't let them take his leg off. 'Make me right, Val, am I a proud man?' No answer needed for that so I just nodded. 'Imagine what would happen if I was half a man. Every gutless coward I've ever come up against would be queuing up to kick my crutches away from under me. Life wouldn't be worth living. Promise me again.' So I did. But inside I was thinking, 'What would I do if I really have to make that decision? Promise or no promise. How could I deprive those two kids of their father? How could I make myself a widow with one word over Lenny's pride?'

I'll tell you what, I never slept another wink until that wonderful day when we were told they'd got on top of that gangrene and everything was going to be all right.

I've already said I'm not religious, but isn't it funny how me and others who say the same thing turn to prayer when there's nowhere else to go? Who saved him? Those doctors and nurses or something bigger? I can't say. A bit of both, perhaps.

When he was discharged a couple of weeks later and he was on the mend at home, I just had to ask him if he'd been really serious about what he'd made me promise or was it the morphine talking. He said, 'My thinking was as clear as it ever was and it wasn't easy, I can tell you, but I wouldn't have wanted it any other way. So let me ask you, Val, would you have kept your promise?'

I said, 'If that's what you really wanted, of course I would.' But thank God I was never put to the test because even today I don't know which way I would've gone.

Of course once it was all over he wanted to treat everybody in the hospital, but I talked him out of that and we settled for buying chocolates and flowers for those nurses that had been involved. Actually they'd already been treated to chocolates, while he was in hospital, and that was down to Alex Steen. Soon as he saw how they were treating his friend Lenny he got Harrods to deliver twenty-four boxes to the hospital. Only there was some mix-up and they went to the wrong ward. Lenny heard about this through one of the cleaners, so as soon as I walked in on a visit he said, 'Val, get yourself down to that ward and bring all those boxes back here.' I told him no way was I going to embarrass myself chasing around looking for chocolates, and anyway what if the nurses had already shared them out? I noticed a look in his face, so I warned him to forget it and we'd order some more. On the next visit I brought in a few bits and pieces for him and when I went to put them in his locker what do I find? Twenty-four boxes of chocolates.

While Lenny had been laid up in hospital I was half hoping that the writer would show up so that it would give Lenny a bit of a boost. Not that he'd mentioned the script but I guessed it was still on his mind. So it came as a real suprise when I opened the door one day and there was this fella clutching a bundle of papers like they was the crown jewels. Lenny was home by then and his face lit up when he found this was what he'd been waiting for.

It was left with us, stuck under the coffee table, and there it stayed until he came round again. We never even opened it. He's saying to Lenny, 'Well, what did you think of it, then?' and Lenny's going, 'Blinding, fucking brilliant.' And the writer's face lit up like Brighton front. If only he knew. Lenny asked him, 'Right, what now then?' and he said, 'All we need now is about ten mill and we're up and running.' Lenny looked at me with his eyebrows raised as if he was saying, 'This bloke's got his head in the clouds,' but all he said was, 'Go on then, son, I'll leave it to you,' and like every time before it just went all quiet and nothing happened.

Why Lenny never actually bothered to read the script wasn't lack of interest, more that if he took somebody on board to do a job he expected it to be done. If somebody's a writer that's what they do, same as a plumber or electrician, and he didn't feel he had to check it out. At least that's what Len thought. What with things dragging on I'd started to get a gut feeling that this film business was going nowhere, though I didn't say too much. He knew how I felt but didn't really want to know. He was typical of lots of men, when it came to certain things. He wouldn't ask questions because he knew the answers might not be what he wanted to hear. But I did.

We went to the writer's home a couple of times for meals, and one of these times I said to him, 'Have you done many other film scripts or books?' I wasn't deliberately putting him on the spot, I was interested because I'd already mentioned his name in a couple of places and they couldn't come up with anything, though that didn't mean he hadn't done a few things.

Lenny shot me one of his looks and this writer screwed his face up while he tried to remember how many scripts and books he'd churned out over the years. Eventually he said, 'Er . . . I haven't actually had anything published yet, but I'm always scribbling away. Doesn't the script speak for itself?' Lenny dived in with, 'Course it does – blinding, brilliant,' and it all passed off.

As time went on Lenny got more and more obsessed with the idea of this film, and carried it about like a puppy does a soft toy or bone. Anybody who had two minutes to spare got it stuck under their nose. I'm convinced nobody actually ever read it until it got into the hands of a woman called Sheena Perkins. I don't even know what she did in the film business, and the first I heard of her was Lenny telling me some bird that works in the 'cow shed' was having a look. I didn't know whether I was supposed to laugh or not, so I just looked at him. He said, 'What? I dunno, that's where she said she worked and I was going to make a crack but I didn't because she's a bit posh.' It turned out that 'cow shed' was a studio expression for the wardrobe department, or props or something like that.

As usual Lenny expected her to be on the phone first thing next morning, but people don't work like that, so then he's on the phone to her every five minutes. Every time her answer was 'Still reading.' It was all right for her, it was me that had to put up with his moaning, 'Fucking woman must be reading one word a day,' then as weeks passed I got, 'That's it, down the fucking happy road again' – something he always said when he thought he wasn't getting anywhere.

Then this Sheena came round saying she had 'certain reservations' about the script. Lenny said, 'What's that in English – all bollocks?' She said, 'No, it needs some changes here and there.' He called the writer round and I was surprised that he didn't lay into him because he hated it if he thought people didn't come up with the goods when he felt he'd done his part. All he did was point out the marked-up bits that needed changing and said to him, 'Go on, son, quick as you like.' So that was weeks and weeks before we saw the script again.

Personally I couldn't care less if we never saw it again because already I was fed up with every conversation we had coming round to film, film, film.

I wasn't really all that surprised that Lenny had got himself all caught up in the idea, because he'd loved films all his life. People of his generation and before didn't have much else for a bit of escapism when they were growing up. Now, I think there's too much – telly, videos, computers, DVDs, you name it. Kids only have about two seconds in their lives to use their own imagination. At the same time, whether it's film stars or pop stars, every one of them is so ordinary it's like there's no magic left.

But when Len was a kid the actors on the big screen were from another planet – they were special and people really thought a lot of them, and from day one I'm sure he fancied that one day he'd be up there alongside John Wayne and his hero Victor McGlagen. Perhaps not too seriously, but it was in the back of his head, that's why he was always doing impressions then asking, 'Good? Very Good? Or Brilliant?' No matter what, we always gave him 'Brilliant' for an answer.

Len himself always put forward that there was one conversation that made him take up acting, and that was with Mike Reid when they were visiting Reg Kray in prison, and he said Lenny should take it up. I don't doubt it was said, but the seed was already well planted in his head long, long before that.

Anyway, Sheena Perkins eventually came back and without messing about she said, 'Lenny, I've been through this script a hundred times and I've shown it to various people in the business. My honest opinion is that you should put it in a drawer and forget about it. Perhaps in years to come your kids might be able to do something with it.' So what she was saying was it would never happen in our lifetime.

I could see disappointment written right across his face and my heart went out to him. He'd been so sure it would all work out once those changes were made; he hadn't prepared himself for a knock-back. I must admit I wasn't too happy with her knocking his dream as blunt as she did, but she had something else up her sleeve otherwise she might have been a bit more diplomatic.

One minute Len's looking a bit defeated, and the next he's back on top raring to go when she said, 'On the other hand, from what you say you have a life that sounds more like fiction than anyone else's reality, so what I will suggest is we try to find a scriptwriter of note who can do your story justice.' She'd given him a big gee about his life and that's what he wanted to hear. Anything else after that he could handle. Even when she said it could cost a hundred thousand it didn't affect his enthusiasm. The last thing he said to her was, 'You find the right person and I'll find the cash.'

When she'd gone I said, 'You know we haven't got that sort of money at the moment, don't you?' because like I said before, he never had a clue whether we had fortunes or nothing.

He said, 'Don't worry; I know loads of people who are just waiting to buy a piece of the action. I'll make some calls.'

Strange, really, if you put a deal up for buying a piece of land for development, or an investment scheme for some product or other, people would be shaking their heads and looking for every guarantee under the sun. But mention film and for some reason real caution goes out the window, so Lenny was right. Within days he had a group of friends lined up and ready to put their own money up.

Months and months later a copy of this new script was delivered from Brian Clemens and Stephen Lister, and according to Lenny once again it was 'Blinding. Brilliant.'

I said, 'Len, you've only just flicked through it. How do you know if it's any good or not?'

But his answer was, 'Well, it's gotta be, hasn't it?

These people have written loads of films.' I didn't know about that but the thought did cross my mind that it should be brilliant when you consider the price of it – that same money could've bought two nice houses at the time.

Sometimes it must read like I'm cynical about everything, but I think realistic is a better word. Though I would've loved everything to go ahead the way everybody seemed to be talking that it would, unfortunately I was proved right time and time again, until really I couldn't get excited about any developments that came up. I'm not knocking anybody's enthusiasm at the time. I'm sure they all thought they were on a winner and made every effort in trying to pull it off, but no matter what, no interest could be raised with the people who held the big money. So after laying out all that money we were no further forward than we had been with that first script.

Then, although the finance had still to be sorted, Sheena started holding auditions for the part of playing Lenny in the film.

I went along with Len to see what sort of people she had in mind. End of the day absolutely none of the young fellas that turned up came anywhere near the sort of character Lenny really was, though I don't mean this as a criticism of them.

As it was Craig Fairbrass got chosen for the part that was never going to happen, and he was another nice young man. Day one told me he'd never be the right person to impersonate Len and nothing ever changed my mind. Not even when he became a television star overnight when he got a part in *EastEnders*. Shame, really, because I have to hand it to him, he really knocked himself out to prove to Len he was the right man.

His uncles were the Dixon Brothers, who'd had more than their fair share of aggravation from the law. But that was a long time ago and since then both Allan and George have become legitimate businessmen. But what I'm coming to is that George Dixon had grown into the most uncanny likeness of Lenny. I hadn't seen him for years, not since him and Alan had become good friends of Len's, and before they went their separate ways.

Peter and his wife Shirley had been out to Spain, and when they came back Peter said to me, 'You won't believe this, Val, but we saw a man out there who was so like Lenny it upset us for the rest of the day.'

All I could say was, 'Life can be strange. They do say everybody's got a double somewhere in the world.'

Then I met George at a charity do and straight away I knew this was the man Peter had seen. And even more so when George said he had a villa in Spain. I told him how much he looked like Lenny and he said, 'You wouldn't believe the amount of people who tell me that.' Though the funny thing is he never looked a bit like Len when they knew each other years before.

I always felt sorry for people like Craig, who got all keyed up about this film and then nothing happened. I know most of them were either looking to double their money or make a name for themselves, but that doesn't take anything away from the fact they all put a lot of time and effort into making it happen. Nobody blamed Lenny, but I knew he always felt gutted that in a way he was letting people down. Yet he did everything that was humanly possible to raise that money – even going so far as to fly over to New York again to get Mafia money interested.

Before, when he went for that fight, he was full of it, like I said, phoning home every five minutes to tell me he'd seen the Empire State Building, or how big their sandwiches were. This time he phoned as much but was very subdued. He'd set off with the writer thinking he was going to come back with a suitcase crammed with dollars, but it turned out that the Mafia, if that's who they were, could be as long-winded as anybody back home.

He called me about four one morning to tell me he'd just bollocked the man from Canterbury. I told him he shouldn't have done that because he'd only been trying to help, and he said, 'You're right, babe. I shouldn't have lost me rag, but you don't know how they're jerking me around over here. I'm coming home.'

One thing about Lenny was you could never keep him down for very long. He got in with a face like a kite. Every American was a mug, the script was shit and all writers could fuck off. Next morning he's raring to go again, but this time on something else.

'I've been thinking. What if we park up the film for a bit and I try me hand at a bit of acting. Good idea or brilliant?'

I was always the one that had to look after realities and slow him down before he got all wrapped up in something then got a knock-back. So I said, 'Well, it's something you've always wanted to do, but if you remember what Craig said, if you don't have one of those Equity cards you won't get any work.'

He said, 'Well, you don't need a scrap of paper to be an extra, you just turn up and do the business.'

I looked at him. 'D'you really see yourself standing in a crowd or drinking a pint in the background of some film? Because knowing you, you'd have to be the centre of attention or nothing.'

He gave me what he would've called 'the old cross-eye', but he knew I was talking sense. 'Ah,' he said, 'I'll make myself busy – then look out.'

That was something about Lenny; he always needed something to focus on. He had his work at the Hippodrome, he had more than he could handle doing paid favours for anybody who phoned, and he had his family. But he loved nothing better than to chase something until he got it under control, and if he had his way, whatever it was had to be done yesterday.

He made a few enquiries among friends and got pointed in the right direction of an agency. They were impressed with the look of him, and they couldn't be otherwise, but they told him he had to have a certain number of hours or weeks under his belt, of things he'd done in show business, no matter what it was.

That stumped him for a bit, then he said to me, 'Know what, babe? Everything I do at work is an acting job. I reckon that should count for something.' I knew what he meant. He didn't just stand around in the clubs he looked after like a lot of them, he made an effort to look somebody. Not all, but a good number, of the bouncers or doormen, whatever you want to call them, parked themselves up, looked mean and kept an eye on their watches until knocking off time. Lenny made himself a presence. He was always suited up nice and you could see your face in his shoes, and I should know because I polished them up every day. He didn't slouch about playing the tough guy. He knew what he was so didn't have to put on a show to prove anything.

So he was right, he was acting a part in a way, but as I pointed out, I didn't think that would count with whoever gave out those work cards. So what he did was go through to different club managers and get them to write a letter saying he'd been doing a strong-man act in their clubs for years. As he told me, he said to them, 'Look, I've done me strong-man bit every night slinging out the agg merchants, so it ain't like you're telling lies.'

That's all it took, and weeks later Lenny got his Equity card. We found out later that if he'd known where to go he could've bought one and saved himself a lot of running about. It's probably not generally known, but when you think that little card can open doors to make a regular living for years, then it's worth good money and to change hands at two or three thousand pounds a time wasn't out of the way at all.

An actor might retire so he wouldn't need one any more, but more often than not one might get down on his luck, sell his card, then if he got any offers, put in for another one saying he'd lost the first. Len said they're a bit like passports – it's only one in a hundred that gets looked at properly.

Everybody wants to get into film or TV work, or so it seemed, and once Lenny got his Equity card all kinds of fellas would ask him if he could get them one.

Going back to his younger days, no matter what he was doing or how much money Lenny had, he couldn't resist making a bit on the side, and he preferred it if whatever it was was a scam. So what he'd say to these people was, 'No, I can't get you one of these cards because they have to be earned, and that ain't easy,' suggesting that he deserved such a thing and they didn't. They'd look disappointed then he'd say, 'But what I could do for you, and I'm taking a bit of a risk 'ere, is get you what they call a green card, and that would entitle you to be an extra in any film in the country.' To get a chance like this was a dream come true for most of these people and no matter what the conditions might be they were going to have one. So when Len adds he's got to pay somebody through the back door, 'if you know what I mean' and it'll cost them two and a half, three hundred, they can't pay him quick enough.

The only thing was, if they'd known how the system worked, they could've taken themselves up town, gone to the office, filled out a form and walked out with the same card for about ten bob.

I was with him more than once when somebody would ask, 'Got my card yet, Len?' He'd say, 'Tomorrow afternoon without fail.' Then they'd say, 'Only I want two more for my mates,' and they'd hand over the cash. Best of it was Lenny didn't even put himself out to do the business. He'd give the details to a friend and let him do the legwork.

I'm saying how seriously he took his job in the Hippodrome and he did, but occasionally a laugh came out of it. Some young man came up to him one Saturday night when the place was packed and said, 'Excuse me, I've lost five pounds.' There were two ways he could've handled that. A simple 'fuck off' or pointed him in the direction of lost property. Not Len. He jumped up, called one of the doormen over, this was Robert Lopez, and told him to sit this young man down and give him a drink – 'Put it on my tab.' Then from the top level of the club – and if you've been there you'll know how high it is – he went all the way down different flights of stairs, across the floor and up on to the stage.

He signalled the DJ to cut the music then started to tap on the microphone. Almost every one of these people knew Lenny so it all went quiet. I can imagine they're all looking at each other and thinking something big's going down. He waited a bit, then in that big voice of his said, 'Now, listen. We've got a problem here and nobody leaves until it's sorted. There's a geezer up top who's in tears 'cos he lost a fiver. He's come to Big Lenny and asked me to help him, so I want you all to line up – '

three thousand people – 'and empty your bags and pockets. Then after we've searched you, I want you all to stand to one side while we take the carpets up.'

According to Robert, who told me this, there was a deathly hush, then the whole place went in an uproar of screaming, laughing and cheering. How the poor fella who'd lost the money felt I don't know, but I should think he crawled out on his hands and knees.

I knew it would happen once he'd signed up with the Chuck Julian Agency, and I wasn't wrong. He phoned them every day to see if they'd got him any work. He was as polite as could be when he was talking to them, but as soon as he put the phone down they were a load of lazy bastards sitting about with their fingers up their arses. It was unfair but that was Len – and again it was me that took all the flak.

I came in one day and he told me he'd put his name down with another firm. I said, 'Oh, Len, give Chuck a chance, you've only been with him a fortnight.'

He said, 'No, I haven't dumped him, but two agents could mean twice as much work.'

I said, 'Who are these new people, then?' and I could've fell over when he told me they were called Ugly. When I fell about laughing the look on his face was funnier than the name of the firm. I said, 'Since when did you think of yourself as ugly?' which I knew he didn't because if ever there was a mirror handy, he'd be checking himself out.

He said, 'No, that's a gimmick, the sort of people they take on have to have interesting faces. Y'know, lived in.'

Eventually they sent him through the card they'd use for advertising, and really it made nonsense of that Ugly name because he looked warm and friendly and – maybe I'm biased, but – bloody good-looking. That was something else for him to carry around until people must've got fed up looking at it and it fell to pieces. I kept one to myself, though, and I've still got it.

I don't remember them ever getting anything for him, but it wasn't too long before Chuck came back with an offer. He phoned up and asked Len to go up to the office to talk about it, and before he left Len had convinced himself this was the big one.

I'm sure he had it in his head that he was up for a remake of *Gone with the Wind* or something, because he ran through his impressions, sang songs and pulled faces at himself in the mirror. I was glad when three o'clock came and he took off.

When he got back even he couldn't help laughing when I asked him what it was all about. First off though, he said, 'Chuck only wants to put me up for the main role in a big TV series.'

I said, 'You're joking.' That's when he laughed.

'Yeah, I am. I'm down for a toilet-paper advert.'

He had to audition for this part so he talked me into going with him and we turned up at the studio just off Charing Cross at about eleven in the morning. There were about half a dozen big fellas sitting in this waiting room, and they all looked at us as we walked in. Lenny gave them one of his looks and every one of them quickly studied the floor. Half a minute and he started on the stage whispers. 'Bunch of wankers.' I didn't know where to look because they must've heard him. 'Look at 'em. Not one of 'em's got a tear-up in 'em.'

I whispered back, 'Keep it down, Lenny, please, they're not here for a fight.'

Luckily it wasn't too long before we got called in. Once we got in this big room with a camera all set up, straight away he wanted to take over. 'Right, where do you want me? What d'you want me to say?' A nice young girl explained that she wanted him to face the camera, and then while he's pulling at a length of toilet roll, make a face and pretend it's too tough for him to break. He says, 'Who's going to fall for that?' He was taking the piss really because by then he couldn't care less about the advert.

She said, 'It isn't a case of anyone falling for it, it's an advert. People expect that sort of thing.'

He gave her a look that said he wasn't convinced and I could tell by his attitude he couldn't wait to go home. 'Go on, then, short stuff, set it up.' She looked down her nose at being called that, but handed him the tissue. Somebody said, 'Rolling,' and Lenny broke the toilet paper. Straight away he said, 'Told you, didn't I?' Give these people their due, they were patient. Then he started growling like he would in a fight while he's tugging at the paper, so they had to stop again and tell him, 'No sound. It's all in the facial expression.' They gave up in the end, but they made a big show of checking that they had his agent's address correct and yes, they'd be in touch within the next few days.

We never heard another word. Chuck wasn't too pleased because he got a bollocking from the advert people, but he didn't go too strong with Len. Just said, 'Perhaps that one wasn't for you. I'll have a look round for something else.' He did explain that though these adverts might seem a bit silly, that didn't matter. What was important, as he put it, was to build up a portfolio and get Lenny's face seen by millions, then work would pour in.

Len took this on board, behaved himself at the next audition and got the job. And he hated it.

Like you would have seen on the cover of his book, he had a face that immediately caught your attention, and that was what was wanted. So all you got when this advert was eventually shown was Lenny in close up, sniffing a bottle of disinfectant. It took all day to film, mind you, because he never pulled the same face twice. I thought it was good but he made me throw the copy they sent us in the bin, so unfortunately that's gone for ever.

What always surprised me was that nobody saw the potential he had as an actor. I used to watch him when he got calls from Ruby Wax, Derek Jameson and loads of others, because he gave them one hundred per cent entertainment. Lenny loved it because he was talking about himself and the centre of attention, and this real-life gangster knocked them out. We knew the term 'gangster' wasn't true, and he never did like to hear the word, but he went along with it because he knew that's what they wanted to believe.

Because he never got offered a serious acting role, back then anyway, he started to get fed up with it. I knew he would because if something didn't take off at a hundred miles an hour, he'd want to park it up. 'Babe,' he said, 'I've had a gutful of this fuckin' about. Seems everybody in that game's a poof or a ponce – not my cup of tea at all. I'm going to move on.' And he did.

What put the next idea in his head I'll never know, but he was always one for doing things on the spur of the moment. He'd been paid out on a deal he'd been working on so he was carrying a lump of cash, and I could only think it was burning a hole in his pocket.

He pulled into a garage in Southgate Road, just off of Essex Road, and right beside it he noticed that a shop was up for sale. He got his petrol, left his car on the forecourt, then without giving it too much thought, did no more than walk next door and buy the shop outright. I suppose he'd heard that small local sweet and tobacconist shops are goldmines – and perhaps they are. But not the way Lenny ran it.

People had been used to it opening at about seven in the morning, so they could buy their bits and pieces on the way to work. Overnight it got to opening any time from then up to ten o'clock because Lenny couldn't be bothered to get out of bed – though to be fair, he often didn't get in from the club until three in the morning. He treated it like a hobby and that's no way to run a business. He was too soft and he didn't have an ounce of patience.

One morning he couldn't get the till open. Instead of calling somebody in to sort the lock out, he picked it up, smashed it on the floor and for the rest of the day put in and took money from it while it was still laying on the floor. Another time we had a delivery of crates of lemonade. No time to bring them in perhaps two crates at a time. He carried eight, tripped over something and broke every bottle, except two, all over the place. Times like that he'd look at his watch and realize he had to be somewhere else 'lively'. So who got left with the cleaning up and re-ordering?

I remember a little girl coming in one day. She had one of her mum's dresses on, all scraping along the ground, high-heeled shoes, lipstick, powder – you name it. She was about four or five and with a basket over her arm. She walked round the shop, picking sweets up like a little old woman. Lenny's looking at her and going, 'Ah, look at that, Val – ain't she a little doll.' When this little doll came up to the counter, she dug in a purse and handed Len about twenty pence for three pounds' worth of chocolate bars. He looked at me, saying, 'What can you do?' took the money, told her to mind the road, and she walked out with the profit on fifty packets of cigarettes.

That didn't happen the once – every kid in the neighbourhood got to know that if I wasn't around they could get a free ice-cream from Lenny just for the asking.

It couldn't last and it didn't. All I can say about it now is that it was an experience, but I was glad to see the back of it. So it was good to see Lenny back at doing what he was good at, and me looking after the house without the aggravation of playing shopkeepers.

It had never been about making money. How could it, when for an hour's 'growling', as he put it, or a day spent evicting some firm or other, he could bring home more cash than the shop ever took in a couple of months? And it was after one of these jobs that really did pull in a lot of money that he decided we should take off to Spain for a few weeks.

We took off for Fuengirola and had a fantastic time, which doesn't mean we tore around all over the place sightseeing or doing anything special. Fantastic to me meant doing nothing at all but soak up the sun and laze around the pool.

Strange, looking back in hindsight. While we were both getting a tan and relaxing, something was getting closer and closer that would change Lenny in a lot of ways and turn our life on its head for years to come. Still, right then we'd no idea what the future held, and it's just as well.

No wonder the papers call the part of Spain we always went to the Costa del Crime. It seemed that some days we couldn't walk five yards without some cockney voice shouting out, 'Big Lenny.' We bumped into Clifford Saxe, who used to own the Fox just round the corner from us – he was on the run for supposedly being involved in a Security Express robbery, some bloke on the run for involvement in the Brinks Mat bullion robbery, and loads of others – too many to mention.

Ronnie Knight was another one, looking good for his age, all done up in a white suit.

But what struck me about all these people, who were living a life ordinary working people can only dream about, was for two farthings they'd jump on a plane right then, just for the chance of pie and mash in Cooksies on a wet Saturday afternoon. None of them could – and I got the impression none of them were particularly happy. That must say something to anybody out there who's thinking about doing some big crime then escaping to the sun. It's obviously not all it's cracked up to be.

It's funny how a little throwaway line can come back to you later on. Lenny said to one of these fellas, 'If you've got the arsehole living here, why don't you wipe your mouth, go home and face it?'

Of course the other one's giving it, 'What then, do five or ten in the Scrubs? Leave it out.'

Lenny said, 'Listen, it's lovely here, but it's like you're telling me it's your prison. OK, do your bit of bird an' after that you can do whatever you want. Make me right? How hard is a spot of prison time? Piece of piss, I can do it standing on my head.'

The fella wasn't convinced because he's still living out there today. Later on Lenny would find out that being behind bars wasn't the doddle he said it would be, though that was for a different reason than he meant at the time.

I suppose it must've been about four o'clock on the Saturday afternoon by the time we got back to Strahan Road. We sorted out the bits and pieces we'd brought back for the kids, had a cup of tea then went for a lie down for a couple of hours. By the time we got up my head was still in Fuengirola, but as far as Lenny was concerned it was all behind him and he was raring to do something.

I thought we'd have a nice night in front of the telly with a bottle of wine and those picky bits you always end up bringing back off holiday, but no. 'Two minutes, babe, that's all I'll be. Gonna shoot up the club and get me bit of scratch.' If he didn't pick up his wages owed for six months, we still wouldn't be waiting for it, so that was just an excuse to get out and catch up with whatever had happened while he'd been away. I didn't argue – I was too tired.

He came to bed in the early hours, and as usual I woke up and asked if he was all right. All I got was, 'Couldn't be better – sound as a pound.'

The phone went about seven. We didn't have one in the bedroom then so I went downstairs to answer it. It was Val Anderson to tell me her Ritchie had been arrested while we were away for stabbing some people. I wasn't surprised, and nor was she really, but it was still bad news. I told her I understood how she must be feeling (I thought I did) and said I would tell Lenny as soon as he woke up.

I'm never at my best until about nine o'clock in the morning, so thought I'd fill the washing machine and go back to bed. That's when I found a shirt with blood spots down the front. It wasn't the first time but so much for 'sound as a pound' some hours earlier.

It seemed like I'd only closed my eyes when the phone rang again. This time I nudged Lenny in the back and said, 'Your turn, I can't move,' and unusual for him he got up without puffing and sighing. It was lovely just lying there dozing, listening to people walking past, the birds singing – yet in two minutes my life was going to be torn apart.

I heard Lenny banging up the stairs and was just thinking, 'Nice cup of tea, babe,' when he came in shaking his head and sat on the bed beside me. I could tell by his face that there was trouble, but I wasn't prepared for him telling me he'd killed somebody. It was like I was hearing something I'd been waiting to hear all our lives together. That makes it sound as though I'd always looked on him as a killer, or somebody capable of murder, but I never did. It's just doing what he did, law of averages said one day someone he took on wasn't going to get up again.

I wasn't a lot of help to him as he sat there looking puzzled and shaking his head. I cried. I just couldn't help it. He gave me a cuddle and said, 'You know the first thing that went through my mind when Mick told me? I'll tell you. It was to jump on the first plane back to Spain and kip down with Ronnie, like he offered.'

I said, 'Please, Len, you can't run away from something like this – we'll face it.'

'That's exactly what I thought, babe, but it won't come to that. Somebody's got it all wrong.'

Then he swore to me that the night before all he'd done to a young man who was high on drugs was give him a slap to bring him to his senses. And I believed him. Why should he lie? He knew that he could tell me anything, and most of the time he did. He said, 'I'm sorry I frightened you, Val. I should've held back a bit, but it was a shock. Tell you what, I'll have a word with Ritchie. He's got his ear to the ground – be sorted in one minute.'

Then I remembered. 'Oh, Len, Ritchie's in Brixton. They reckon he stabbed a couple of men.'

He just went, 'Oh, fuck me. What's happening?' For once he didn't go tearing off, mainly because he could tell I was really shaken. But he spent most of the day on the phone. All Mick Theo, the friend who'd rang him first, could tell him was that a mate of a mate who was in the Fire Brigade had somehow put Lenny's name in the frame over some man they'd picked up. That's all it was. Nothing official, just rumour among mates.

Nobody else knew anything and by the end of the day Lenny was back to his old self, singing his head off – though I think that was more with relief.

As for me, I couldn't get rid of the knots in my stomach no matter how much it seemed we'd been scared for nothing. I knew Len so well. He wasn't cut out to be caged up. Not that anybody is, I suppose, but he had to be doing something all the time. He wasn't like normal people who are content to sit in front of the telly night after night – he thought that was a complete waste of time. And as for being ordered around or told what to do, God help anybody who tried.

That's why the thought of prison frightened me. He'd end up doing something that would get his sentence extended over and over again, and he'd never get out. People he knew had ended up like that. They start with five years, then as time gets added on for causing trouble behind the bars, they finish with twenty. Seems crazy, but some people can't help kicking against the system. And you don't have to look any further than Frankie Fraser to see that.

Luckily Jamie and Kelly were heavy sleepers, like most kids their age, so never heard a word of what went on that morning. They might have wondered why we were both a bit preoccupied but they never said anything.

Monday and Tuesday passed. Lenny went back to work, and the Sunday started to seem like some horrible dream. Then it all unwound.

Seems like I'm in bed every time something happened in our lives. The reason for that is, anything that was going to happen usually did while Lenny was at work, so I'd hear about it late at night. Or if the police were involved and wanting to break our door down, it was always going to be early in the morning.

So yes, I was in bed. I vaguely remembered the door going and somebody coming in the house, and I found out later that it was Ronnie Joyce, a friend of Lenny's who often popped in early for a chat with Len. For a minute I lay listening to their mumbled voices and bursts of laughing then I dozed off. It seemed like I'd no sooner closed my eyes than there was a loud banging on the door, raised voices, footsteps on the stairs and Lenny burst into the bedroom, shouting back down the stairs, 'I've warned you, don't fucking move.' Then he said to me, 'I'm lifted, babe – over that bloke that died up West. They reckon I fuckin' well done it.'

It was like a punch in the stomach and on came the tears again. Somebody shouted, 'Come on or we'll have to come up,' and Lenny looked like he'd explode. He was grabbing his suit out of the wardrobe. I got out of bed and we had a cuddle that was saying 'be strong' from each of us. As he went to go he whispered, 'Lose that shirt I had Saturday,' and I said, 'Washed spotless,' and he made a kiss, said, 'Good gel,' and he was gone. I felt like getting back into bed and pulling the covers over my head, but that would've been letting him down and he had enough on his plate without thinking I was going to pieces back home.

Ronnie was still in the kitchen when I went downstairs, and trying to make me feel better he said, 'Don't worry about it, Val, they're trying it on. Bet you a tenner Len'll be back here in time for his dinner.' I should've taken his bet.

They wouldn't let me in to see him until well late in the day. As if I wasn't strung out enough, I was treated like I was of no value at all. Not by the ordinary coppers at Vine Street station, but by the higher-up ones. One, they wouldn't tell me anything apart from he was being charged with murdering somebody called Humphries, and on top of that they spoke to me like I was guilty of something, or somehow involved.

By the time they let me have a few minutes with Lenny I'd got myself into a state, so when they led him into a little side room where I was waiting, I was crying my eyes out again. If he was upset himself he certainly didn't show it, not even when he tried to explain, as gently as he could, that this time they really did have a case against him – and he didn't stand a chance.

— TEN —

When Lenny told me the bad news all I wanted to do was to cling to him, but some inspector, cold as you like, came in and told me to leave.

Mick Theo and his wife Helen had driven me to Vine Street because I wasn't in a fit state to get myself there. They'd waited in a cafe opposite, and I don't remember leaving the station or crossing that busy main road. All I can remember is Mick holding me with my back to a wall to stop me sliding to the ground. I'd already rung my sister Marie, who lived opposite, asking her to go over to the kids and make sure they didn't put the radio on, just in case it was on the news.

By the time I got home my voice sounded like it was coming through a broken microphone – half my words came out, half didn't. Kelly and her best friend Karen were waiting with my sister. I managed to make myself understood and explained what was going on. The two girls burst out crying, and with that on top of everything else I just collapsed. Marie, thinking I'd had a stroke, called the doctor and he called an ambulance. While we were waiting for the doctor Marie took me into the garden and made me breathe with a paper bag over my mouth. Lucky for me that she knew what to do when somebody is hyperventilating in panic.

So half an hour after getting in, I was being driven

through the East End with sirens going. How Marie coped I don't know, because with Lenny up for murder and me apparently dying, Kelly and Karen just went hysterical. Some neighbour must've heard them screaming, so next thing the police turn up to investigate. It was complete and utter chaos.

Once I was in the hospital they gave me Valium and I calmed down a lot. The doctor said I'd suffered the 'classic reaction to a bereavement'. Talk about a pill reversing my state of mind. I went to hospital in the deepest depression you can imagine, then laughed all the way home. It couldn't have been natural laughing, but whatever, I just couldn't stop myself.

The girls had calmed down because Jamie had come in by then. Seeing me get out of the ambulance laughing the way I was, he said to them, 'Why've you brought her home? Take her back, she's gone mental.'

Eventually the drugs wore off, and with all the terrible trauma of the past twelve hours we all just slumped in armchairs and looked at each other. What now? By the time we woke up in the morning we'd all come to terms with what was happening in our own different way. Jamie went into denial. 'Dad'll be OK, won't he? Dad'll be back in a few days,'

I keep referring to my two kids, and I'll still be saying that when I'm seventy, but they weren't babies by a long way. Jamie was twenty and Kelly was a year younger, so they knew what life was about and that, guilty or not, their dad could be behind bars for the next twenty years.

Kelly put a brave face on it, but inside she was torn to bits. As for me, I just wanted someone to turn the clock back. But as I knew that could never happen, made up my mind to do what Lenny said and be strong for everybody. It was hard though, specially as my voice kept coming and going, so half the time I couldn't even comfort my kids without writing down what I wanted to say.

All over again we had to suffer policemen and forensics tramping through our home. They turned the place upside down, yet not one of them would tell me what they were looking for. I know my asking must've sounded like 'Wha ... y ... loo ... or,' with my vocal cords seized up. But they understood me all right.

If Lenny had killed that man up West, what's that got to do with inside my home? What evidence did they expect to find emptying all my cupboards and lifting carpets up? They were already treating me like I was a criminal because I admitted washing Len's shirt, not that I mentioned the blood on the front, but apart from that nothing indoors could help solve why that young man had died.

That was something else that upset me apart from worrying about Lenny. Somebody's son had died, for whatever reason. While I was crying over what was going to happen to my husband, somewhere out there a mother and father were crying over the loss of their son. His death would mean pain and worry for all our family, but that never stopped me wondering how his parents were coping with such a terrible thing.

The worst part in those first days was trying to come to terms with the real fact that Lenny had killed somebody. Though he couldn't understand how a simple slap could've caused somebody to die, he accepted that with all the facts he had, that it was a possibility and he even told me that he'd put his hands up to it by the time I was allowed to see him again.

I'm no lawyer, but if only through watching crime programmes on TV I knew you never admitted you were guilty, no matter what, and I told him as much. Then he said, 'I'd no choice, babe. That copper said they'd charge

Robert Lopez if I didn't cough, because he reckons if it weren't me it must be him. I ain't never known that kid to shove anybody, let alone kill 'em. So how could I let him do that?'

In my croaky voice I encouraged him the best I could, saying things like they'd soon realize their mistake, and that once he was in court he'd get bail and we'd fight it from the outside. But in my heart I already had Len locked up for life and was trying to imagine how all our lives would be. Strange, the doctor telling me I was suffering from bereavement shock, because that's exactly how I felt. Like he'd already been taken away from me for ever. I can remember thinking, 'This is how so and so felt when her husband died,' or even how my mum had felt when she lost my dad at twenty-three.

I must've been so naive, but back then I'd nothing to compare it with. Now I have, and I wish with all my heart that Lenny was locked up in Durham or Maidstone instead of not being around at all. Selfish I know, because a life sentence would've drained the life out of him, but at least I'd see him every week or so, instead of only having a photograph to talk to.

I went to his remand hearing and it was all over in two minutes. Name, address, charge – murder, remanded to Brixton.

We had a thirty-second kiss and cuddle, and he was taken away in handcuffs. And that was a horrible thing to see. My husband; my friend; the person I loved – chained up like an animal and being led away. It broke my heart completely.

After that I knew I couldn't go any further down, so the only way was up. And what helped me towards that was when I had a meeting with our lawyer, Martin Lee. Suddenly things didn't seem so clear cut as the law seemed to think, and if there's anybody left out there who hasn't read *The Guv'nor*, I'll just run through what he told me.

Gary Humphries had a mental condition. He'd been let out of a mental home or a hospital and from then on, like a lot of people do in that situation, he didn't take his medication. That'd caused him to get in a state and once that happened he didn't know what he was doing. He ended up in the Hippodrome, and I'll never understand how he was let through the doors, unless once he got inside he had a drink and that took him over the edge. Either way it wasn't too long before he stripped his clothes off. He climbed on the stage and somebody knocked him off, so already before Len even got near him there was a possible injury.

After that he ran among the crowd naked. And knowing what I know now it's heartbreaking to think, like I said before, that this was somebody's son, lost and confused. But nobody knew that then and taking his carry-on as just the behaviour of another drunk or druggie, that's when Lenny and Robert stepped in.

In a nutshell, he was chased, caught and put in a store cupboard out of sight of all these young girls. Len slapped him to bring him to his senses, partially dressed him, then saw him out of a side door. Straight away a policeman spoke to him because he looked spaced out and dishevelled, and I don't suppose it was the first time the copper had seen somebody leaving the club looking like that. He spoke to him, got an answer, and as he seemed perfectly all right had no reason not to let him go about his business.

Some hours later he took his clothes off again and dodged in and out of traffic until the police caught up with him. He tried to fight them off but they held him down. Witnesses seemed to think they used excessive force, but he was a strong lad and I doubt very much whether they intentionally hurt him. But he died suddenly shortly afterwards.

I said to Martin, 'Put the way you've just explained it, no way did Lenny have anything to do with his death. Go and tell them that. Get him out.'

He said, 'If only it was that simple, Val. What you have to consider is that's why we have courts. Both sides will have a chance to put their side of the story, then a jury will decide – guilty or otherwise.'

My spirits went right up at the thought that in a matter of weeks it could all be sorted, but how many weeks exactly? His answer knocked me down. 'Could be a year, at worst eighteen months, before it comes to trial.'

I went into one because he said it so matter-of-factly. 'This isn't some dispute over a fence in the wrong place, this is a man's life we're talking about here. He didn't do it. You've just told me he couldn't have done it, yet he's got to rot in prison until they decide it's convenient? I'm going to take this somewhere.'

He said, 'There's nowhere to take it, this is the law and neither you or I can do anything to alter it.' I was as down as I could possibly get, so when he added, 'Due to Lenny's ... er ... past lifestyle, I feel there is pressure from somewhere to make this one stick,' it hardly registered.

So that's what we had to look forward to for the next year and a half. Lenny locked up in some stinking prison and me and the kids trying to hold our lives together without him. What I do know is we couldn't have got through it without the support of friends and family. The least of our worries was money, yet we had offer after offer of cash from all kinds of people, and I think the reason for that was there was nothing else they could do. No matter what any of them said or tried to do, nothing was going to get Lenny out of the situation, so they did the only thing possible. It meant a great deal to me. Not the money but the thought behind it.

Something I'll never forget is that Arthur Thompson phoned me almost every day of Lenny's sentence. Not only that, he wrote to Len every day as well and the only time he didn't get in touch with us both for a while was when his son was murdered.

Prison visiting is as much of a degrading experience for them going in as it is for those already inside. From the minute you hand over that visiting order slip, you're treated as though you're beneath contempt because you're a friend or relative of a con. Never mind that they're innocent until proved guilty. Looking round at all the other visitors I couldn't help being struck by the thought that it didn't matter if you were a duke or a dustman, we were all in the same boat.

My handbag was searched, I had one of those metal detectors run over me, then I had to wait until everybody had been treated the same. We were led like sheep into the visiting room. You take a table then wait while the prisoners file in. I got all choked up as Lenny appeared in the door, but I'd told myself, 'No more crying.' He had enough to worry about without seeing me in a state every time he saw me.

If ever a man looked out of place it was him. I mean I shouldn't generalize, but looking at some of the men that came walking in, they looked what they were. Pale, tattooed, shaved heads – the sort of people you'd sooner cross the road from than walk past. And there was Len – big, strong and every inch the Guv'nor. He stood out like a sore thumb.

Once we got all the small talk out of the way I asked him how he was finding it. 'Piece of piss. Grub's terrible but it's a break from all the agg outside.'

I said, 'Len, it's me you're talking to. How do you feel?'

He sort of looked round to see if anybody was listening, then said, 'Val, it ain't this place. It ain't the screws and it ain't half these mugs I've got to rub shoulders with. It's what might happen, and it's tearing my guts out.'

Strange how when one half of a partnership weakens the other half gets stronger. Up until then I'd felt really crushed, and though I supposed I'd carry on feeling like that I made up my mind never to let it show again. So I told him that everything was looking good as far as the law was concerned, and while he'd have to sit it out, it would all come right in the end. He said, 'That's good news, babe, I won't worry about it no more.' What I didn't know and never found out until it was all over was that he was humouring me. I should've known but obviously wasn't thinking straight.

Ralph Haeems had told Lenny exactly what Martin told me. It wasn't looking good and someone was out to get him sent down for a very long time.

Prison visiting's a lot like hospital visiting. You want to be there, but after a while you keep looking at the clock because you've run out of things to talk about. I think I said before, he wasn't a great one for small talk, and nothing had changed. He went along with me prattling on about ordinary everyday things, but I would see his eyes wandering around the room waiting for me to finish so he could ask, 'What did the solicitor say again?' And I'd have to repeat word for word a telephone conversation I'd had with him the day before.

In the same way Peter would do when he put the phone down and lied about what the other person had said about Lenny, I found myself making up bits and pieces just to keep him happy. I'd no choice. Although he insisted I rang every day to find out what was happening, most of the time I didn't. What was the point of wasting their time or mine, when I didn't think there was very much they could tell me anyway?

Lenny was locked up. His papers and the evidence for and against him were sitting on a shelf. Everything was on hold until the wheels of justice ground along as slow as they could.

So with us two having the least to say among the hundred other people in the room, we were the ones to get a visit twice as long as anybody else. I've just said Lenny didn't have a lot to say, but on the other hand he didn't want the visit to end. And it didn't until he was good and ready. A whistle would blow and after about fifteen minutes of 'Come on now,' all the other visitors would reluctantly file out, leaving just Lenny and me. Time would go by and a screw would come up all apologetic, 'Excuse me, Lenny,' and he'd be tapping his watch. Lenny would say, 'D'you mind? Two minutes,' and that would go on for two hours until I really did have to make some excuse to break it up. I suppose from their point of view it was easier to leave us alone than risk a flare-up.

Another thing was he didn't want anybody else coming in to see him except me. And that was awkward because people were queuing up to visit him, thinking they were doing him a favour. Good people and very close friends, but he wouldn't have it. Perhaps he couldn't stand to be seen by anybody that he knew in a situation where he wasn't in control. The screws might have been intimidated by him, but with the law behind them and weight of numbers, whether he liked it or not Lenny was a number and no different from every other prisoner.

He did ask me to bring his sister Lorraine in, but that wasn't so much for himself as for his cellmate. He said, 'I've got a kid in my berth and he never gets one visitor, so bring Boo in for a visit and it'll be nice for him.' She didn't mind and came in quite often.

For a while this prisoner didn't say anything about Lenny, what with knowing she was his sister. But when he found out that she wasn't under any illusions about how her brother could be, he said to her, 'You know what? He's driving me completely round the bend. All he wants to talk about night and day is his case.' Boo knew this from me already. He said, 'I'm frightened to open my eyes in the morning because I know he's sitting waiting for my eyelids to flicker. Soon as I look up he says, "Good, now you're awake let's run through my papers again." We had a lock-down the other day and he kept me reading his papers from seven in the morning right through until eight at night. When I said, "Let's have a look at mine, because I'm in court next week," he said, "What, after the day I've had? Nah, too tired," and went to sleep.'

When I was on a visit to Len a short while after this he said, 'You won't believe what them bastards have done. They've only ghosted my mate out of the cell while I was having a medical. I bet he's gutted.' What he didn't know was this fella had begged to be moved to another wing.

Sometimes Boo would give me a break and sit with Lenny and I'd go outside the visiting room, after telling him I was going to pay some cash into his canteen account. It wasn't true, I just had to get away, because after two hours I was like a limp rag and feeling like I'd done ten rounds with Mike Tyson.

When we came out of the prison we'd go and have a coffee. We'd look at each other and she'd say, 'An' what did the solicitor say?' and we'd both go hysterical. We weren't really laughing at Len, but when you've heard that a hundred times on a visit, you either laugh or go off your head.

On one visit I couldn't help noticing that he didn't seem with it all. He was vague, didn't have anything to say and looked like he was going to fall asleep any minute. I went over to the canteen in the corner to get some tea and on the way back one of the prisoners who'd seen me with Len said as I passed him, 'Bastards, ain't they?' I said, 'Excuse me?' and he said, 'Ain't he told you? Them screws come for him mob-handed last night and stuck 'im with a needle – took ten of 'em, I 'eard.' I never got a chance to ask any more because one of the guards started walking over.

When I got back to Lenny he was fast asleep with his head on the table. I didn't wake him up because quite honestly I was glad of the rest from his questions. My whole life revolved round those visits, and he never thought for a moment of saying, 'Give it a miss every now and then.' I had to make that journey every day, seven days a week. I think prisoners get very selfish. All they see is you sitting in the visitor's room. They never question how you got there. Never question perhaps you didn't feel well that morning, or the effort it might have taken. If there was any hold up on the way I used to panic because I knew he'd go into one. I got a puncture one morning, but I was so worried about being late I drove the rest of the way on the rim, with people tooting and pointing every five yards. With him asleep in front of me I just thought he was exhausted with the worry of it all, and never for a moment dreamed he was drugged up.

At the end of the visit I shook him awake and asked him if he'd been beaten up by the guards, but he just looked vague and said he'd like to see them try. If he'd said yes I would've taken it further, but as it was I didn't want to cause trouble for him over nothing.

This state he was in went on for a good while and I just carried on with the assumption that he wasn't sleeping at night so did it during the day. We've all been there. You toss and turn all night, yet you can sleep for Britain any other time.

Then I was walking to the main gate with all the other visitors when one of the guards stopped me. He said, 'Lenny McLean's wife, yes?'

I said, 'Yes, what's the problem?'

He looked all round then said, 'Look, you didn't get this from me but I want to warn you Lenny's being doped up on Liactol. And if you don't get something done about it, they'll nut him off and you'll be visiting him in a mental hospital.'

I was horrified. I couldn't imagine this sort of thing going on or being legal, so I said, 'What can I do about it?' And he told me to make an appointment with the probation officer.

Before I could do that I caught Lenny in one of his more lucid moments and asked him if he was being given pills or anything. He said, 'Yeah, we all are. They feed us on shit so we have to take vitamins to hold us together.'

I said, 'Don't make a fuss but in future make out you're taking them, then throw them away, because one of the guards has told me that those pills are strong tranquillizing drugs.'

In a way it was lucky he had that Liactol floating about in his bloodstream, otherwise there would've been murders. As it was he took what I said quite calmly. Just as well I warned him, because as far as the probation officer was concerned the use of drugs was quite normal in dealing with dangerous prisoners and nothing to worry about. Lenny was classed as an A-category prisoner because he was being held on a murder charge and because of his background, classified as dangerous. Prisoners on the As don't always get drugs to calm them down but all it took was a few flare-ups from Lenny and that was all the excuse they needed. In the end Lenny solved the problem himself when a doctor asked for his help.

I've got a feeling that it was suspected Lenny wasn't taking his pills, so they found other ways round it. I know he had a supposed iron injection, then once he was confused again they could dose him up in drinks or whatever. He was changing from the Lenny I knew into a stranger.

I started to worry about his mental state when his sister Boo told him a funny story. Come to think of it, it wasn't really that funny but when you're under stress the silliest things can seem hilarious. It was something to do with her asking Jamie if he wanted afters. She was in the kitchen shouting through to him, and as they're always having a laugh with each other, for some reason he's shouted back, 'Bollocks.' Quick as anything she's shouted, 'Is that with custard?' Well, we thought it was funny, anyway.

Next day, scraping the barrel for conversation, she told Lenny. He never cracked his face, just looked at me saying, 'But you didn't laugh, did you, Val?'

Luckily I caught on to what he meant and said, 'Oh no, not me, Lenny.' That pleased him.

'Good girl, babe. I didn't think you'd be laughing with me stuck in this poxy 'ole.'

Another time and it was Boo again. She told him we'd had a lovely barbecue in our garden. And we had. It was a scorching hot day so my sister Marie, her husband

George, Boo and the kids had had a nice afternoon. When she told Len his face dropped and again he said to me, 'But you didn't sit out in the garden, did you, babe?' I lied because it was obvious he wanted me to be as much a prisoner as he was. It was crazy thinking and I really began to think I'd lost him. Then he asked me to meet one of the prison doctors outside the walls and he'd explain what it was all about.

After a few phone calls I met the doctor in the Star Bar in Bethnal Green Road. It seemed that a well-known actor was sexually abusing the young son of a friend of the doctor and Lenny had agreed to arrange a beating to get it stopped. In return the doctor had said he would smuggle in a mobile phone if I supplied it. I thought he was getting his problem sorted out on the cheap, so I said to him, 'You're the top doctor in there, aren't you?' When he said yes I said, 'Right, how you do it I don't know, but I want my Lenny off those drugs starting today. And if I don't see an improvement soon you'd better start looking for another job.' I thought he was going to argue but he just said, 'Take it as done.'

Whether I was getting paranoid I don't know, but there was something strange about the whole business and I didn't trust him one bit. It struck me that there were two things going on. The abuse was right enough, and I do know Lenny had it dealt with. But I think the doctor also had a deal going with the prison authorities over the mobile phone, because he asked me all kinds of incriminating questions I didn't answer because I felt he was wired up.

I got hold of what they call a cloned mobile so it was untraceable, and before I handed it over I polished it while I was wearing gloves so they wouldn't get my fingerprints, if that's what they were after.

Once Lenny got the phone it was like when he was in America all over again. Calls every hour day and night. He didn't have a bill to pay so he rang everybody he could think of. More than once I got a call around two-thirty in the morning asking if there was any news from the solicitor.

With nothing ever secret inside a prison it couldn't last, and it didn't. One of the cons who the law had set up to grass on other prisoners told everything he'd heard to the chief officer. They turned over Lenny's cell, found the mobile and sent him straight to Belmarsh Prison in Woolwich. No matter what they threatened, Lenny wouldn't say where it had come from and no way mentioned the doctor. But as always it all came out and I think it must've been the shock and the disgrace that finished the doctor because he died before he could get prosecuted. Still, being a new prison, conditions were much better, and as far as I was concerned the travelling was easier for me. Like they say it's an ill wind.

Something he never forgave himself for was that he was in prison when Jamie became twenty-one. I used to tell him that it wasn't his fault, but he still felt bad about it. He'd say, 'My boy turned into a man and I wasn't there to give him a hug.' We had a party for him but you can imagine none of us felt like celebrating, specially as Lenny had a date for his trial by then and nothing seemed to have changed to make us think a 'not guilty' was guaranteed.

In the weeks of the run-up to the trial Lenny changed from day to day. He went from being very worried to anger, frustration and irrational behaviour. He really was under a lot of strain and I was the only one he'd admit it to. As he walked through that door and back to his cell I should think on the outside he was every inch the Guv'nor, but inside he was in pieces.

I noticed as well that early on he'd wanted me to walk away and forget him if he got a life sentence, but as time crept by that was all forgotten and he wanted constant reassurance that I'd stick by him whatever happened. I would've done anyway, no matter what he said.

One day I arrived and he was even angrier than usual, if that was possible. He said, 'When you go out of here I want you to go to the main desk and pick up a packet I've left for you.' Prisoners weren't allowed to bring anything into the visiting room.

I said, 'What's that, then?'

He said, 'You'll see what it is, and what I want you to do is take it out in the garden when you go home and burn it until there's nothing left.'

I thought, 'I'm not sitting here for four hours wondering what the package is,' so I said, 'What is it? A knock-back on your trial date?'

He said, 'No, the writer has sent me in another draft of that filmscript and that c*** has let me right down. He's written something that makes my whole family look like mugs and I want to kill him.'

I did pick up the envelope, but I didn't burn it and it's still in the back of a cupboard somewhere, though Len never knew. Why I've kept it I don't know, because Lenny was right. It didn't make his family look good at all. In fact, from the words in that script I wouldn't have recognized any of them. Still, it took his mind off of his trial for a few hours.

If there's a more intimidating place than the Old Bailey, then I've never seen it or want to. I suppose that was the intention when it was designed – to make everybody who has to appear in it about an inch tall. If you're ever unfortunate enough to be brought to trial there and you think you'll stand in the dock and lie your way out of it, you'd better think again. Because though

I can't explain it, there's something about the place that must force you to tell the truth, like it or not.

Lenny said it about himself in his book and I'll say it again – all the legal talk went completely over my head. It's strange to say that it was boring when the rest of Lenny's life hung on every word, but there's no other way to describe it. Throughout the days of both sides giving it this and that, I went home every night to cry myself to sleep, convinced it was only a matter of time before I was sentenced to life without him.

If support was enough to get a 'not guilty', they should've let him out there and then, because friends and family packed the gallery. Apart from us, reporters and official people, the rest of the court was filled with the general public. I couldn't help looking at them all and thinking, 'This is just a bit of entertainment to you lot. Something to do, like visiting a museum or the Tower of London.' And I'll bet every one of them was hoping for a 'guilty' to add a bit of drama to their day – something to talk about in the pub later. Did any of them understand what it was like for me and Lenny? Did any of them care?

Somebody had told me that Newgate Prison used to stand on the same site as the Bailey, and less than a hundred and thirty years before people would be trying to get a good view at a public hanging not far from where I was sitting. Nothing changes, does it?

Of all the people in the court one man stood out among them, as somebody who looked to me like he was enjoying every minute of it, and that was the DI who'd arrested Lenny. He seemed to smile through every day. When the prosecution put Dr Lannas on the stand to say she'd known of six cases of death by broken jaw, his smile turned into a grin like a Cheshire cat. No wonder Lenny said in his book that if he got a guilty he'd be over the rail to smash him. I felt like slapping that look off his face more than once. That was a bad day because I could see by the jurors' expressions they were taking in every word she said.

Lenny kept looking over at me and shaking his head, as much as to say, 'It's all over.'

I mouthed back to him, 'Don't worry,' though I felt physically sick myself.

I never slept that night. I sat up smoking and drinking tea that I didn't really want.

The following day everything was turned on its head like something out of a film script, and that was down to Professor Gresham. He was the most unassuming man you could meet, yet his evidence – given as cool as you like – made fun of everything Lannas had said. The jury had to take notice because he was one of the most respected pathologists in the country, and to this day I think Lenny and me owe that man everything, because it was down to him alone that we got the verdict we had prayed for on bended knees.

The case against Lenny was that he'd broken Gary Humphries' jaw when he supposedly beat him up inside the Hippodrome. Didn't matter that he'd walked out of the club under his own steam and had a brief conversation with a policeman who would surely have noticed if his jaw was hanging open. I'm not saying he didn't end up with this break but it never happened because of Lenny. Dr Lannas gave evidence saying she'd seen a number of cases where people had died after getting an injury like that, but then the more experienced Professor Gresham turned that all upside down when he went in the dock and said he'd never heard of such a thing. The most damning evidence he gave, though, was against the police, when he said that in his opinion he thought it more likely that Humphries had died from a stranglehold given to him by one of the officers on the scene. That straightened up a few faces on the other side, I can tell you.

Sometimes innocence isn't enough – you need an expert to prove it. Nothing was guaranteed, though, not even after what he'd said, so it was a bad night again before the final day. No wonder the jury filing back into court ready to give their verdict is such a popular drama in films and on TV. The tension that built up was unbelievable. I looked at Lenny standing in the dock. Shoulders back, almost standing to attention, looking proud and defiant, and I knew if he heard the worst he was going to take it like a man. He blew me a kiss and I blew him one back.

In the space between the foreman being asked for a verdict and him answering, not one person breathed – and it seemed like minutes were ticking by instead of seconds. One word would mean Lenny spending the rest of his life in prison. Two words and all my prayers would've been answered. And that's what we got. 'Not guilty.'

In films the court goes wild with cheering and shouting and everybody hugging each other. But in our case the relief was very quiet. A few handclaps and quiet cheers, because like I said, the place intimidated all of us. Not Lenny, though. He gave that big grin of his and put his arms out to me in a hug across the courtroom, then to everybody's surprise started to sing 'Always Look On the Bright Side of Life'. I looked at the judge to see if he thought Lenny's behaviour was in contempt, but he was laughing as well as he said, 'Take him down.'

I was laughing and crying all at once, and couldn't wait to get outside to give Lenny a big cuddle as he stepped through those big doors. I got a big disappointment, though. We hung around outside for about an hour and didn't think nothing of it because no doubt paperwork had to be sorted and his stuff packed up and all that. Eventually Martin Lee came out to tell us that Lenny wasn't coming home. Once the court was cleared and the dust had settled he'd been brought up again and given an eighteen-month sentence for ABH. With the time he'd done that meant he had a couple of months left to serve. My first reaction was: 'You bastards. It's been proved beyond doubt that he didn't kill Gary Humphries!' Didn't even contribute to his death, but they just couldn't admit defeat and let it go. No, they had to punish him for giving a slap to what he thought of at the time as a hysterical drunk. Something he must've done a thousand times before.

Still, having just swapped the possibility of twenty or twenty-five years alone, those remaining months were nothing. I was disappointed that I couldn't take Lenny home with me there and then, but on the other hand I was so elated he was coming home at all I never let it get me down. I accepted the way things had to be, even though it was unfair, and that was just as well because I didn't have any choice.

One thing I'll never forget is the look on the inspector's face when that 'not guilty' was read out. All the way through the trial he'd seemed to be smiling at us, but once that verdict wiped the smile off his face he looked like a spoilt child who hadn't got its own way. His mouth was turned down so far it's a wonder he didn't trip over it. He wouldn't look at any of us, but if he had he would've seen us all deliberately beaming at him, instead of the other way round.

With that terrible weight lifted off of all of us, those next months just flew by. When he stepped through the door in Strahan Road we had a big welcome home party waiting for him and it was wonderful to have him back indoors. But I don't think him or me were ever the same again. Individually I mean, because though our relationship got a bit rocky for a while all that sorted out eventually. We never really talked about it much afterwards, but buried inside both our heads there was this dark memory where neither of us could forget that experience.

Strain like that over a period of eighteen months has to have some effect, and I feel sure that health problems I have even today go back to that time. Strange too that when Lenny was diagnosed with cancer, his doctor told me that tests had shown his lung cancer had started some seven or eight years before. Is it just coincidence that that's when he was in prison?

A strange thing happened days after he came out. I was sitting in the kitchen and he was on his way down the stairs when somebody knocked on the door. He opened it and I heard him shouting, 'What the fucking hell's this?' Then a man's voice said, 'Sorry, mate, nothing to do with me, I'm just delivering it.' The door crashed shut and next thing he's walking through holding a wreath. What is it about a wreath in the wrong place that turns your stomach over? He slung it on the kitchen worktop and we both just looked at it lying there. No message – nothing. Lenny kept shaking his head and saying, 'Cowards, gutless cowards.'

After a bit I said, 'Who've you upset, then?'

He said, 'Upset? I've been banged up for eighteen months. But you know as well as I do that a lot of people got the hump I never got lifed off.'

We never did find out who'd sent it, but we both had a good idea.

We just put it out of our minds and started to look forward to the holiday I'd booked for us in Fuengirola.

Before we went he said to Karen, ''Ere, Kall, get 'old of some pens and paper. Lenny's got a little job for you.'

Karen was Kelly's best friend and had been in and out of our house for years. When Lenny was arrested she moved in to give us all support, and she's still doing the same today. She was like a second daughter to Lenny and he loved her to death. You couldn't find a more easy-going person, and of course he took advantage of that, so whenever he wanted something doing, Karen always got the job.

The thing was Lenny had made a lot of friends inside, and typical of him, when he was released he would've told them all to keep in touch and he wasn't going to forget that. So he sat Karen down and dictated long letters for her to write to these prisoners. This would go on for hours. She'd come through to get him a cup of tea and say to me, 'Val, my fingers keep cramping up. I must've written twenty letters this morning.'

I said, 'Well, tell him you won't do no more,' but she wouldn't do that.

Knowing what I was doing Karen knew she was wasting her time right from the start, but Lenny never had a clue. Just as well because if he'd found out I was only posting a few of them he'd have gone up the wall.

Being Lenny, he described every one of these people. 'See him,' he'd say, 'stabbed his missus to death, but a lovely geezer really.' Or, 'Young kid 'ere killed some boy at a bus stop – gotta feel sorry for 'im, though.' Well, he might have but I couldn't bring myself to feel the same way. One, I didn't want people like that to be encouraged to visit our home when they got out, and two, most of them sounded nasty pieces of work. I could understand what Len was saying about not judging them, but I'm a mother and the thought of somebody stabbing my son, then getting sympathy for it, made me feel sick. So after all Karen's efforts, apart from a few letters to a couple of decent fellas, all the rest went in the bin.

Rightly or wrongly, I never even felt guilty when a week or so later Len would be moaning, 'D'you know what, Val? After me writing all them letters I've only had a couple of replies. Not one of them other slags have even bothered to get in touch.'

I'd say, 'Well perhaps they aren't worth bothering with,' and he'd say, 'You're right, babe – fuck 'em.' And that was a relief to me.

Whether it was those drugs he'd been put on or just the stress of waiting day after day to be sent down for a recommended twenty years, Lenny came out a different man from when he'd gone in. He was angry at the system for what it had done to him, but what could he do to hit back? Nothing. So he took it out on those around him – and me in particular.

We took off for Fuengirola with me thinking that it was just the sort of break we needed after what we'd been through, but the anger he took with him spoilt it completely. Right from the start he was horrible towards me. And this wasn't in private – he didn't care what he said or where he said it.

In the airport going, if there was a queue it was my 'fucking fault'. When he couldn't get a seat in the smoking area it was my effing fault. As we boarded the plane he was well in front of me, almost like we weren't together, and some man came up beside me and said, 'How do you put up with that?' nodding towards Lenny. It frightened me to death, because if Len had overheard him, in his state of mind he would've killed him without a second's thought, and we'd have been right back to square one.

It got worse. On the beach in Spain where everybody

was relaxed and happy in the sun, he sat stone-faced and miles away. Though not so far away that he didn't notice some good-looking young foreigner glance over at me, or so he thought. He said, 'See him, see that slag – he's eyeing you up.'

I said, 'Don't be daft, Len. Have a look round – there's about a thousand eighteen-year-olds laying out in the sun and most of them are topless. Why would he look at a forty-year-old?' He just mumbled something.

A couple of hours later I thought I'd have a paddle in the sea before we went for something to eat. Len was asleep so I didn't say anything. I was nearly at the water when I bumped straight into the same young fella he'd made the remarks about. At the same time, from right behind me, I heard Lenny screaming, 'Oi, you dirty slag, what's your game?' He'd followed me down the beach and was having a go at the man. The only good thing was that he didn't knock him spark out there and then. This man didn't speak a word of English, but he didn't have to to get the message, what with the way Lenny was going off. Everybody was looking, so I just grabbed Len by the arm and walked him back to our deckchairs.

He couldn't understand why I was so upset; he just kept saying, 'I was looking after you, babe.'

We had some nice moments and I'd start to think he'd relaxed and everything was back to normal. Then all it took was a waiter leaning over his plate and he'd be off again, effing and blinding, and then the same to anybody that happened to catch his eye. It was a nightmare. In those two weeks I went from trying to be understanding to not liking him, to hating him, then back to trying to work out what was going on inside his head.

Looking back, that holiday was the worst thing I could've done. I should've waited and let him work out his aggression at home or work, instead of throwing each other together twenty-four hours a day. I'd lay awake at night looking at him sleeping beside me and think: 'Is this it from now on? Have we been through more ups and downs than most people can think of since we were kids, for it all to end like this?' Then he'd wake up in the morning and the first thing he'd say was, 'Love you, Val,' and mean it, yet an hour later he'd be screaming at me because he couldn't find his shorts.

Back home things improved once he got back to work, though he found that he was finished at the Hippodrome. I'm sure he wasn't the first or last to find out that once you come up against the law, it touches your life in all kinds of ways apart from just spending time behind bars.

Lenny would have been the first to admit that he was guilty of many things that he never got pulled for, but that doesn't mean you have to, in his words, wipe your mouth and accept punishment for something you didn't do. I know the police have the attitude that if we can't get you for something we know you did, then we'll get you for something you didn't. I suppose that seems fair in their eyes, but it's not.

It doesn't matter that Lenny had been fighting and hurting people since he was a kid – he never hurt Gary Humphries. That young man could've behaved ten times worse than he did that night and Len still wouldn't have broken his jaw. It was against his nature and everything he stood for to hurt someone who wasn't big enough to take what he knew he could hand out.

Who would the police have pulled in if our flight had been delayed and Lenny hadn't turned up at the club? Gary Humphries died when he was in their custody and they must've thought they'd struck gold when Len's name got put up. I believe that young man died by accident and nobody would say otherwise.

As Len said time after time when he got away with some crime, 'I bet they've got a book on me down the nick. You watch – they'll 'ave me one day.'

Something that did upset him was that regardless of the evidence given in court that pointed the finger away from him, the Humphries family still believed he was guilty. Whether it was them or somebody sympathizing with them I don't know, but when BT got a complaint in 1992 about using a murderer to advertise their telephones, they took Lenny's advert straight off the screens.

He never did have any luck with the adverts he made for television. The last one he made, and the only one he really liked, never even saw the light of day. It was to do with commemorating Enid Blyton on stamps and there he was, looking like he was enjoying himself having a fight with Big Ears. He used to tell everybody to look out for it when it was due to be shown, then Princess Diana was killed, and though I couldn't see any connection, the Post Office pulled the plug on it.

So, going back to the repercussions of waiting all that time to prove his innocence, Lenny came out with mental problems – there's no doubt of it. His TV work was affected and he got sacked from the Hippodrome. Luckily he had a good friend in Mick Parker, who managed the club, and though he couldn't stop the sacking, at least got him fixed up in Cairo Jack's just round the corner in Dean Street. It wasn't that we needed the money, but without something to do where he felt he was doing the business, Lenny would've cracked up completely.

As time went on he became more and more like his old self, but he wouldn't lose that terrible anger inside him until he started working on his book some years later.

Once he got his head together, out of the blue he

started to talk about his film again. I'd been hoping that he'd forgotten all about it, especially after what he'd said about the script while he was in prison. But that was Lenny – nothing ever got forgotten until he was sure it was stone dead.

A good while after he came out of prison he suddenly said, 'Was that Perkins woman in touch while I was away?'

I had to think who he was talking about for a minute, then remembered she had been the person who'd read the film script and brought it back to Len. I said, 'I would've told you if she had.'

He just said, 'Oh, I thought you might've forgot.' He knew I wouldn't have forgotten something as important as that – he was just hoping I might say, 'Yes, and they're starting shooting next week.' He sat and thought for a bit then said, 'Right, that's it. I'm going to shoot down to Pinewood an' give her a tug; she might've had second thoughts after all this time.' Grabbed his jacket and the film script and took off without saying any more.

When he came back late that afternoon he was full of it. The woman he was after had moved on so he never got to see her, but while he was having a cup of tea, he happened to bump into two 'Blinding fellas. Top film people – got their own office in the studio down there and they want to do the film.'

You never got all the details from Lenny unless you did a bit of digging, and me, as cynical as ever, said, 'How much are they paying, then?'

He gave me a look that I knew meant: 'Why do you always have to ask awkward questions?' 'No,' he said, 'it doesn't work like that – at first. They reckon if I put up ten, they can have it steaming ahead in about nine months.'

I was taking a chance when I had a dig and said,

'What, ten pounds? That's cheap enough,' because he was still liable to flare up at the slightest thing. But he didn't – just quietly said, 'Ten thou,' and covered that quickly by saying, 'They'll turn that into ten million once it gets made.' And that was the start of a long trip 'down the happy road' as Len would say, and the beginning of years of aggravation that took over all our lives.

I was going to say I couldn't imagine what Lenny could've said over a cup of tea in Pinewood's canteen, but on second thoughts I know exactly. He would've poured out the whole film business to these two. The price of the script – how his friends had come up with cash – every detail – and they would've picked up on his enthusiasm, or desperation. Even today it makes me sick to think they used my Lenny's dream to make money without ever getting within a mile of a camera.

Once it all started there was nothing I could say to him that would make him stop and see he was being used. In every other part of his life people would say, 'Never cross Lenny McLean, because he never forgets until he's made you pay one way or another.' Yet with those two he allowed himself to be ripped off. Him – who never really trusted anybody. He swallowed all the rubbish they fed him, all the 'next week', 'next month', 'next year', because he couldn't bear to think it would all come to nothing.

By the time he admitted to himself the film was going nowhere it was too late and a quarter of a million pounds of our money and his friends' money was down the pan. I wish I could print the names of those people in letters a foot high, but like I said at the beginning, I'm tired of aggravation in my life and I want to move on. Not spend time in court defending myself when I've only told the truth. That's how the law works in this country.

Somebody can steal a fortune from you and nothing can be done about it. As Lenny found, threaten justified violence and the police are there in two minutes. Publish the truth and there's a writ on the doorstep before the ink's dry.

Though it was a small consolation for those friends of Lenny's who'd backed him financially all the way – in those last months before he died he managed to ruin the career of one of those men. Lenny sat for hours in our conservatory working out a plan, and when it came off it was a sting that any con man would've been proud of, and it worked perfectly. One minute this fella was a high flier in the film and TV business, the next he's on the skids, and I'd no sympathy for him whatsoever.

Once that was out the way he went after the other one, and this time his plan was even more complicated because it involved drugs and dirty money, plus the help of reporters dressed as Arab millionaires and lots of other things you'd only find in spy books. Unfortunately he died before he could put the last piece in place, and that person got away scot-free – for now, anyway.

Strange, isn't it? Lenny, physically the most powerful man in the country, and possibly one of the most danger-ous when you consider what he was capable of, turned over by two weak and cowardly men. Most people would never get over something like that. They'd burn inside with anger and frustration for the rest of their lives. But Lenny put it in the back of his mind and got on with his life. Like I said, he never forgot – not even when he had the biggest thing in his life to contend with; but he never let it fester away at him – just calmly did what had to be done when the time was right.

— ELEVEN —

I suppose it's safe to say that Lenny retired from organized fighting once he came out of prison. I know that before he went away he'd more or less given it up, but in his mind there was always the thought that if the right challenge came along he'd take it. But afterwards, and I think he gave it a lot of thought when he was locked up, he said, 'I know I've said it before, babe, but this time I mean it. I'm finished with the ring and the cobbles.'

Considering he was putting a full stop to something that had been his life since he was a kid, I didn't know what to say, so I said, 'Does that mean in the clubs, as well?'

He went, 'Nah, not likely. Any mug wants to try me they can have it for nothing.'

I looked at him and saw his hair was thinning, and even though he still trained every day he was getting a slight spare tyre that comes to most men in their forties. So I thought, 'Yes, he's beginning to feel he's not the man he was.' Women don't rely on strength to get things done, so it's never obvious that they're getting weaker. But with men who've been lifting and carrying all their lives, it comes as a shock once they're approaching middle age that they can't do it any more. I didn't say that to him, and just as well, because a couple of weeks later he proved me wrong.

We'd parked up in town where he had a bit of business, had some lunch then when we got back to the car we found we were wedged in completely. Lenny effed and blinded and looked up and down the road hoping somebody would come back, then he said, 'Right, I'll show that fucker.' For a minute I thought he was going to damage the car in front, but he just said, 'Hold me coat, Val,' and started to lift the back of this motor. There was just enough room between the bumpers for him to get his legs in and what he was doing was lifting the car sideways inch by inch. First the back, then the front, until slowly he managed to get it on the pavement.

Taxi drivers were slowing down and shouting, 'Go on, Len,' and 'Nice one, big fella,' and a crowd was building up as they all watched him. Getting it on the pavement wasn't enough, though. He lifted the back completely off the ground and pushed it along like a wheelbarrow, parked it against the railings, and walked back to me saying, 'He'll think twice about doing that again once he's paid his fines.' I'm not talking about a Mini car – this one was a family saloon, and what do they weigh? Half a ton? Anybody who thinks he was giving it some flannel about bench-pressing five hundred pounds should've been there.

We all do it at some time – wish we could look into the future. Whether it's wanting to know the Lottery winning numbers or as simple as wanting to know if it'll be sunny for a weekend barbecue. Wouldn't it be nice if we could see what's just round the corner? On the other hand, wouldn't it be horrible?

We'd reached a time in our lives when everything was just right. We had a nice house, the kids were settled in good jobs, we'd no money worries like you do when you're young, and the big thing for me was that Lenny wasn't earning a living by putting himself up for offer in the ring. It's funny, when you're in your teens you look at people in their forties and think their lives are over. But when you reach that time in your own life it's the exact opposite – and really life is just beginning.

So we were well settled and looking forward to every year getting better and better. Just as well then that we couldn't see into the future, because that thing inside Lenny was sitting there like some sort of timebomb, and every day it was growing a little bit more. Right then, though, he was as fit and strong as he'd ever been, and if I'd been betting on him living to be ninety I'd have put everything I had on it.

He still hadn't got over being in prison and what it had done to him mentally, and every now and then he'd go into one over nothing at all. A word out of place or a phone call that frustrated him, and something would end up getting smashed. The phone or a cup would be thrown up the wall and he'd curse me into the ground. And all I could do was sit it out knowing it would pass and he'd be full of apologies. People who saw him in rages like that, or had heard what he was like, must've thought that I lived in fear or that behind closed doors he raised his fist to me. But that never, ever happened, and not once was I ever frightened that it would. Luckily those flare-ups of his didn't happen too often as time went on, and I think the reason for that was that he started to fill his life up with the thing he'd wanted to do for years – his acting.

At first it wasn't proper acting, like being in a film or a series, or anything like that. But when he appeared on different TV chat shows he acted his way through them so it amounted to the same thing. Over the past few years villains' faces have somehow got respectable and they pop up all the time on television. But back then you rarely saw them, so when they caught onto Lenny as what they called 'the real thing' he went down a bomb.

Half the time they got their research all wrong and had him down as a minder for the Kray Twins. The truth is he never had any involvement with them when they were around in the sixties. He knew of them, like every-body did, and every now and then he'd see them in different pubs. But he was only about sixteen or more then and didn't take a lot of notice. His connection with them didn't happen until Reg got in touch with Alex Steen and asked him to bring Lenny in for a visit.

Why Reg wanted to see him was to get his brother Charlie out of a bit of bother. So much for the gangland empire the Krays were running from inside prison. A bit of trouble and they turned to Lenny. Charlie, thinking he could trade on the family name, had run up a few debts with the wrong people – people who didn't care one bit about what they'd got up to thirty or more years ago. As it happens Lenny was owed a few favours from the firm that was after Charlie so he didn't have to do much growling to get it sorted.

He had a lot of time for Charlie and often told him, 'Park up them two, 'cos they've given you nothing but grief all your life.' Lenny knew the twins had a big public following and wasn't going to rock the boat, but privately he didn't really have too much to say for them. And why he visited them both so often was more out of respect for other people who were too blind to see what they really were.

Prisoners are totally selfish and I know that first hand – particularly long-term ones. What they all desperately want are people outside to become friends with them, then con as much out of them as they can. Somebody like Reg would keep an eye on the TV and papers, see who was up and coming, then invite them to visit him. They'd think they were important because this world-famous man wanted to see them when really all he wanted was somebody to supply him and his friends with trainers, drink and money.

Lenny never fell for it. I lost count of the times we got early morning phone calls from Reg asking Len to bring in boxing gloves or training equipment. Len said the same thing every time: 'No problem, Reg – get the cash dropped round and the stuff's yours.' No money turned up and Lenny ignored it. Didn't stop Reg trying again, but he never got anywhere. Others who fell for it weren't so lucky and ended up paying bills that ran into thousands. The last straw was when he rang up saying one of the cons who was due for release wanted to buy a small club up West. Len saw an earner for himself and a way of doing a favour for a friend who had a club to sell.

The two of them went to Maidstone Prison with all the details, so he told me after. When he asked Reg where the buyer was, he called over some spotty kid. Len said, 'How much cash you got?' and this kid said, 'Errr – none at the moment. I was thinking—'

Len said, 'Fuck thinking. You've wasted my time and you've wasted my mate's time. I should knock your fucking 'ead off – and yours,' he said to Reg, and walked out.

When he got in he was still fuming, but more about the change that had come over Reg than the wasted time. 'That's it, Val,' he said. 'I don't want to know any more. I've always given him ten out of ten for keeping his head up all these years. Now he don't make no secret that's he's gone the other way and it makes me sick. I could get banged up for fifty years and I'd never go down that road, so in the future don't answer that phone.'

How could I not answer the phone? We didn't have

one of those caller displays then, so it could be anybody. At eight in the morning we were in bed, what with Len working late. Most times we ignored the ringing but sometimes I forgot and answered it, then had to make excuses to Reg that Len was out. This went on for weeks until one morning Len did his nut. He jumped out of bed, flew downstairs and grabbed the phone up. Reg must have wondered what had hit him. I'd heard him screaming down the phone, 'Don't you ring this fucking number no more and don't send any of your poxy firm knocking on my door or I'll break their backs! Now piss off.'

For the next two mornings the phone went at eight o'clock and again we ignored it, but Len said, 'Babe, get this number changed before I lose me temper.' That was a laugh considering how he'd let off the other day at Reg, but I didn't make a comment. And that was the end of Reg as far as we were concerned.

Before all that happened, though, he did do Lenny one favour, and that was a first for him, although at the time he thought he was doing himself a bit of good. He sent a fella round to us at Strahan Road to collect some stories from Len to put in a book he was doing. That was typical of Reg. Pick up a hundred thousand on a book deal, then get other people to fill the pages.

This was Peter Gerrard, and Len and him hit it off that first meeting. Apart from making cups of tea I left them to it in the front room and sat in the kitchen reading. But I couldn't avoid hearing Len because he always did have one of those voices that carried through walls. He spoke about Reg for about half an hour, and most of what he said he genuinely believed – but then again a lot he didn't. Though show me anybody who told the truth about the Krays before they died and you can bet your life they'd be kidding themselves.

Once he'd given Peter what he came for he wasn't going to waste a brand-new audience so he was off on all those stories about himself. I saw Peter and his friend Steve out of the door about four hours later, and they both looked dazed. Well, anybody would after Lenny bending your ear for that long.

When I came back to the front room Len said, 'All done. We've got a deal.'

I said, 'What's that?' and he said, 'That fella seems to know what he's doing, so I've asked him to do my book.'

Thinking of the other writer and the still unmade film I said, 'Why should this time be any different?' and he said, ''Cos this fella's on the firm.' He meant because he was in with the Krays, and I thought, 'That's some reference.'

'So like before you'll be spending another six months talking about your life and all for nothing?'

'No,' he said. 'He explained all that. Yeah, I do a load of talking, but as soon as he sorts out a deal the publisher shells out cash up front. Different, see!'

I said, 'Oh, look, Len, a pig just flew over the house opposite.'

He shot his head round going 'Where?' then laughed saying, 'Take the piss, but you'll see.'

Now Peter's writing this down for me and I know he's thinking, 'I didn't know you thought like that,' but I did and it wasn't personal or nothing. It's just that my Len had allowed himself to go 'down the happy road' so often in the past, I couldn't bear to see him get a knock-back again.

Two weeks later they had a contract for the book and from then until his dying day that book became his life. He never forgot the film and he was looking forward to some proper acting parts, but getting his life story into print was real and he put everything into it. From the word go his idea was to tell nothing but the most violent and sometimes nasty things that he'd ever been involved in. He wanted to show the world he was the toughest man in the country, and as always, 'A fuckin' raving lunatic.' At the same time he had it in his mind that his book would be a good way to pay off old scores with people who'd upset him over the years.

At night when Peter wasn't there he'd take himself off into the front room, warn me not to come in, then talk into a tape recorder. Like I said, I didn't have to go in to hear what he was saying. Lists of names, dates and places like '. . . And then there was—, runs one of the biggest companies in the country and I knew him when he was an errand boy for the Krays . . .', '. . . This actor by the name of—', 'I want everybody to see him on the telly and go, "We know what you done, you dirty slag . . ."' This went on and on.

One night after working on the book all day he said, 'It ain't goin' to work.'

I said, 'What?'

He said, 'The writer – he's going down the wrong road.'

That didn't surprise me. With Len there was only one road and that was his. Still, I said, 'Why's that?'

He said, 'He keeps asking me shit, like how did I feel when me dad died? How did I feel about Irwin? Did I love me mum? It's all bollocks. What's that got to do with being the toughest minder in the country?'

I enjoyed reading books, but when it came down to putting one together I didn't have a clue. But I'd never been happy with what he'd been saying so I thought then was the time to tell him how I felt. I said, 'I don't know if I'm right or wrong, but this book isn't just about you.' The eyebrows came down as much as to say 'Who else, then?' and I said, 'It's about your life, but it's about everybody else that came into it as well. I mean, you missed your dad when he died.'

'Yeah.'

'And you did love your mum.'

'Course.'

'And you love me as well?'

'You know I do, babe.'

'Well, then, say so, and cut back on all that stuff you've been saying about people and tearing faces off and all that.'

He wasn't convinced, just shook his head saying, 'You and 'im don't understand what people want,' and we left it there.

I think Peter had gone home to Lincolnshire for a few days so Len had time to think. Before he was due back Lenny said to me, 'I've been thinking, babe. P'raps I should tell 'im a bit about what life was like when I was a kid. Y'know, fill it out a bit.' Just like him – take on board what I'd said then think that he's thought of it.

I just said, 'That's nice, Len. Just tell it like you told me all those years ago.'

He did and it worked. If violence was all it took to sell half a million copies, then every book of its kind that came out after would've done the same – but they didn't.

I said a lot more to him than the few lines I've just put down, and most of it I've forgotten. But I know I spelled out the way he'd been behaving since he came out of prison. His rages, him smashing things in temper – and how I'd had to put up with being verbally abused every time things didn't go right for him.

Looking back it's something I should've done years before, and strange now to think that one conversation could change him almost overnight. His book was so important to him – that's what swung it. If I'd had a row about how he'd treated me it might not have gone in the same. But tying what I had to say in with his book made all the difference, and he never looked back after that.

I'd love to know what went on in his mind after I gave him some home truths, but whatever it was it made him rethink a lot of things, and I feel that's when he got tired of dealing with, as he put it, 'low-lifes and druggies' and wanted to start moving on with 'proper' people.

With his book in good hands he made up his mind to concentrate on getting a career on the screen. He got himself a new agent and sat back and waited – and waited. In the end he said, 'Fuck this, Val. I'm taking over the reins meself,' and he started putting himself about.

A mate of Jamie's was a good friend of Martine McCutcheon and he used to pop in with her every now and then. Her and Lenny got on well, and though she'd nothing to do with it, I think just seeing how well she was doing in *EastEnders* gave him the idea of trying to get a part in the soap.

How he blagged his way past the security at Borehamwood Studios I don't know, because even the famous faces had to show a pass – but that was him. Nothing to do with intimidating the people on the gates, but the size and presence of him gave the impression he was somebody, whether he was or not. He got to see the director or casting people, and at first I think they were quite interested. But though the show is supposed to be real East End life, I think he was just a bit too real, so they turned him down.

He already knew a lot of the cast because he'd minded them at different functions they'd had, so after his meeting he toured the set saying hello to everybody. By all accounts he turned the place upside down wandering all over the place, and they even had to stop filming when he took it into his head to walk across the set to talk to June Brown. Everything was turned on its head that day. Instead of the cast being the celebrities, they all turned into fans that wanted to see the Guv'nor. I think if they'd given him a part their ratings would've gone through the roof, but on the other hand he might've been more trouble than they could cope with.

Another girl who often came to our house was Victoria Adams. She was another friend of Jamie's mate and, same as with Martine, he'd bring her in to our house if he was passing. I'd love to be able to talk about long conversations we had or little secrets she told me, but she wasn't famous at all then and was about as ordinary as you can get. Nice girl. A bit shy and didn't have a lot to say – ordinary teenager, really. Now I look at her as Mrs Beckham, or Posh Spice as they call her, and can't help thinking how far she's come since then. Her husband David told my Kelly that he took *The Guv'nor* on honeymoon with him and couldn't put it down. Lenny was gone by then but it was a lovely gee from one of the most famous men in the world.

Going back to *EastEnders*, after they turned him down he thought he'd put our Kelly's name up. I knew he was wasting his time because even though she's got everything going for her if she wanted to be an actress, but what with looking a lot like Patsy Palmer, especially with her red hair, she never had a chance from the start. The only way it might've been done was if they'd stuck her in as a long-lost sister, but they weren't prepared to do that so it came to nothing.

No sooner did one door close than Lenny was looking round for another one to open. He had loads of friends and acquaintances in the business, but when it came down to it, no matter how famous their faces were they didn't have any pull when it came to casting – though a lot of them put themselves out to help him. He tried *The Bill* next, and you would've thought he would be perfect to play a villain because that's what the show's all about, but no luck. Personally, and I'm not being biased, I think they were frightened that somebody like him would overshadow the regular cast, and in fact that was proved later on.

He was always puzzled as to why nobody seemed to want him. I remember him standing in front of our full-length mirror in the bedroom. He just had shorts on. He flexed his muscles, turned this way, turned that way, until I said, 'For God's sake, stop admiring yourself.'

He said, 'I'm not. I'm trying to see what those casting people see when they look at me.'

I said, 'It's nothing to do with the way you look, you're fine.'

He carried on. Then he said, 'I know what it is, it's this,' and he patted his stomach. 'Make me right, babe, do I train every day?'

I said, 'Yes, without fail.'

'Yet I can't get rid of this poxy spare tyre.' That's all he needed – a reason, and that was enough for him to brood on it.

A few days later he sat at the kitchen table with a load of newspapers spread out in front of him, ticking off adverts in the back pages. When I looked I saw he was underlining adverts for liposuction clinics. I said, 'You're not?' He said, 'Look at this,' and showed me a picture of a woman who looked eight months pregnant. In the other picture, supposedly taken two hours later, she had a stomach like an eighteen-year-old. I said, 'Please don't mess about with yourself, Len. It's all a con – it's not natural.'

Nothing I said would stop him once he saw the possibility of knocking twenty years off his waistline.

Usually when a phone call had to be made it'd be, 'Val, ring this number,' like I was his personal secretary. But this time he rang the clinic himself and made an appointment. Afterwards typical woman, I had to ask 'How much?' and, typical man, he said, 'Just over two grand.'

'How much over?'

'Er . . . a grand over.'

The next thing I knew it was all going ahead and he asked me to pick him up that afternoon. Before he left he hummed and sang. Never whistled, though, because he hated the sound of that more than somebody eating.

It was a different story when I arrived at the clinic up some back street in the West End. His face was grey and he was lying on a filthy stained bed you wouldn't let your dog sleep on. As he swung his legs off the bed and stood up, this horrible yellow stuff was running down his legs and dripping on the floor. Looking at his stomach, it didn't look any different than it had before. In fact it looked a lot worse because it was all lumpy. I called a nurse, if that's what she was, and she said it was perfectly normal and would smooth out in a few weeks. It never did and he was in pain for months. That was something in itself because Lenny had the highest pain threshold I'd ever come across. So if he said it hurt, you can bet your life it would be agony for somebody ordinary.

Did he go back and smash the place up? Did he sue them for everything they had? No, he let it go and never wanted to speak about it again.

Before it healed up and he was still feeling uncomfortable Kelly came running in one afternoon saying Karen was getting some agg from a crowd of young fellas. He's jumped up, gone flying round a couple of turnings from Strahan Road, and they were still there messing her about and trying to pull her bag off her shoulder. Lenny didn't even speak, just knocked the biggest one spark out into the middle of the road. The rest ran off.

Karen worked in a local shop and after that he said he'd walk her home every day in case these fellas tried it on again. He said to her, 'What time do you finish?' She said, 'Five o'clock,' so he said he'd be there on the dot. For a couple of weeks afterwards he'd walk in the shop between three and four o'clock. 'All right, Kall, get your coat – lively,' and the manageress would just smile and let her go early.

He didn't mind putting himself out for her but it had to be at his speed. So, as she said, he'd put his hand on the back of her neck and march her down Roman Road. She'd lived around there all her life so knew loads of people, and of course they're all saying hello or wanting to speak. Each time Len would force her head straight, saying, 'No time for talking – home. Nice cup of tea.' She was glad when the threat from those lads disappeared and she could walk home at her own pace.

His agent got him a spot on a programme called *Arena* about a young bare-knuckle fighter who was starting off in the game. It turned out to be a con against the TV company, but Lenny didn't know that and gave a brilliant interview filmed in Kenny Mac's car showroom, showing this kid the ropes and giving advice. Afterwards this supposed fighter was shown up as an actor pretending to be something he wasn't, but Lenny got a few quid and an appearance on TV so it didn't do him any harm. But he wanted more than that. He wanted to show off his acting abilities, not do endless interviews.

He'd sit watching the telly, commenting on all the characters that were pretending they were tough guys. 'I'd fuckin' well show 'em. One belt and that bloke would be on his back.' I tried to tell him they weren't supposed to hit for real, but he wasn't listening. Then *London's Burning* came on and he's going, 'There's Craig, there's Glenn – there's Helen Keating – tell you what, I'm going to shoot down there and get myself fixed up.' Same as before, didn't matter that he was friendly with half the cast, he got turned down.

He was starting to get the hump and suddenly all producers are a bunch of wankers who don't know their arse from their elbow. Paul Knight wasn't one of them, though Lenny didn't know it at the time. Paul had made a note of him when they'd met on the set of *London's Burning*. He was planning a series to be called *The Knock* and thought Lenny would be perfect for one of the villains. To cut a long story short, he approached Len and, against a lot of argument from casting and others, gave him the part that could've been written for him – and probably was.

At last he'd got the thing he'd dreamed of for years – a proper acting role. Like he had with that *Guv'nor* film script, he carried this one around with him wherever he went and every spare moment you'd see him studying it with his mouth moving but no sound coming out.

That first day on set he thought he'd have everybody jumping around and doing things his way, but he had a lot to learn. He wanted to change the dialogue to what he thought was more natural. Like saying, 'A real villain wouldn't say that, he'd say, "Listen, you c***, don't f— around."' They'd agree with him but point out that TV wasn't ready for that sort of language, especially on a Sunday night, and eventually Lenny learned to do what he was told.

When the series was screened the media couldn't get enough of Len. I said before that I thought he might overshadow the stars in any show. As it happens he didn't in the series because he'd learned to be a bit more low-key, but off camera he put every one of them in the shade with newspaper articles and magazine write-ups.

Me and Peter went with him to Planet Hollywood, where the producers held a preview of the first series when filming was all over. It was Lenny's first real acting part and he turned into the star. Looking round the main bar I could see that the less well-known actors didn't mind at all, but some of the real stars, like the main actors, definitely seemed to have the hump. They were sitting or standing around on their own and you couldn't even see Len because he was in the middle of a crowd of journalists and TV people. They couldn't get enough of him and he played right up to them with all his stories. I knew he'd eventually come out with, 'That poxy murder charge,' and when he did I laughed inside to see the way their eyes opened up and they all stepped back. I suppose most of the time all they ever did was go through the motions of interviewing another actor from another run-of-the-mill series. Then all of a sudden they've got the real thing standing in front of them.

Paul took a gamble on Len and it paid off in a way he could never have dreamed of. Everybody wanted to see this 'real' tough guy. The only time this had been done before was when they put George Raft in films, and he had Mafia connections, or Leslie Grantham in *EastEnders* after a guilty on a murder and John Binden who got a not guilty for a similar charge. But these last two hadn't begun to live the sort of life Lenny had, so you could say he was the first and the last of a kind.

He was proud of that series. The only part he wasn't keen on was right at the end when his character Eddie Davies got arrested. If you didn't see it, what happened in the scene was him and some other fellas were in a big warehouse when customs police burst in and grabbed them all. I think about four men had a fight with Eddie but eventually they overpowered him, then two fellas, who only came up to his shoulders, led him away. Even I found it funny to see Lenny in that situation because it could never happen in real life.

He watched it on video more than once and he'd say, 'See that, Val, that was the hardest bit of acting I had to do the whole time.' What he meant was it was against all his instincts to let himself be put down, and most of the actors that took him on were comparing bruises in the green room afterwards.

His contract had been for one six-week series but because he was so popular and had got a lot of publicity for the programme, Paul Knight got the scriptwriter to give him a suspended sentence so they could bring him back for the next.

About this time we left Strahan Road. Why after a lifetime in the East End Lenny suddenly decided we should move out into the country, I don't know. Though, thinking about it, I suppose it was all part and parcel of him wanting to get away from mixing with the low-lifes, drunks and druggies, as he put it. When I say country, I mean an East Ender's idea of the country, that's any-where away from London and not necessarily miles of fields and trees.

It seemed that no sooner Lenny came up with the idea than we were moving into a house a few miles through the Blackwall Tunnel. When the traffic was light you could drive from Strahan Road to our new front door in ten minutes, yet to both of us it was like going into a different world. The roads were wider, the houses bigger and the people were what Len would call 'proper' people. That's not knocking those we grew up with; it's just that suddenly our neighbours were accountants and office workers. Straight-goers, if you like, and we weren't used to that.

Lenny was proud of that house because it meant he'd pulled himself up from being a scruffy East End kid who'd had a bad start to life, through years of living with violence day after day, to end up in a tree-lined avenue successful and – very important to him – respectable.

He was well pleased but no sooner was he saying to me, 'We're on the up, babe,' than he got a knock-back with his book.

There were all kinds of reasons why that particular publisher decided they didn't want to do it any more, but I think the main one was they'd somehow tied it in with the film and with that going nowhere they thought what was the point of waiting.

One way or another Lenny had this need to make his mark on the world. In a funny sort of way it was almost like he knew his time was short and wanted to leave something behind. Whether it was a film about his life, a name as an actor, or a book – didn't really matter as long as there was something. So he accepted the disappoint-ment over the book because his mind was taken up with acting and he didn't have enough time to sit around brooding about it.

No way was he going to let it go, though, so all he said to Peter was, 'I'll leave it to you, son – get another deal, lively. You know this is too good to walk away from.' Easier said than done. Letter after letter went out to all the biggest publishers and every one of them turned it down. 'Not a story with much public interest...' 'Mr McLean is not high profile enough...' 'Not suitable for our lists...' 'Not up to scratch...'

None of us gave up, but I've got to say the whole business got stuck on the back burner. Particularly with

Len, because once the second series of *The Knock* was all over he got asked to audition for a new Bruce Willis film, and the thought of acting in a proper movie instead of just TV put everything else out of his mind. When he came back from the audition and I asked him what it was all about, he pulled a face and said, 'Know what, babe? I haven't got a fucking clue.'

I said, 'How can you take on a part if you don't know what it is?'

He just shrugged his shoulders. 'I ain't said yes, yet – 'cos they might have me down for a poof or some sort of nutcase.'

As it turned out the part they had him down for was nearly as bad in his mind. 'Old Bill, Val. Can you believe it? I told 'em to fuck off – I can't be Old Bill, I'd never live it down.' A few days later when the producer personally phoned up and explained that with the script being set well in the future he'd be nothing like the law, as we know it, he gave in and accepted the part. I've watched *The Fifth Element* since, and to be honest if you blinked you'd miss Lenny, because I think a lot of the scenes were cut. He enjoyed himself making it, though.

I said before that big stars didn't impress Len and he didn't make any exception for Bruce Willis and that was obvious when he settled himself in Bruce's dressing room one day. He'd been having a wander around the studio and as usual came across a door with a big star stuck on it so he's gone inside. By the time Bruce had finished a scene and come back he found Lenny stretched out on his settee.

As Len said that night, 'Should've seen his face, babe – wasn't used to somebody taking the piss. I said to Bruce, "You're a bit of a tough guy in all them films where you wear the same vest all the time – how about you and me having a straightener over who gets this posh pad and who gets the poxy little cupboard I'm stuck in?" Know what he said, Val? "OK, Lenny, as long as I can have an AK47 and two hand grenades." Good stuff. One of your own, even though he's a Yank.'

Something else he did on set was treat Lee Evans as a gopher and tea-boy until he found out who he was. What with Lee acting the boyish idiot all the time – and that's what he was famous for – Len took it that he was a studio runner and had him backwards and forwards getting him lemonade and teas. From what I heard Lee went along with it and thought it was a good laugh. Never took offence or nothing, just took it with good humour and accepted that was the way Lenny was.

The strange thing is the film that made his name all over the world is the one he never had a lot to say about. It was only looking back afterwards that I realized that during the filming of *Lock, Stock* he must've felt more ill than he ever let on.

The first thing he said to the producer Matthew Vaughn and the director Guy Ritchie when he was given the script was, 'You're going to have to change that title – it don't make fucking sense to me.' Then without reading it he wanted his character's name changed. 'Barry the Baptist? I mean, do I look like a fucking vicar?' As it was they did change the name to Harry the Hatchet but that wasn't down to Len. As far as he was concerned it was a very low-budget movie that would be a job for a few weeks and bring in a few thousand.

But from beginning to end he was plagued with 'the flu' and though he never, ever let them down when he was due on set, some days he didn't feel like it at all. So with that and not having too much interest I never got much out of him, like what he'd been up to in the day. We'd sit there at night and I'd say, 'Good day?' and he'd say, 'Not bad, babe – not bad,' like he used to years before when he might have been up against guns or the IRA a few hours before.

What he didn't tell me was he was having difficulty breathing when he was shooting scenes that meant climbing a few flights of stairs.

We all know how a heavy cold or flu can really bring you down, specially if it drags on for a while, but what I wasn't noticing was he gradually looked less well as filming went on. I suppose there's technical reasons for shooting a film back to front, and that's what they did. So if you watch *Lock, Stock* you'll see that Lenny looked better at the end than he did at the beginning because they shot that last. You'd think that once the film was in the can, as they say, Lenny would've been full of it and talking about it coming out in the cinemas. But like the fight with Roy Shaw, once it was done it was all over and not worth talking about.

Things went a bit quiet. He was still working in the club but when it came to straightening out the tearaways he was leaving that to the fellas that worked under him. If things got too out of hand his reputation was enough that all he had to do was show his face, give a bit of a growl and it was sorted.

Same with jobs he was still being asked to do. All he had to do was pick up the phone, say who he was and the trouble went away.

A couple of fellas turned up one night looking for help because they'd lent some money out, then when it was due with interest, they'd been told to eff off because whoever had borrowed the money was backed up by a North London firm so he thought he could get away with it. They told Len this and he said, 'You ain't looking for favours, are you?'

They said, 'No. Whatever it costs, just say the word.'

Because I think they were out by forty thousand,

Lenny thought, then said, 'Tell you what; you've come through a good pal of mine so you must be all right. Call it two grand and I'll square it off.' They couldn't pay him quick enough.

As soon as they went out the door he made a phone call. Twenty minutes later a very big black man turned up. Lenny said to him, 'I want you to slip down to Essex and square this off – it's all on this bit of paper. Make sure you let 'em know Big Lenny sent you, and pick up some dough. 'Ere's three hundred notes wages – gimme a bell when it's done.' As I came back in the room after seeing the fella out, Len gave me seventeen hundred pounds saying, 'Get yourself a new blouse, babe.' That's all it took. The debt was settled the next day.

Seems like easy money, but don't forget to get to that position where a word was enough to settle anything, Lenny had gone through things the ordinary man couldn't even think about, so you could say he was reaping the benefits of thousands of fights and of suffering the occasional shooting and stabbing.

Our kids were grown up and both doing well. We had a lovely house and never had to give money a second's thought, but something was missing. Not in my life – I couldn't wish for anything more, but then I'd always been satisfied with what I had – Lenny wanted something more.

He'd been out all day trying to get money back from the film people who'd taken a lot of money off him and his friends. He had no luck – in fact when he fronted one of them up the police had been called so he didn't have any choice but to walk away, and that got right up his nose. He said, 'Can you believe it, Val? The toughest faces wipe their mouths when I give them a tug, and that fucking straight-goer gets the law on his side and takes the piss.' What could I say? If you've struck a deal with your own and there's a problem, it can be sorted one way or another. But with the straight world you didn't have any comeback, apart from going through legal channels, and Lenny didn't want to know that.

He said, 'Make me right, Val, the film's gone down the pan.' It had, but I'd always felt it would come to nothing. 'An' me book – nobody wants to know, do they?' It seemed that way. 'An' you know what? I thought I'd be getting bundles of parts after that *Lock, Stock* thing, but not a whisper, babe – fuck 'em. Let's have a nice holiday, somewhere warm – get rid of this poxy flu.' He was right. A bit of a break would set us both up.

Somewhere warm meant Fuengirola and we both took off a week later. I don't suppose we were in our apartment more than an hour when he started to cough and couldn't stop. I don't think either of us got a wink of sleep that night, and by morning I wanted to book a flight home. Lenny wouldn't have none of it, just said, 'Something's gone down the wrong way, that's all.' I said, 'What, for twelve hours?' but he said, 'Be all right once I get the sun on me chest.' And it did ease off eventually.

Usually when we were in Spain he liked nothing better than to wander about doing nothing in particular, just going from bar to bar – coffee in one, orange juice in another. But this time all he wanted to do was sleep. When I did talk him into going out he complained his knees hurt, and for him to admit to anything hurting was right out of the ordinary. When we'd arrived I must've gone into the hotel ahead of him because I wasn't aware that he didn't carry the cases in. But when we were leaving at the end of the week I saw him lift my case (the heavy one) and put it down again – he was puffing a bit. Just then the taxi driver turned up and he said to him, 'Go on, son, pick them up lively,' then said to me, 'He might as well earn his tip.' Any other time he would've carried both cases and slung the taxi driver over his shoulder if he'd wanted to, but even then I didn't think much of it.

On the flight home he dozed most of the time and hardly spoke at all, though he did say, 'Remember that time we came back from 'ere and I ended up behind the door for eighteen months? Never know what's round the corner, do we, babe?' and went back to sleep again.

Usually when we got back after being away he'd either have to go out or spend hours on the phone catching up on the news, but he didn't seem to have any energy or interest in anything.

I was washing up when the phone rang so I told him to answer it and I heard him talking in a very 'couldn't care less' sort of way. 'Yeah ... Nah ... Not bad ...' Then he changed. 'Do what? Fucking blinding. Never mind that – we're in the driving seat now, son, set it up.' He was a different man walking back into the kitchen singing all the way, something he hadn't done for weeks.

I said, 'Who's that? We won the lottery?'

He said, 'As good as. That was Peter the book man – he's only got us a definite deal – shit money but that don't matter.' That's all it took to pick him right up and he was like his old self again.

Suddenly he dug up energy from nowhere, put a tracksuit on and told me he was going for a run round Danson Park. 'Five miles, babe – sweat this flu out, 'cos me and Peter 'ave got work to do.' I felt really pleased for him. Like he'd said, you don't know what's round the corner and from thinking nothing much was happening in his life, one phone call had turned everything round. Best of it was, this was a definite deal. Not if, not perhaps, not next year – seven months ahead his book would be on the shelves.

He'd never been one for doctors and apart from injuries he'd got through his business I don't think he'd ever been to one for minor illnesses. So it took a lot of effort from me to talk him into going for a check-up on that persistent cold he had. Colds and flu can hang on for weeks but never months, so I wanted to get to the bottom of it. First thing he told our local GP was he felt 'Top of the world – strong as a bull,' so the doctor must've wondered why we were there at all if that was the case.

Between listening about the bestseller that was going to be published soon, and the film that never was, the doctor examined Len and found he had a chest infection. He prescribed antibiotics and we went home feeling a lot easier knowing it would be cleared up within ten days. A fortnight later nothing had changed, in fact he was a bit worse. Nothing serious enough to worry about but every now and then he'd have one of those coughing fits and he was more breathless than he had been.

All I thought was that he needed stronger pills, so back we went to the doctor's. This time he was a bit more concerned and booked Lenny in for tests at St Mary's Hospital in Sidcup. They kept him in and that week was bad for me. Trouble is today most people, me included, can't help the thought from flicking across your mind that illnesses you can't explain might be that disease that we don't even want to mention.

Night-times were the worst. I'd lay in bed thinking this and that and getting myself in a right state. Then when I'd visit Len all those silly negative thoughts disappeared because he'd be sitting up in bed looking as fit and well as ever. To him the whole thing was a nuisance and a waste of time. 'Heard from Peter? Did you find them photos for the book? What date's it coming out?' That's where his mind was, not worrying about something as trivial as a chest infection.

Somebody mentioned his symptoms seemed a bit like pleurisy and I clung to that like a drowning man to a straw. Hospitals never take a guess at what they think might be wrong, and I can't blame them for that, but no matter who I asked all I ever got was: 'We'll know at the end of the week.' I didn't think it then, but afterwards I realized that week was almost the same as what I'd gone through at the murder trial. One half of my mind was telling me everything would be all right – the other half trying to avoid the thought of: 'What if the result isn't the one I'm praying for?'

I had a morning visit, then when I was leaving a nurse said to me that the doctor wanted to speak to me. If Len hadn't been looking so well I might have worried. As it was I just thought, 'Oh good, the results are through. They'll be able to treat the problem and we can move on.'

She didn't beat about the bush but all I heard was 'Afraid – cancer,' because the rest was drowned out by the sound of blood rushing to my head. I got a pain in my stomach like it was being screwed into a knot and I felt weak. She was looking at me for some reaction and all I could say was, 'He's only forty-eight,' as though that would make her diagnosis wrong.

I felt like I was drugged. Perhaps that's nature's way of protecting your mind in situations like that. I didn't cry. What she'd just said put me way beyond that. I knew Lenny didn't know yet because I'd just left him, so I just said, 'Don't tell him until I'm there,' and I don't remember anything else until I found myself at home.

I sat and thought of him in the hospital at Sidcup. Having a laugh with the nurses, making a nuisance of himself – telling everybody near enough to hear all about his book. Looking forward to 'being in the driving seat', as he put it, when things were going well, and not knowing the terrible thing I was going to have to find the strength to tell him.

I'd eventually make a more painful journey, but at that time those few miles to St Mary's that afternoon was the worst I'd ever made in my life. On the way I couldn't help looking at people and thinking I'd give anything in the world to swap places with them. I didn't know what problems they had in their lives but all I could think was no matter what they were none of them could've been like mine.

I opened the ward door and there was my Lenny, sitting there in bed like he didn't have a care in the world. My heart sank as I thought, 'That's all going to change when I tell him what's wrong with him.' He saw me and his face lit up. 'All right, babe? Bad news, I've got cancer in the lungs and in the brain.'

They'd done it again, like when he had gangrene in the leg – they'd gone against what I said and told him. I cried then for the first time. I cuddled him and he put his arms around me saying, 'No need for that, babe, me and you'll fight this all the way.' We didn't know it then but he'd been given a death sentence and he was comforting me.

Once he was back home, sometimes I could almost forget what we had hanging over us. Life went on, as far as he was concerned. He had some radiotherapy treatment, but in hindsight I think the doctors were just trying to show they were doing something, rather than with any hope that it would do any good. Those cancers were too far gone for any treatment to slow them down. They told us his lungs had been infected for seven years and his brain for about two. It just shows his strength that carrying that about for all those years hadn't slowed him down a bit.

Sometimes I'd look at him and he might be rubbing

his forehead. I'd say, 'Got a pain, babe?' and he'd say, 'Tiny headache, that's all,' and I'd know that for anybody else they'd feel like their skull was cut in two.

One thing that bothered him was the book. 'I reckon they'll dump me book when they find out I won't be here to promote it.' I'd say, 'Course you will be, Len, give that radiotherapy a chance and you'll be as right as rain.' I didn't believe it myself and I don't think he did but we pretended to each other that things would work out, even after we were told at best he only had months to live. I kept looking for signs, because we all know what cancer does to you when it gets a hold, but he never changed. I expected his weight to drop off but it never happened. That gave me hope even though it was a false one.

We were all invited to a private showing of *Lock, Stock* but I couldn't bring myself to go and see it. Lenny went with Jamie and Kelly, but I made an excuse about not feeling too well. The truth was I just couldn't face the party spirit that goes with a first showing. Everybody's excited, they've worked hard for months and they're all keen to see the finished film. On top of that they'd all be talking about what they'd go on to from there, and as far as Lenny was concerned we all knew too well where that was going to be. At the same time I knew the script off by heart, and the thought of seeing my Lenny killed off at the end and laying back in a chair stone dead would've torn me to pieces.

Three times Lenny went to see it and though every time he said it was 'fucking brilliant' I'm not sure he was all that interested, because that's as far as his comments went. If I'm not putting it too mildly, perhaps inside he was disappointed that he'd never get the benefits from a success that all the other actors would. To be honest at that time all he thought about was his book.

Eventually, in the August, when it went on public release and was straight away an enormous success, I did go and watch the film with the kids and Lenny's brother Barry, who had come from Australia for the funeral. But what with Lenny only been gone a month, I had too much grief filling my mind for me to really appreciate what a good film it was.

To settle Lenny's mind about whether his book might get knocked back, Peter got in touch with the publisher and told them about his illness. Straight away, without any argument at all, they decided to bring publication forward from September to July and that was only three months away. They didn't do it for commercial reasons – in fact it messed their schedule up a bit – but simply so Lenny could hold that dream in his hand.

Even then it was a worry he might not be able to hold on that long, so Peter and Shirley's daughter Vicki arranged for a printer in Cambridge to make up four books, one for each of us, so Lenny could write in them. These people were one of the few firms who could've done such a small run because they were used to making up a couple of copies a time for university students' theses. He was given them in April at our twenty-ninth wedding anniversary party, and he couldn't have been more pleased. He said over and over again, 'This is the best present I've ever had.'

Sometimes I'd listen to him and think he hadn't really taken on board that time was running out for him. Like overhearing him saying to Peter, 'Listen, son, we've got to make as much out of this death as possible' – 'this death' as though it was somebody else or another angle for publicity. But he knew, all right. He kept himself strong for everybody around him who seemed to be taking it worse than he was. I don't remember a single one of his friends going out of our front door without

tears in their eyes after a visit. Every one of them wondering if they would be half as strong if they were in the
same position.

He never gave a thought to himself. He never complained, and not once did he say, 'Why me?' His only
concern, apart from his book, was about me and the kids.

He made arrangements for me to be protected when
he wasn't around – pulled debts in off the streets and
looked round for ways to make us financially secure.
Apart from close friends nobody knew he was terminally
ill, so to break the news nationally he got a good deal
from one of the papers to do a feature. As always with
something like that it has to be kept secret until the day.

His cousin Johnny Wall, who I mentioned earlier,
died of a brain tumour and Lenny went to his funeral
with Kelly. What might have been going through his
mind knowing his own wouldn't be too far away? But
on top of that everybody there who'd heard he'd been in
hospital wanted to know how he was. He gave nothing
away, just told them he'd had a chest infection and would
be back on the cobbles in two minutes. They must've
been shocked when the truth came out the following
weekend.

Over and over he was 'strong as a bull', but out of the
public eye he wasn't at all. As the cancer grew inside his
head it affected him down one side, so that by the time
he was invited onto *The Littlejohn Show* he had to wear
a plastic caliper to support his leg. I couldn't bear to go
with him but I sat at home watching him on the telly,
crying along with the audience as that big tough man
limped on leaning heavily on the ebony cane Jamie had
bought for him. He never asked for sympathy but even
sitting at home I could feel it pouring out of that audience. None of them could've known the effort it had
taken him just to get there. He'd slept most of the day

just to build up enough strength. But he'd said, 'I'm going even if I have to be carried on a stretcher.'

Same as with his first book signing. He'd read out of the paper that some famous person couldn't do a signing because they'd hurt their knee. He said, 'See this, babe – fucking sore knee. He oughta be ashamed. I'll do mine if I have to crawl on me hands and knees.' And he meant it.

But before that he'd been sitting and looking a bit thoughtful, and I was wondering where his mind was taking him. Eventually he looked up and said, 'I wanna ask you a question, babe.'

I said, 'Go on, then.'

'Have I been an all right husband, a good husband or a very good husband?'

For a second I thought of all the ups and downs he'd put me through, but then answered honestly, 'The best I could've wished for.'

That pleased him. Then he said, 'If you had your time over again would you still marry me?'

I said, 'Yes,' and I was knocked out when he said, 'Marry me again, then.' What had brought that on I don't know, but it meant something to him and a lot to me. You can't get married twice but you can do what they call 'retake your vows' and that's what we did at a little church in Sidcup. Even now it's too emotional to talk about, so I'll just say it was a good day for both of us.

I kept it to myself but it was heartbreaking when I thought that twenty-nine years before we'd made the same vows as we started our lives together, full of hopes and dreams. On that day at Sidcup, the best I could hope for was that we could be together for a few more months.

As one day slipped into the next his strength started to go, though really it was only me and the kids who noticed, because whenever friends called in he found something inside him that got him on his feet to put on a normal front. Most times it took a lot of effort.

One of those days he said, 'Got to slip up West later, babe.' He'd slept for twelve hours and getting down the stairs was difficult for him so I said, 'Can't it wait until you're a bit stronger?' but he said, 'No, I've just remembered. When I was filming I promised Guy and Matt that I'd take 'em up Hatton Garden an' introduce them to a pal of mine – him with the shop, 'cos they want to use it in their film *Snatch* or something.' If he'd promised there was no way he would go back on it so I didn't try to argue and off he went.

Same as I didn't bother trying to stop him when his book was delivered at last with a suggestion of doing a signing at Dillons in Oxford Street. The publisher couldn't have known how bad he was at this stage or they wouldn't have asked.

By now he had a lovely MacMillan nurse coming in to look after him. She happened to be the sister of Karl Housman, the actor. I asked her if it was all right for Lenny to do this signing, hoping she'd say no, but she said, 'From what he says to me, apart from his family this book is the most important thing in his life, so we can't take that away from him. Just don't let him get too tired.'

It was a special day for him and I made it even more special by hiring a limousine to take him there in style.

I could've cried in the shop as I watched him. He was sweating with the effort of writing his name, and between having a word or a joke with 'his public' he sat with a faraway look in his eyes. What was he thinking? He couldn't have dreamed of a better turnout. People queued all round the store and out into the road.

I thought, 'I wish all those publishers who turned him down could be here to see this.'

If he'd been asked he would've done the same every day. As it was another one was set up for a fortnight later in W.H. Smith's at Liverpool Street Station. He kept saying this one would be bigger and better because he'd be that much stronger by then. I don't think he pretended to himself that he wasn't going to die, but every now and then he spoke of 'when I shake this off' and 'I'll do so and so when I'm better'.

As desperately as he didn't want to let anybody down, he never made it.

In those next two weeks Karen must've read *The Guv'nor* to him a hundred times. He spent most of his time in bed, though still dug up reserves of strength to get up if a friend rang the doorbell.

His legs and feet hurt him so he got Karen to massage them and read to him at the same time. She'd get to the end of his book and he'd say, 'Just a couple of pages from the front,' and then wouldn't let her stop. She was kneeling at the bottom of the bed, knees aching, eyes drooping, but every time she dozed off he'd waggle his toes on her nose or in her mouth saying, 'No time for sleeping – Lenny's waiting.'

On the Monday night we had a nice long talk. I can't go into all that because it's too painful and too personal, but it touches me today remembering him saying, 'What am I going to do without you, Val?'

He'd said often enough that he wasn't afraid to die, and I don't think he was. The only thing that bothered him was leaving me.

The second signing was booked for the next day (Tuesday, 28 July 1998), and this time he knew he had nothing left. He said, 'Val, don't let them people down, you go with Pete and Shell and tell 'em I'm sorry I couldn't be there.' I said I would because I knew it meant a lot to him. Then he said, 'I'm a bit tired now. Love you, Val,' closed his eyes, and though I didn't realize it then, he wouldn't open them again because overnight he slipped deeper into a coma.

The next morning the nurse warned me and the kids that his end was very near, so we sat on the bed talking to him. He knew we were there because every now and then he'd flutter his eyelids, but he never woke up. Obviously, as much as he'd wanted me to I didn't go to the signing – just sat with him the whole time. About twenty to two I gave him a cuddle, told him I loved him and saw his eyes move under his lids. Then I kissed him and said, 'Lenny, I'll be all right – you can go now,' and he did. My strong Lenny, the only man I'd ever loved, had waited for me to give him the word before slipping out of my life.

Soon after I finished this book I laid my Lenny's ashes to rest with his mother. Now I'll take a line from his book, where he said what he'd do about his mum after she died, and do the same myself. Tuck him into a little corner of my heart and carry on my life without him. What else can I do? I don't have any choice.